ENCODED ARCHIVAL DESCRIPTION:
CONTEXT, THEORY, AND CASE STUDIES

EDITED BY
JACKIE M. DOOLEY

THE SOCIETY *of*
AMERICAN ARCHIVISTS
Chicago

Seventh Printing 2006

Encoded Archival Description: Context, Theory, and Case Studies has also been published as the *American Archiv* volume 60, number 3 (summer 1997) and number 4 (fall 1997), published in August 1998 by the Society American Archivists.

Cover design by Gael-Image.

The Society of American Archivists, 527 S. Wells St., 5th Floor, Chicago, IL 60607-3922 USA
312/922-0140 • fax 312/347-1452 • info@archivists.org • www.archivists.org

Library of Congress Cataloging-in-Publication Data

Encoded Archival Description: context, theory, and case studies /
edited by Jackie M. Dooley.
p. cm.
Published also as v. 60, no. 3-4 of the American Archivist.
Includes bibliographical references and index.
ISBN 0-931828-43-0 (alk. paper)
1. Encoded Archival Description (Document type definition)
I. Dooley, Jackie M. II. American Archivist.
Z695.2.E53 1998
025.3'24--dc21 98-46827
CIP

Table of Contents

Introduction

JACKIE M. DOOLEY

ENCODED ARCHIVAL DESCRIPTION (EAD) first sprang onto the archival scene at the Society of American Archivists 1993 annual meeting in New Orleans, where Daniel Pitti presented a paper on the Berkeley Finding Aid Project, a fledgling research and development project (and precursor to EAD) which was barely under way at the time. The project gained immediate momentum the following month, when Berkeley was awarded a major grant from the U.S. Department of Education to develop both an SGML-based encoding scheme for archival finding aids and a database of finding aids encoded using the new scheme. In the ensuing five years, the momentum that began in 1993 has not abated for a moment, and it can be argued that the development of EAD has generated more interest in both the U.S. and international archival communities than any other technological development in the thirty or so years since the automation revolution began to change the way in which cultural repositories of all kinds conduct their business.

Why has the development of EAD captured the attention and enthusiasm of so many archivists, librarians, software designers, and other information professionals throughout the world? Within the U.S. archival community, surely this can be attributed to the inherent appeal of a standard for structuring and automating finding aids. Despite a somewhat traditional penchant within the profession for the development of unique solutions to common problems (and a concomitant resistance to various types of standardization), many archivists instinctively are attracted to a technique that promises to reduce the need to reinvent the finding aid wheel in every repository, or to rekey or edit data every time a software upgrade is necessary, and which also demonstrates clear potential to radically improve access to archival materials by facilitating structured access via the Internet.

But why the strong interest in EAD beyond the American archival community? Two reasons come immediately to mind. First, in selecting Standard Generalized Markup Language (SGML) as the metalanguage environment within which the EAD data structure (or Document Type Definition [DTD], in SGML parlance) would be developed, Pitti made a deliberate decision to position his finding aid encoding scheme somewhat "ahead of the curve" in terms of existing library and archival software applications. As a result, the World Wide Web environment is coming of age to facilitate full use of the sophisticated capabilities of SGML, through development of the new XML standard, at virtually the same moment that EAD is approaching its first official version 1.0 "release" (once XML is in place, archivists will no longer have to "dumb down" EAD finding aids into HTML in order to present them on the Web).

Second, within the context of the revolution in access to all types of information that has been enabled by proliferation of the Web, librarians and other information professionals have sensed the potential of hierarchically structured finding aids for providing access to many such resources. Thus, they are watching EAD closely as either a tool for direct use or as a potential model for development of similar DTDs.

The twelve chapters in this book were originally published in two consecutive issues of the journal of the Society of American Archivists, the *American Archivist* (volume 60, numbers 3 and 4), and are intended to introduce readers to the key issues that led EAD's developers to design an encoding standard for finding aids, as well as to reveal the experiences of six institutions that were "early implementers" of the "beta" DTD prior to the release of EAD version 1.0 in August 1998.

Part I: Context and Theory. Taken as a group, the first six chapters reveal the context within which EAD was developed, its intended purpose in an integrated system of archival description and access, the essentials of its structured approach to encoding finding aid data, and the role that EAD is meant to play as an archival descriptive standard, both in individual repositories and for the profession as a whole.

The first two chapters, by the principal architect of EAD and by the preeminent spokesperson for American descriptive standards, respectively, lay the conceptual foundation for EAD as a logical outgrowth of earlier work both in archival theory and in library and information science. First, Daniel Pitti outlines important characteristics of the broader information storage and retrieval environment within which EAD resides, describing how his understanding of that environment contributed to his vision of an encoding scheme for archival finding aids. Pitti felt strongly that such a scheme could enable archival description to play an effective role within today's rapidly evolving and increasingly integrated information universe. In a related chapter, Steven Hensen refers back to the work of the National Information Systems Task Force (NISTF) and the development of the USMARC Archival and Manuscripts Control format (MARC AMC) in his description of the evolution of archival descriptive standards and practice and of the important role that he sees EAD playing in the future.

These background chapters are followed by two lucid analyses of structured encoding schemes. Steven DeRose, an internationally recognized SGML expert and software developer who contributed his expertise to the development of EAD, outlines the characteristics of structured information that enable powerful navigation, retrieval, and control of textual data. DeRose's straightforward analysis serves as a prelude to Janice Ruth's presentation of an overview of the most important structural characteristics of EAD itself. From her chapter, archivists who have not yet been introduced to the specifics of EAD will obtain a clear picture of how numerous elements of traditional finding aid structure have been incorporated into this new encoding scheme, as well as of the potential that EAD presents for utilizing that information in powerful new ways. Even those archivists with no plans to implement EAD will find value in her clear overview of the elements of an effective finding aid. Ruth's writing is informed by expertise gained during many years as a finding aid author and editor in the Manuscript Division of the Library of Congress.

The final two chapters in Part I, written by the descriptive experts who have team-taught more than twenty two-day EAD workshops in four countries from 1996 to 1998, serve to assist archivists in thinking about the roles that EAD can play as a tool both for individual repositories and for the international archival profession at large. Michael Fox, a distinguished archival administrator and technical expert, offers guidance regarding the types of questions managers should ask in deciding whether and/or how to incorporate EAD into their local arsenals of technical tools for enhancing the efficiency of finding aid preparation and the effectiveness of archival access systems. In the second half of his chapter, Fox describes five general scenarios for choosing encoding software and outlines some of the workflow implications of each. In her chapter, Kris Kiesling describes the important role that EAD can play as a shared international standard for archival description.

As the Chair of both SAA's Committee on Archival Information Exchange and the EAD Working Group during the key years of EAD's early development, she is well qualified to bring perspective to the importance of standards development and maintenance for any mature profession.

Part II: Case Studies. The six case studies in Part II describe the experiences of archival repositories that began experimenting as "early implementers" of this new descriptive standard as early as 1996. Each of these institutions leaped into the pool while EAD was still under development, two or more years before it was a finished, stable encoding scheme, ready for use by all archival repositories. Such pioneering activity is not for the fainthearted! When these archivists began applying EAD, documentation had not yet been published; software tools were not yet stable, affordable, or easy to use; and the structure of EAD itself was in a considerable state of flux. Even so, archivists at these institutions saw the potential of EAD to standardize their finding aid practices and, in so doing, to improve the quality and functionality of their archival information access and delivery systems. Who are these pioneers, and what perspectives do they bring to the archival community's understanding of EAD?

Dennis Meissner's chapter on the Minnesota Historical Society's project to "re-engineer" its finding aids in preparation for EAD implementation should be required reading for all archivists planning to make their collection guides available within a distributed information environment such as the World Wide Web. He succinctly describes some of the ways in which we all must rethink the nature of our finding aids when they are to be delivered electronically to remote searchers rather than handed to researchers within the context of an in-person reference interview.

Leslie Morris, leader of the Digital Finding Aids Project at Harvard and Radcliffe, describes the careful approach that her team took to the analysis of data elements as a prelude to the development of a "pan-Harvard" finding aid system. Because this group of repositories had never before used a common finding aid standard, this approach presented considerable challenges, but as Morris describes, it has served the project very effectively.

Much like the situation at Harvard, archivists at Yale also used EAD to bring together several discrete repositories for implementation of a university-wide on-line finding aid system. Nicole Bouché describes characteristics of the overall project with a focus on the Beinecke Library's participation. She particularly emphasizes the fact that rigorous use of a consistent database structure and format in past years made Beinecke's conversion of thousands of pages of "legacy data" a veritable breeze.

Archivists in several divisions of the Library of Congress have been extremely active in testing both the technical and intellectual capabilities of EAD. In their detailed explication of the various approaches taken at LC, Mary Lacy and Anne Mitchell describe a variety of finding aid types and approaches to EAD conversion within an environment fueled by the considerable expertise and resources of LC's National Digital Library Program.

As director of the University of Virginia's Electronic Text Unit, David Seaman was encoding texts in SGML using the Text Encoding Initiative DTD for several years before the emergence of EAD. As such, he brings the special perspective of a seasoned SGML veteran to his oversight of Virginia's EAD efforts. This experience is apparent in the advice he offers on matters such as documentation, workflow, and development of efficiency-enhancing software tools.

To close this section, Elizabeth Dow of the University of Vermont describes her one-person implementation of EAD in a relatively small repository. Her story evokes one's childhood memories of *The Little Engine that Could!* Dow's cautionary tale of advice sought, lessons learned, and how she would do it next time should be of great interest to the numerous archivists who cannot dream of commanding the institutional resources available to the other authors.

Numerous other archives in the United States and elsewhere already are implementing EAD, and one expects that our professional literature increasingly will be filled with reports of the particular challenges faced and lessons learned by each. For example, my own repository—Special Collections and University Archives at the University of California, Irvine—is a participant in the Online Archive of California (OAC), the consortial implementation of EAD by the nine-campus University of California system. Under development for less than two years, OAC already has been effective in raising the profile of archival collections university-wide by virtue of their early inclusion in UC's digital library. Three features of the UC project are of particular note. First, an explicit training component was included to ensure that EAD is successfully adopted as a standard technology in all UC repositories, both large and small. Second, participants were required to link to each EAD finding aid from a USMARC catalog record in UC's MELVYL® online catalog, in the same fashion that links are made to other types of electronic resources. And third, an invitation was extended to non-UC archival repositories throughout California to contribute their finding aids to be marked up by project staff and made available via the OAC database. In addition, the UC project has successfully confronted the obstacles inherent to a geographically dispersed consortium that includes repositories of widely varying size and automation expertise. Such project management issues will be reported upon following a formal evaluation phase led by Anne Gilliland-Swetland of UCLA's Department of Library and Information Science.

As the authors of these case studies would no doubt agree, cooperative endeavors of this type may well be the key to implementation of EAD and other new technologies, not only for large multi-repository institutions and consortia, but for many small and chronically underfunded repositories that are home to little-known cultural riches. As you read the case studies in Part II, and about EAD in general, think about your own natural allies and partners, and how you might work together to utilize technology to further your own mission and to make your archival riches ever better known to the audiences you seek.

Part I

CONTEXT AND THEORY

CHAPTER 1

Encoded Archival Description: The Development of an Encoding Standard for Archival Finding Aids

DANIEL V. PITTI

As Encoded Archival Description (EAD) nears completion and formal release as a standard, it seems useful to recall the long-standing problem that it seeks to address, to survey the technology that it employs, and to recount the process by which its nature and structure have been defined.

Successful innovation does not take place in a vacuum. The intellectual inspiration for innovation comes from tradition, even if at the same time the innovation seeks to transform past practice. The chief motivation for developing EAD was to provide a tool to help mitigate the fact that the geographic distribution of collections severely limits the ability of researchers, educators, and others to locate and use primary sources. Modern attempts to overcome the obstacles presented by the geographic distribution of resources date back to at least the middle of the nineteenth century,[1] and the library and archival communities have been trying in various ways since then to tackle this problem. EAD represents but the most recent and certainly not the last endeavor in this ongoing tradition.

Attempts to address the problem of the geographic distribution of materials have focused on providing universal *intellectual* access. Attempts to solve the problem of universal physical access to the materials themselves, or, more accurately, to their intellectual content, are in their infancy, as the technological means for doing so have only recently emerged. As we began to work toward a standard computer-based data structure for finding aids—the textual analytic guides that control and describe archival collections—we believed that such a standard would be an important contribution toward realizing the long-sought goal of universal intellectual access, but also would set the stage for providing access to the intellectual content of the physical materials themselves.

N.B. "Encoded Archival Description: The Development of an Encoding Standard for Archival Finding Aids," by Daniel V. Pitti, co-published simultaneously in the *American Archivist* (The Society of American Archivists) vol. 60, no. 3, pp. 268–83; and *Encoded Archival Description: Context, Theory, and Case Studies* (ed.: Jackie M. Dooley) The Society of American Archivists, 1998.

[1]Charles C. Jewett, *On the Construction of Catalogues of Libraries, and Their Publication by Means of Separate, Stereotyped Titles* (Washington, D.C.: The Smithsonian Institution, 1853).

There is a close relationship between endeavors to overcome geographic obstacles and the emergence of technological innovations; all efforts to improve access have been inspired by new technologies that suggest promising new solutions.[2] EAD is not different from its predecessors in this regard. Emerging computer hardware and software technology, combined with advances in standards and network communications, have stimulated the imaginations of those involved in the development of EAD.

In addition to being an intellectual and technological undertaking, the development of a standard is also a political exercise; it is a community-defining and -building activity. A successful standard must reflect a community's interests, and the community must be directly involved in the standard's development if its interests are to be served. From the beginning of the development of EAD, we have sought to involve the archival community.

Universal Access via Printed Catalogs

The attempt to overcome the geographic distribution of primary sources places EAD development squarely in the mainstream of a major movement in both the library and archives communities that has been making its relentless way throughout most of the current century. Well before the emergence of international networked computing and on-line catalogs, the library community was working steadfastly to overcome the challenge presented by the geographic distribution of collections. Initially, these efforts were directed toward providing union access to published materials. In 1909 the Library of Congress began a catalog card exchange arrangement with several major libraries. Herbert Putnam, then Librarian of Congress, described the plan and its purpose as follows:

> The Library of Congress expects to place in each great center of research in the United States a copy of every card which it prints for its own catalogues; these will form there a statement of what the National Library contains. It hopes to receive a copy of every card printed by the New York Public Library, the Boston Library, the Harvard University Library, the John Crerar Library, and several others. These it will arrange and preserve in a card catalogue of great collections outside of Washington.[3]

This was the first tentative step toward what would eventually become the *National Union Catalog.* Other libraries joined the effort, and by 1926, the Library of Congress had compiled a file of nearly two million cards. In 1948 the file was officially named the *National Union Catalog* (*NUC*), and the libraries that had been only selectively reporting acquisitions were asked to report comprehensively.

Gathering the titles together was only the beginning of the effort to create a useful union listing. In order for it to be universally useful, it needed to be universally accessible. It would take until 1956 for the library to develop a solution to this problem by reviving the book catalog, a format which had not been used by most libraries for fifty years. In 1946 the library published *A Catalog of Books Represented by Library of Congress Printed*

---

[2]Stereotype printing was the technological development behind Jewett's plan to develop a universal catalog. Instead of metal plates, however, Jewett intended to use clay. When the plan failed, it was derisively referred to as "Jewett's Mud Catalog."

[3]*The National Union Catalog Pre-1956 Imprints* (London: Mansell, 1968), vol. 1, vii.

Cards Issued to July 31, 1942. Ten years later, at the urging of the American Library Association, the Library of Congress applied this approach to the *National Union Catalog* and began issuing in book form the titles acquired by the reporting libraries. This eventually led to the publication of the more than six hundred volumes of *The National Union Catalog Pre-1956 Imprints*, the largest single publication ever produced.[4] For the first time, the library world and the public it served had a system for building a national union catalog and making it universally available. But this union catalog, significant as it was, provided access only to published materials, and not to the nation's rich collections of primary source materials.

In 1951 the National Historical Publications and Records Commission (NHPRC)[5] began to compile a union register of archives and manuscript collections held by the nation's repositories. The objective was to provide central, intellectual access to the nation's primary source materials. The effort initially focused on collection-level summary description rather than on in-depth subcollection or item-level description. After gathering collection-level data from thirteen hundred repositories nationwide in the 1950s, the commission published *A Guide to Archives and Manuscripts in the United States* in 1961.[6] The commission decided to revise the directory in 1974, but, after assessing the situation, found that the number of repositories and records had increased so dramatically in the thirteen years that had elapsed from the publication of the first directory that compiling collection-level descriptions would be prohibitively expensive. The commission decided to change the focus to repository-level information and thereby provide a coarser level of access. Despite this shift in focus, the commission continued to envision a "national collection-level data base on archives and manuscripts."[7] For a variety of reasons, the idea was abandoned in 1982.

In 1951, the same year that NHPRC began planning the directory, the Library of Congress began actively to plan the *National Union Catalog of Manuscript Collections* (*NUCMC*).[8] *NUCMC* was intended to be for manuscripts and manuscript collections what the *NUC* was for printed works. Winston Tabb at the Library of Congress has described a major factor in the decision to develop *NUCMC:*

> Scholars, particularly in the field of American history, were instrumental in urging the establishment of a center for locating, recording, and publicizing the holdings of manuscript collections available for research. They had long been frustrated by the difficulties of locating specific manuscripts and even of identifying repositories possibly containing primary-source materials.[9]

It was not until late in 1958 that the Library of Congress began to implement its plans with a grant from the Council on Library Resources. In 1959 the Manuscript Section was established in the library's Descriptive Cataloging Division and was given responsi-

---

[4] *The National Union Catalog Pre-1956 Imprints*, vol. 1, x.

[5] At the time, the NHPRC was named the National Historical Publications Commission.

[6] This account is based on Richard A. Noble's article "The NHPRC Data Base Project: Building the 'Interstate Highway System,'" *American Archivist* 51 (Winter/Spring 1988): 98–105.

[7] Noble, "The NHPRC Data Base Project," 99.

[8] This account is based on the "Foreword" to the *Library of Congress National Union Catalog of Manuscript Collections: Catalog 1991* (Washington, D.C.: Cataloging Distribution Service, Library of Congress, 1993), vii–ix.

[9] *Library of Congress National Union Catalog of Manuscript Collections: Catalog 1991*, vii.

bility for initiating and maintaining the *NUCMC* program. The union manuscript catalog would provide collection-level description for collections held in U.S. repositories and, for particularly important manuscripts, item-level descriptions. Like the *NUC*, the catalog would consist of catalog cards and was to be published in book form, available by subscription. The first volume of *NUCMC* was published in 1962, one year after the NHPRC's *A Guide to Archives and Manuscripts in the United States*. After thirty-two successful years, the library announced in 1994 that volume 29 would be the last *print* publication of the *NUCMC*.

The elimination of the *NUCMC* print publication in no way suggests that it is no longer important to build union catalogs to provide access to our intellectual and cultural resources. Instead, this change was the logical and prudent response to the realization that *NUCMC*'s objective would be better served by using powerful networked computer technology instead of print technology.

Universal Access via On-line Catalogs

The advent of machine-readable catalog records, coupled with the emergence of nationally networked computer databases, provided the archives and library communities with the means to build centralized union catalogs that would be available everywhere, all the time, and in doing so, set the stage for the development of standards such as EAD. For the first time, technology enabled archives and libraries to provide universal access that was not geographically and temporally constrained and thus was far more accessible and effective than printed catalogs. Technology also has greatly facilitated the compiling of union databases. Over the course of the 1980s and 1990s, the OCLC and RLG databases, by aggregating millions of machine-readable catalog records, emerged as *de facto* union catalogs to not only the nation's bibliographic holdings, but to a good share of the world's as well. Scholars, educators, and the general public, using networked computers in offices, homes, and libraries, could discover what published materials existed and where copies could be found.

As of 1983, the records in these national utilities almost exclusively represented published print materials; the primary source materials in the nation's archives and manuscript repositories were not represented. This was all to change with the work of the National Information Systems Task Force (NISTF) of the Society of American Archivists. From 1981 to 1984, NISTF paved the way, both intellectually and politically, for the development of the USMARC Archival and Manuscripts Control (MARC AMC) format.[10] The AMC format made it feasible for archives and manuscript repositories to provide brief, synoptic surrogates for collections in their care in bibliographic catalogs. The AMC format by itself, however, only specified content encoding standards; it did not provide standards for the actual content of the records themselves, and without such standards, the format was simply an empty vessel. The archives and manuscripts community found the *Anglo-American Cataloging Rules*, second edition (*AACR2*) inadequate because its chapter on manuscript cataloging abandoned longstanding archival descriptive principles. In response, Steven L. Hensen, then working at the Library of Congress, developed an alternative set of rules that was to complement the AMC encoding standard. These rules,

[10]For a short history and evaluation of the work of NISTF, see David Bearman, *Towards National Information Systems for Archives and Manuscript Repositories: The National Information Systems Task Force (NISTF) Papers 1981–1984* (Chicago: The Society of American Archivists, 1987).

entitled *Archives, Personal Papers, and Manuscripts (APPM)*, coupled with the AMC format, have enabled the archives and manuscripts community to contribute more than 475,000 records to the Research Libraries Group's RLIN database.[11] Through these utilities, scholars now have access to a growing accumulation of brief descriptions of the nation's archival and manuscript collections.

As important and revolutionary as these accomplishments have been, however, they represented only one major step toward enabling researchers to easily locate primary source materials. The generalized descriptions found in AMC records can only lead a researcher to a collection which *may* have individual relevant items. The researcher must next consult the assortment of inventories, registers, indexes, and guides, generally referred to as finding aids, with which libraries and archives have achieved administrative and intellectual control of archival materials in the form of in-depth, detailed descriptions of their collections. Finding aids provide hierarchically structured description, proceeding in defined stages from the general to the specific. At the most general level, they roughly correspond in scope to collection-level catalog records. At the most specific level, they briefly identify individual items. In between, in varying degrees of detail, they describe subsets or series of related items. Finding aids are the detailed maps that lead one from the main highway to the byways, and from those to one's ultimate destination, the item itself.

MARC AMC collection-level records and finding aids are intended to work together as parts of a hierarchical archival access and navigation model. At the top of the model, the AMC record represents a collection in the on-line catalog and leads, through a "finding aid available" note (field 555), to the more detailed information in the finding aid. The finding aid, in turn, leads to the materials in the collection.

In this three-tiered model, the descriptive information in the collection-level record is based on and derived from the collection's finding aid. Only a very small portion of the information contained in the registers and inventories finds it way into the bibliographic record. The summary nature of the collection-level record is dramatically illustrated by the finding aid and catalog record for the *National Municipal League Records, 1890-1991 (bulk 1929-1988)* in the Auraria Library in Denver, Colorado. The finding aid comprises more than fourteen hundred pages and thirty thousand personal names. By comparison, the AMC record for this collection is approximately two pages long and has nine personal names as access points!

Thus, as positive a development as the AMC format has been, it was not the final step in the drive for universal access to primary sources. Nevertheless, AMC was an excellent prologue to the final act. AMC records whetted our appetite for more information and, almost immediately, made us aware of where we should look for it: in the detailed inventories and registers from which the collection-level catalog records had been derived in the first place. It was clear, then, almost as soon as AMC had triumphed, that the next logical step to facilitate scholars' easily locating relevant primary source materials without buying a plane ticket or putting the completion of a research project at the discretion of the U.S. Postal Service was the creation of yet another encoding standard to complement the AMC standard, a standard for the finding aids themselves. And it was equally clear that this standard would lead to the creation of union Internet access to the nation's finding aids for archives and manuscripts.

---

[11]RLIN database statistics were provided by Ann Van Camp at the Research Libraries Group and reflect the RLIN database as of August 25, 1997.

The Value of Standards

But why insist on the development of a standard? The success of AMC itself should obviate any need to argue the necessity of standards to the archival community, but recent experience has shown that the lure of simple techniques can lead us to ignore lessons already learned. In an era of tightening budgets, it can be difficult to remember that we exploit the new information frontier best if we bring enduring value to it. In the current atmosphere, it is critical to remind ourselves of the importance of standardizing our own time-honored practices rather than rushing to embrace ephemeral digital fashions that will not stand the test of time.

MARC has successfully demonstrated the value of a community-based standard in realizing the goal of universal access to primary resource materials. We are steadily and inexorably moving toward providing comprehensive, universal intellectual access to both primary and secondary resources. This remarkable effort would not be possible without the library community's pioneering work in developing content and structure standards. With the development of AMC, the archival community joined in recognizing the paramount importance of standards. Having grown accustomed to the benefits of well-designed, community-based descriptive standards, it was inconceivable that the archival community could accept proprietary, nonstandard, or worse, substandard approaches to providing universal access to finding aids and the resources they document.

Standards are the foundation upon which individuals sharing common interests form communities, enabling them not only to coexist but also to cooperatively build shared and enduring works. While many archivists were skeptical about the adaptation and use of bibliocentric library standards, the desire to make archival materials available to users more effectively motivated them to work with the library community. Archivists share with librarians the compelling objective of making information concerning the existence, availability, and nature of the materials in their care more readily available to users. Thus, when the means was found to create surrogates for archival collections in on-line public catalogs, enabling users to locate and identify relevant primary resources more easily, the archival community embraced it.

The Lessons of MARC

Many of the design features successfully demonstrated in MARC are also desirable in an encoding standard for finding aids, and the developers of EAD looked to MARC as a model from the very beginning.

An encoding scheme such as MARC, a computer-readable system for representing the unique, intellectual structure of cataloging data, was absolutely essential if we were ever to build large networked databases that could support sophisticated and effective control, searching, display, and navigation of library collections.[12] Merely transferring complex catalog records into networked computers as unstructured text would not in itself have enabled computers to exploit the complex distinctions and relationships among the elements of descriptive cataloging records.

Cataloging is an "order-making" activity by which complex rules are applied to a defiant, unruly information universe in order to "whip it into shape," making it appear

[12] "Control" is here intended to mean "knowing what we have and where it is."

orderly to the users of catalogs.[13] Catalogers determine the identities of authors, works, and items, and the relationships among them. To be usefully exploited by computers, all of this complex order-making data must be explicitly represented in a manner that allows machines to process it with intended, predictable results. Computers cannot reliably perform complex processing on flat, unstructured text, because programmers cannot instruct machines to process that which has not been identified. To take full advantage of network computer technology, it was thus necessary to have an encoding system for catalog data that rendered the boundaries of its intellectual components explicit to programmers and computers alike.

The original designers of MARC saw it primarily as a method for automating the production of printed catalog cards, but they wisely invented an encoding system that would support more than this one use. Given the many uses to which cataloging information would eventually be put, it was important that the encoding scheme developed be sufficiently flexible to support all potential uses. The best way to accomplish this objective was to make the scheme descriptive rather than procedural.

Procedural encoding tells the computer what to do with specified components of a text; by its very nature, it is dedicated to only one use of the information. But as we know, cataloging data is subjected to multiple forms of processing in order to provide effective control, searching, display, and navigation. To support application of multiple procedures, each component could be encoded with multiple processing instructions. This would be highly inefficient, however, because it involves a great deal of redundancy and also forecloses on new processes unforeseen at the time the encoding scheme was developed.

An alternative approach, and the one wisely chosen by the developers of MARC, is to descriptively encode the information. Descriptive encoding involves designating *what* each important component is: a catalog record, an author, a title, and so on. If we know what a data component is, then it is possible to apply different procedures to it based on explicit knowledge of its nature. The decision to make MARC a descriptive markup system ensured that information could be exploited in multiple ways, *and* it left the door open to apply procedures unforeseen in the early stages of development. In addition to faithfully representing cataloging data, MARC's developers also recognized that the system they were designing had to be a publicly owned standard to ensure that cataloging information would endure in an ever-changing computer environment. A standard must not be based on any specific hardware or software platform if it is to endure in our rapidly changing technological environment.

The descriptive nature of MARC encoding, in addition to supporting flexible processing, also supports MARC's long-term survival through means such as mapping MARC data into other computer representations. In fact, most existing MARC systems do not store and use MARC in its native form; to comply with the standard, they simply import and export MARC records. Mapping MARC into a successor standard, if and when one emerges, will be a simple export procedure. MARC's successful survival of the unbelievably rapid transformation of computing over the course of the last thirty years is a testament to the wisdom of its designers. These aspects of the design of MARC—the fact that it is descriptive markup and that it is publicly owned—strongly influenced the developers of EAD and determined the nature of EAD's design to a large extent.

---

[13]David Levy, *Cataloging in the Digital Order*, <http://csdl.tamu.edu/DL95/papers/levy/levy.html>.

Early in the development of EAD, we surveyed options for the encoding of finding aids. The primary selection criteria were (1) that the system chosen had to be a standard, which is to say, a formal set of conventions in the public domain, not owned by and thus not dependent on any hardware or software producer, and (2) that it had to be capable of faithfully representing the complex intellectual content and structure of finding aids in a manner that would enable sophisticated searching, navigation, and display.

Because of MARC's design qualities, its success in capturing the intellectual content of bibliographic description and the fact that it had been used successfully by archivists for providing collection-level summary access to collections, MARC immediately earned consideration as an option. It was a standard in the public domain. But was it capable of representing the complex intellectual content and structure of finding aids?

After careful study and deliberation, we decided that MARC was not the best available scheme for three principal reasons. First, MARC records are limited to a maximum length of 100,000 characters. This represents approximately thirty 8½-by-11 pages of 10-pitch unformatted text stored in ASCII. Since many finding aids are longer than this, the size restriction was a prohibitive obstacle. Second, and even more significantly, MARC accommodates hierarchically structured information very poorly. Since finding aids are inherently hierarchical documents, the flat structure of MARC makes it unsatisfactory. As archivists are painfully aware, MARC was primarily designed to capture data describing a discrete bibliographic item; complex collections requiring descending levels of analysis quickly overburden the MARC structure. At most, a second level of analysis can be accommodated, but the kind of information supplied is limited.[14] The third reason for not using MARC for finding aids involves the marketplace. It is a gross understatement to say that libraries, archives, and museums are generally not resource-rich institutions. To put this into perspective, the cost of one B-2 bomber would fund the Library of Congress for well over three years.[15] Lacking large amounts of capital, MARC's user community has been incapable of driving state-of-the-art hardware and software development.

SGML, HTML, XML, and EAD

After determining that MARC would not provide an adequate representation of finding aid data, we shifted our attention to Standard Generalized Markup Language (SGML). SGML provides a promising framework or model for developing an encoding scheme for finding aids for a number of reasons. First, like MARC, SGML is a standard (ISO 8879). It comprises a formal set of conventions in the public domain, and thus is not owned by and thereby dependent on any hardware or software producer. Second, unlike MARC, SGML accommodates hierarchically interrelated information at as many levels as needed. Third, there are no inherent size restrictions on SGML-based documents. Finally, the SGML marketplace is much, much larger than MARC's.

[14]One possible way around this problem is to employ multiple, hierarchically interrelated and interlinked MARC records at varying levels of analysis: collection-level, subunit, and item. The use of multiple records, though, introduces extremely difficult inter- and intra-system control problems that have never been adequately addressed in the format or by MARC-based software developers. Even if the control issues were adequately addressed in the format, the control required to make multiple record expression of hierarchy succeed would entail prohibitive human maintenance.

[15]According to the United States Air Force Web page, the unit price for one B-2 bomber is $1.3 billion. Various other sources place the figure at closer to $2 billion. The 1997 Library of Congress budget is $360,896,000.

While SGML is both standard and generalized, it does not provide an off-the-shelf markup language that one can simply take home and apply to a letter, novel, article, catalog record, or finding aid. Instead it is a markup language metastandard, or in simpler words, a standard for constructing markup languages. SGML provides conventions for naming the logical components or elements of documents, as well as a syntax and metalanguage for defining and expressing the logical structure of documents and relations between document components. It is a set of formal rules for defining specific markup languages for individual kinds of documents. Using these formal rules, members of a community sharing a particular type of document can work together to create a markup language specific to their shared document type.

The specific markup languages written in compliance with formal SGML requirements are called Document Type Definitions, or DTDs. For example, the Association of American Publishers has developed three DTDs: one for books, one for journals, and one for journal articles. A consortium of software developers and producers has developed a DTD for computer manuals. The Library of Congress currently is testing a draft USMARC DTD. The Text Encoding Initiative has developed a complex suite of DTDs for the representation of literary and linguistic materials. DTDs, when shared and followed by a community, are themselves standards.

While MARC is devoted to structuring a specific kind of data, namely cataloging data, SGML is very general and abstract. It exists formally over and above individual markup languages for specific document classes. Because SGML syntax and rules are formal and precise, it is possible to write software that can be adjusted with relative ease to work with any compliant DTD. Typically, an SGML software product has a toolkit that allows the user to adapt its functionality to a specific DTD. As a result, all SGML users, not just library and archival users, comprise the market that drives SGML software development.

Similar to MARC, SGML is intended to support descriptive rather than procedural markup of text.[16] As discussed above, procedural markup specifies a particular procedure to be applied to a document component, while descriptive markup defines each component, leaving the processing routines up to applications.

It is useful to distinguish two kinds of descriptive markup: structural and nominal. Descriptive structural markup identifies document components and their logical relationships. Structural elements generally are components that warrant distinct visual presentation: examples include chapter titles, paragraphs, lists, and block quotes. Descriptive nominal markup identifies named entities, both concrete and abstract: examples include corporate names, personal names, topical subjects, genres, and geographic names. While a specific visual presentation of them may be desirable, such elements usually warrant being indexed in particular ways to provide access to some aspect of the document. It is also possible to use SGML to treat the descriptive components of finding aids as named entities. EAD, for example, distinguishes scope and content, biographies and agency histories, chronological lists, various types of administrative information, and many more components of archival description. By explicitly identifying these components, software

[16]For a detailed description of different types of markup, see James H. Coombs, Allen H. Renear, and Steven J. DeRose, "Markup Systems and the Future of Scholarly Text Processing," *Communications of the Association for Computing Machinery* 30 (November 1987): 933–47.

can be employed to index, search, display, and navigate each component in particular ways.

SGML also supports referential markup. As its name suggests, referential markup refers to information that is not present; it is markup in the third person, so to speak. Referential markup is most commonly used for hypertext and hypermedia, providing the foundation for dynamic references or links to other text and to original digital or digital representations of manuscripts, photographs, audio and audiovisual materials, drawings, paintings, three-dimensional objects of all kinds, chemical formulae, printed pages, music, choreography, and anything else that can be digitally captured and rendered in some useful form. In addition to its many other benefits, using SGML for finding aids offers the exciting option of providing access to digital representations of the primary resources in our archival collections.

HyperText Markup Language (HTML) is an SGML DTD that has enjoyed enormous success as the encoding standard underpinning the World Wide Web. As a specific application of SGML, the HTML DTD limits itself to simple procedural encoding dedicated to on-line display and hypermedia linking. Because of HTML's relative ease of use and its ability to support on-line display of finding aids, many have suggested that it suffices for the encoding of finding aids. The EAD developers felt strongly, however, that HTML was inadequate because its procedural focus would not represent the complex intellectual content and structure of finding aids in a manner that would enable sophisticated searching, navigation, and display. Evidence of HTML's limited ability to support intelligent searching and document discovery, let alone complex display, navigation, and other processing, is not difficult to find. Many of us have used Web search engines to look for both known items and items relevant to a particular topic, and more often than not, we are overwhelmed by voluminous results. Our patience frequently is exhausted looking for an item or two that satisfies our need.[17]

The success of HTML as a display format for the Web brings into sharp relief the one major weakness in available SGML software, namely the limited options currently available for delivering native SGML over the Internet. SGML software developers have produced very good and affordable tools for SGML authoring and editing, data conversion, and database indexing and searching; they also have produced very good publishing tools for in-house and CD-ROM publishing. Delivering SGML documents on the Web, however, has been a serious obstacle, but the prospects for this changing in the near future appear to be bright.

In 1996 the World Wide Web Consortium (W3C) founded the XML Working Group to build a set of specifications that would make it easier to use SGML on the Web.[18] The working group, in a short period of time, wrote a specification for a simplified subset of SGML named Extensible Markup Language (XML). Both Microsoft and Netscape have committed to fully implementing XML in their Internet browsers.

The motive behind the development of XML is the recognition that HTML will not support complex, community-based use of shared information on the Internet. HTML

[17]In response to this problem OCLC has led an international effort since 1995 to develop a simple, generic descriptive metadata scheme that would make it possible to more intelligently index and search HTML documents on the Web.

[18]The original name was SGML Editorial Review Board. Jon Bosak of Sun Microsystems is chair of the Working Group. Other members include Jean Paoli, head of Microsoft's Internet Explorer development, and Tim Bray, representing both Textuality and Netscape.

hardwires a small set of procedurally oriented tags. Constraining the set of tags has made it easy to build applications that make life relatively easy for authors and Web publishers, and ease of use has been a major factor in the Web's remarkable success. The small, closed tag set, however, has come at a price: HTML has extremely limited functionality. Jon Bosak has identified three areas in which HTML is wanting: extensibility, structure, and validation.[19] SGML is strong in all of these areas, but its strength, like HTML's weakness, comes at a price: SGML is complicated for both application developers and the users of the applications. The W3C's XML Working Group addressed this weakness by identifying and proscribing some features in SGML that are difficult to implement. The result of their work is XML, a simplified subset of SGML for use on the Web.

The ongoing development of XML and closely related standards promises to overcome the last major obstacle to the use of SGML for encoding finding aids: their easy delivery over the Internet.[20] Fortunately, most of the SGML features proscribed in XML were not used in the EAD DTD, and expressions used in EAD that do use proscribed features can easily be expressed in XML-compliant ways. Thus very little modification of the EAD DTD is required to take advantage of future Internet browsers produced and distributed by Microsoft, Netscape, and other vendors, and these changes will have been completed prior to the release of EAD version 1.0.

The decision to develop EAD as an SGML DTD still appears to have been propitious. It allowed us to incorporate MARC's strengths—descriptive markup and public ownership—and to overcome its weaknesses—limited record and field length, hierarchical poverty, and small market appeal. It was an article of faith when we began developing EAD that to become truly robust the Web would have to outgrow HTML, and that the likely successor to HTML would be based on SGML. This was a calculated risk, but it appears to have been thoroughly justified.

EAD's foundation in the mainstream of library and archives efforts to achieve universal access coupled with the use of emerging powerful computing and network technologies, would appear to provide EAD with everything it would need to succeed. But the most important element of any standards process: the community which will use the standard—also had to be brought into play.

Overview of EAD Development

The success of any standard depends upon broad community participation in its development, followed by widespread recognition of the standard's utility. Standards are the products of communities, not of individuals working in splendid isolation, and the development process is as much a political exercise as it is an intellectual and technical undertaking. Thus, to be successful, an encoding standard for finding aids must reflect and further the shared interests of the archival community and of the agencies and institutions that support it.

From the very beginning of the effort to develop an encoding standard for finding aids, those involved realized it would be crucial to involve the archival community in the

[19]Jon Bosak, *XML, Java, and the future of the Web*, <http://sunsite.unc.edu/pub/sun-info/standards/xml/why/xmlapps.htm>.

[20]XML includes three related initiatives: XML, Extensible Linking Language (XLL) and Extensible Stylesheet Language (XSL). For current information on the status of the development and the latest drafts of each, see <http://sil.org/sgml/xml.html>.

intellectual and technical design of the standard. In 1993, when the UC Berkeley library staff was first beginning to contemplate developing such a standard, Jackie Dooley and Steven Hensen both firmly emphasized the necessity of broad community involvement if the effort was to succeed.

The Berkeley Finding Aid Project (BFAP), funded with a grant from the Department of Education's Title IIA Program, began the process that has led to EAD. BFAP's objective was to demonstrate through development of a draft DTD (initially named FindAid), as well as an Internet-accessible database employing the DTD, that an SGML-based encoding standard was both feasible and desirable. To ensure that the prototype DTD reflected the content and structure of the community's finding aids, BFAP staff solicited representative examples of finding aids, regardless of quality, from scores of repositories.[21]

Early in 1995, two developments served to transfer ownership of BFAP's work to the national community. In April the Commission on Preservation and Access (CPA) and the Berkeley library cosponsored a Finding Aid Conference at Berkeley attended by seventy representatives of special collections, archives, libraries, and museums. The purpose of the conference was to evaluate the results of BFAP and to make recommendations about what should be done next. Those gathered enthusiastically agreed that BFAP had succeeded in its limited goals and that the effort should continue, though with the active participation of archival descriptive experts.

The opportunity for engaging archival experts more closely in the project came with the author's successful application to the Bentley Library Research Fellowship Program at the University of Michigan for a team fellowship. The team, led by the author, included noted archival description experts[22] as well as distinguished SGML expert Steven J. DeRose of Electronic Book Technologies. The team met in Ann Arbor in July 1995 to evaluate formally the BFAP finding aid model and DTD and to develop a new model. The team reached early agreement on design principles, which were called the ''Ann Arbor Accords,'' and spent the remainder of the week developing the model on which a new DTD would be based.[23] It was at this time that BFAP was renamed Encoded Archival Description (EAD).

A flurry of activity followed the Ann Arbor meeting. In the next two months, the author wrote the first draft of the EAD DTD. At the September 1995 annual meeting of SAA in Washington, D.C., members of the team began the process of determining appropriate mechanisms for profession-wide adoption and maintenance of an encoding standard for finding aids. The design principles and revised data model were presented to SAA's Committee on Archival Information Exchange (CAIE), and CAIE was invited to become formally involved in the development of EAD. CAIE agreed and created the EAD Working

---

[21]The response to this solicitation provides an interesting glimpse into the standards development process. Many repositories enthusiastically promised to send finding aids, but after several weeks, only a handful had arrived. BFAP staff began to approach each repository that had promised to send finding aids to request them once again. Over and over the response was that, while they wholeheartedly supported the effort, they were concerned about how their colleagues would view their finding aids. The finding aids they eventually submitted tended to be those in which they had the most confidence. Thus the community itself voluntarily began to normalize finding aid practice.

[22]Other members of the group were Jackie Dooley, University of California, Irvine; Michael J. Fox, Minnesota Historical Society; Steven Hensen, Duke University; Kris Kiesling, University of Texas, Austin; Janice Ruth, Library of Congress; Sharon Gibbs Thibodeau, National Archives and Records Administration; and Helena Zinkham, Library of Congress.

[23]''Ann Arbor Accords: Principles and Criteria for an SGML Document Type Definition (DTD) for Finding Aids,'' *Archival Outlook* (January 1996): 12–13.

Group (EADWG) chaired by Kris Kiesling and including representatives from the Library of Congress (LC), RLG, OCLC, and SAA. EADWG was charged by CAIE with: 1) assisting in developing and reviewing a data model for archival finding aids; 2) reviewing the EAD DTD; 3) testing and evaluating the EAD DTD; 4) reviewing application guidelines; and 5) initiating review of EAD by the SAA Standards Board and SAA Council. SAA also agreed to formally request that the LC Network Development/MARC Standards Office (ND/MSO) assume the maintenance of EAD once it had undergone thorough community review and was accepted as a standard. In October 1995 LC's National Digital Library (NDL) sponsored a meeting of the team in Washington, D.C. to review the model and draft DTD.

After the October meeting in Washington, ATLIS Consulting Group, under contract to LC and in consultation with the author, began revision of the DTD and creation of a tag library. In a letter to Susan Fox, SAA Executive Director, the ND/MSO formally agreed to be the maintenance agency for EAD, with SAA responsible for ongoing intellectual oversight and development of the standard.

In December 1995 SAA received funding from the Council on Library Resources to create application guidelines for EAD, and at a meeting at UCLA on January 4-6, 1996, the EAD project team met with Anne Gilliland-Swetland and Thomas LaPorte to review the draft DTD and tag library and to outline the content of the guidelines. Further changes were incorporated into the "alpha" version of the DTD, which was completed and released electronically by ND/MSO for use by early implementers in February 1996. On April 27-29, 1996 the EAD team met in Berkeley to discuss the draft guidelines drafted by Gilliland-Swetland and LaPorte and to review suggested changes to the "alpha" version of the DTD that had been suggested by team members and early implementers. Agreed-upon changes were incorporated into the "beta" version of the DTD, which was completed by the author on June 15, 1996 and after review by the development team, was released publicly that September. The draft guidelines, tag library, and encoded examples of a wide variety of finding aids were made publicly available on the Internet in December 1996.

During the course of the EAD development process, a variety of major research and demonstration projects began implementing EAD. From the earliest stages, UC Berkeley, Duke University, and LC's NDL began encoding finding aids using EAD to test its intellectual and technical soundness. Yale University began working with the alpha DTD as soon as it was released in early 1996, as did Harvard University. The University of California, San Diego successfully began experimenting with exporting into EAD finding aids that had been created in a database. SOLINET decided to incorporate EAD into its Department of Commerce-funded Monticello Project, and the NEH-funded Dance Heritage Coalition also made the decision to employ EAD in its archival access project.

Since the EAD beta public release in September 1996, several repositories have initiated finding aid projects of varying size and complexity. The Public Record Office in London is currently developing a strategy for conversion of its repository guide. When completed, this guide will comprise hundreds of thousands of pages describing several centuries of British public records. Several universities in the United Kingdom, including Liverpool, Oxford, Durham, and Glasgow, have substantial EAD projects underway. In the United States, UC Berkeley, with funding from NEH, embarked on the California Heritage Digital Image Access Project. The goal of this project was to demonstrate that USMARC collection-level records linked to EAD-encoded finding aids could provide effective, useful access to collections comprising more than twenty-five thousand digital representations of pictorial materials documenting California history and culture selected from the Bancroft Library's vast pictorial collections. Significantly, the California Heritage Project's prototype access system is being used in an ambitious UC Berkeley K-12 outreach program called the Interactive University Project, which is funded by a Department of Commerce grant. In this project, a team of faculty and library staff are working with K-12 teachers and curriculum planners from the San Francisco and Oakland public school districts to create a teaching program and lesson plans that will use the digital archives to teach subjects related to California history and cultures during the 1997-98 school year and possibly beyond.

The California Heritage Project also has provided the foundation for two other projects, the NEH-funded American Heritage Virtual Archive Project and the University of California EAD Project (UCEAD),[24] the latter funded by UC's Office of the President as the first in a series of UC-wide digital library projects. In addition to building a UC-wide database of finding aids, a key goal of UCEAD was to train archivists at all nine UC campuses to efficiently implement EAD through the use of customized software ''toolkits.'' The American Heritage Project involves a collaboration between Stanford University, the University of Virginia, Duke University, and UC Berkeley; its goal is to demonstrate that EAD can be uniformly applied to diverse existing finding aids for collections documenting American heritage and culture at the four collaborating repositories to enable building a combined virtual archives. The project is exploring the intellectual, political, and technical issues that need to be resolved to provide integrated access to finding aids from multiple institutions.[25] The centerpiece of this project is the development of ''an acceptable range of uniform practice'' in the application of EAD to existing finding aids. At a meeting in Berkeley in November 1996, representatives from the four collaborating institutions, building on the extensive work of a team of Berkeley technical and archival staff, debated and reached consensus. That consensus was codified in the first draft of the *EAD Retrospective Conversion Guidelines.* Soon thereafter, archivists representing the nine UC campuses met in Los Angeles to launch the UCEAD Project and to further refine the consensus represented by the *Guidelines.* The American Heritage and UCEAD participants, representing twelve university repositories, all agreed to follow these *Guidelines.* These repositories hope that the guidelines will serve as the basis for a discussion leading to a national consensus on ''an acceptable range of uniform practice.''[26]

The Research Libraries Group recognized that development of EAD training was critical to its community-wide acceptance and use. In the summer of 1996, in collaboration with UC Berkeley, RLG developed the Finding Aid SGML Training (FAST) workshop curriculum. Over the course of the following year, with grants from the Delmas Foundation and the Council on Library Resources, RLG held several workshops in the United Kingdom, Canada, and the United States. Taught by Michael Fox and Kris Kiesling, the FAST

[24]The UCEAD Project later was renamed the Online Archive of California.

[25]Given current technical limits, the project is integrating the finding aids into one centralized database. As technology improves for integrating access to distributed databases (a model much preferred for many practical reasons), the lessons learned from this project will inform migration to the new technology.

[26]Citing a 1980 NHPRC report, Richard Noble reports that commission staff projected that 20,000 repositories and over 700,000 collection descriptions would be included in a national database. See Noble, ''The NHPRC Data Base Project,'' 100. The finding aids in the Berkeley database average twenty-seven pages in length. If this average is representative, then 700,000 finding aids would amount to nearly 19 million pages of text!! It is worth noting again that after only eleven years there are over 475,000 records for archival materials in the RLIN database. Since many of the nation's archival collections have never been processed, arranged, and described, 700,000 may be a conservative estimate.

workshops have successfully provided initial training to scores of archivists. FAST and other EAD workshops have led to a number of other repositories, large and small, initiating their own finding aid encoding projects. The University of Iowa, University of Vermont, New York Public Library, North Carolina State University, and University of North Carolina, to name a few, all have projects underway. In August 1997 RLG turned the workshop over to the Society of American Archivists at the Society's annual meeting in Chicago, and SAA has now integrated the workshop into its educational curriculum.

RLG and Chadwyck-Healey both are exploring incorporating EAD into their products and services. Following successful development of EAD training, RLG has formed an EAD advisory group to assist in planning and implementing new services. At this stage of planning, RLG intends to provide union access to finding aids worldwide, both those housed on local servers and those deposited on the RLG server by repositories lacking the resources or desire to mount their own findings aids. The advisory group has identified the need for participating repositories to apply EAD uniformly and, in this regard, has decided to use the *EAD Retrospective Conversion Guidelines* to initiate discussions leading to community-wide "best practice" guidelines. In addition, RLG is exploring the feasibility of hosting a retrospective conversion service that would make use of third-party vendors. Chadwyck-Healey is contemplating a similar service and is considering ways to enhance its *ArchivesUSA* product by incorporating EAD-encoded finding aids. In addition to the activities of RLG and Chadwyck-Healey, a number of software vendors have EAD products under development.

In addition to the successful transfer of the FAST workshop to SAA, there were several other important developments at the 1997 SAA annual meeting. Jackie Dooley, chair of the SAA Publications Board, reported on discussions with LC concerning the publication of the EAD DTD, tag library, and application guidelines. Kris Kiesling, chair of the EADWG, announced that Meg Sweet of the Public Record Office in the United Kingdom had joined the Working Group and that the Delmas Foundation had funded a meeting of the Working Group in fall 1997 in Washington, D.C. At this meeting, the group reviewed revisions to EAD suggested by the international archival community and, after thorough discussion, decided which changes would be codified prior to EAD's public release as a standard in 1998. The Working Group also reviewed drafts of the tag library, publication of which will coincide with the formal release of the DTD.

Conclusion

Prior to the advent of MARC AMC and *APPM*, the archival community had little motivation to develop descriptive standards. The economic benefits of sharing cataloging that motivated libraries were not available to archivists, whose collections are mostly unique. Nevertheless, archivists wanted to make their materials more accessible, a professional objective they shared with their library colleagues. This desire provided the motivation to explore and eventually embrace MARC AMC and *APPM*, the success of which convinced the archival community of the value and importance of encoding and descriptive content standards. Further, archivists were inspired to want to go beyond summary descriptions and to find a way to provide access to the full, detailed finding aids that constitute the heart of all efforts to make archival collections accessible.

The emergence of the Internet, which has enabled the revolutionary transcending of the spatial and temporal boundaries of our information environment, awakened an abiding but dormant aspiration: to provide comprehensive universal access to the world's primary cultural and historical resources. For the first time in history, it is possible to render the absent present. Not only will archivists be able to better serve those we have traditionally served, but we will also, for the first time, have the means to make our collections accessible to educators and students at all levels and to the general public.

EAD and related standards have initiated the realization of an information future in which serious scholars and the casually curious alike will easily find the cultural treasures they seek. In this emerging future, information seekers will follow clearly marked paths from catalogs to finding aids, and from finding aids to a wealth of information in a multitude of digital and traditional formats. We are embarking on providing not only intellectual access to our collections, but also access to digital facsimiles, at least selectively, of the materials themselves.

While we have not yet fully realized this long-sought goal, and much work remains to be done, it is now possible to begin to envision a future even more promising—one which builds new and unprecedented collaborations between scholars, educators, publishers, archivists, and librarians. Over and above the structured database of catalog records, finding aids, and digital representations of primary source materials, it will be possible to create both private and public information spaces that interpret materials from a wide variety of perspectives and disciplines to serve an equally wide array of cultural needs. Archivists will play an essential role in building the networked digital information environment that promises to transform the intellectual community by admitting new groups of people who, prior to its advent, had never set foot in an archives.

CHAPTER 2

''NISTF II'' and EAD: The Evolution of Archival Description

STEVEN L. HENSEN

Introduction

THE DEVELOPMENT OF ENCODED ARCHIVAL DESCRIPTION (EAD) is part of a long process of evolution of archival descriptive standards that had its roots in the early work of the SAA National Information Systems Task Force (NISTF), and which began the integration of archival description into the so-called ''bibliographic mainstream.'' The EAD project is in fact a natural culmination of much that had gone on before; an extension—nay, more of a quantum leap—of standard archival practice that leapfrogs the archival world into the unaccustomed role of being on the ''cutting edge'' of current advances in networked information access.

The EAD project is maturing at exactly the moment when archivists and manuscript curators both need and will be able to make use of it. When Daniel Pitti first started the Berkeley Finding Aid Project, there was little sense of how such a system might ultimately be implemented. No one had heard of the World Wide Web or HyperText Markup Language, and certainly few could have predicted the current explosion of information resources over the Internet. Today, forward-thinking archivists are developing plans and systems for making information about their holdings—and even the holdings themselves—available over the Internet. These systems are almost universally conceived in traditional hierarchical models of archival description: catalog records with subject indexes, linked to finding aids, linked to digital representations of archival objects. Without the Berkeley Finding Aid Project and its evolution to EAD, such systems would not yet be feasible.

The title of this chapter makes a connection between the EAD project and what I refer to as ''NISTF II.'' At the 1994 annual meeting of the Society of American Archivists in Indianapolis, Larry Dowler chaired a session in which I was one of the speakers. The session, somewhat enigmatically titled ''Archival Stonehenge,'' was focused on the tenth anniversary of the MARC AMC format. In commenting on the papers dealing with the past, present, and future of MARC AMC, Dowler remarked that archival descriptive standards and systems had come so far so quickly (and were, in fact, heading even more

---

N.B. '' 'NISTF II' and EAD: The Evolution of Archival Description,'' by Steven L. Hensen, co-published simultaneously in the *American Archivist* (The Society of American Archivists) vol. 60, no. 3, pp. 284–96; and *Encoded Archival Description: Context, Theory, and Case Studies* (ed.: Jackie M. Dooley) The Society of American Archivists, 1998.

quickly into unanticipated new directions), that maybe it was time to convene a new National Information Systems Task Force, or "Son of NISTF," as I believe he called it. In February 1995, at the RLG Primary Sources Forum meeting, Dowler was called upon to summarize the presentations and recommendations of the assembled representatives of this group, and he repeated this conclusion. He has since told me that it was the Berkeley Finding Aid Project, coupled with the explosive growth of new modes of networked information retrieval, that were pushing him towards this conclusion. Moreover, Dowler was recognizing subtle parallels and connections between the dynamics of current developments and his own earlier experiences in archival standards development.

It is thus my contention that the Berkeley Finding Aid Project in many of its goals and ultimate aims was, if not the "Son of NISTF" that Dowler was calling for, such a strong lineal descendant that it deserves immediate adoption, if not actual christening, as "NISTF II." As a quondam companion of Dowler's in much of that earlier work, I would like to draw on that experience and briefly examine the principal themes and history of archival standards development over the last ten years by way of more fully appreciating and understanding the importance of the present project and how deftly and systematically it fits into the overall process.

NISTF and the MARC AMC Format

The work of the National Information Systems Task Force[1] was a lengthy and often contentious process. To be sure, the issues with which NISTF was dealing were complex and controversial and required as much attention as could be given them. In addition, however, the world was a more leisurely place twenty years ago; there was not the pace of progress with which we must contend today, in which fundamental social and cultural changes seem to occur at the same pace as (and indeed are often prompted by) changes in computer software and hardware—which is to say an eighteen-month obsolescence cycle. Two recent projects with which I have been involved—the RLG Digital Image Access Project and the EAD project—were frustrated in trying to proceed towards their respective goals as the ground was almost literally moving under their feet. As a consequence, both projects ended up in altogether different environments than those in which they started.

Among the difficult issues with which NISTF grappled was the seeming hostility felt by many in the archival community towards anything that smacked of librarianship, and the firm belief that since archives were unique, they required unique approaches, and standards could thus never be applied. Add to this mix the sentiment that the methodologies and principles of archivists were somehow fundamentally different than those employed by their more library-oriented "manuscript curator" colleagues—perhaps a vestige of the "archives/historical manuscripts" dichotomy that dates to Sir Hilary Jenkinson in the early twentieth century.

---

[1]NISTF was formed in 1977 by the Society of American Archivists with funds from the National Endowment for the Humanities. Its members consisted of Richard Lytle, chair, and David Bearman, project director, both of the Smithsonian Institution; Maynard Brichford, University of Illinois; John Daly, Illinois State Archives; Charles Dollar, National Archives and Records Administration; Larry Dowler, Yale University; Max Evans, State Historical Society of Wisconsin; Steven Hensen, Manuscript Division, Library of Congress; Tom Hickerson, Cornell University; Charles Palm, Stanford University; and Nancy Sahli, National Historical Publications and Records Commission. For a detailed summary of the work of NISTF, see Richard Lytle, "An Analysis of the Work of the National Information Systems Task Force," *American Archivist* 47 (Fall 1984): 357–65.

Thus, NISTF had to address whether there was any substance in the long-standing dispute between "archivists" and "manuscript curators" over various matters of theory and practice. Towards this end, Elaine Engst conducted a thorough study of descriptive practices in a wide variety of repositories. Her unpublished report, "Standard Elements for the Description of Archives and Manuscript Collections,"[2] clearly demonstrates that there is no significant difference between the descriptive approaches of these two groups and that, in the words of Tom Hickerson, "there are common methods of archival description which could be integrated into a broadly applicable set of standards."[3] More importantly, however, Engst's report helped lay an essential foundation for the subsequent development of a unified data elements dictionary, which was the first step on the road to adapting the MARC format for the purpose of describing (or, more specifically, "cataloging") archives and manuscripts. At the time this work was going on, it was not altogether clear to the members of the task force that it was possible or desirable to describe these materials in the same systems used for describing other library materials, but it was already obvious that the superstructure used by the library community (the MARC formats) could easily be adapted to archival purposes. The result was the USMARC Format for Archival and Manuscripts Control (MARC AMC).[4]

NISTF also came to the crucial realization that the new superstructure must somehow accommodate multilevel archival hierarchy. There is nothing quite so sacred or central to an understanding of the archival worldview than the principle that the *fonds*, whether consisting of personal papers or government records, are essentially organic in nature, i.e., generated as the natural documentary byproduct of the activities or functions of corporate bodies or persons. From this flows the archival principle of provenance (also known as *respect des fonds*), which holds that the arrangement and description of these materials follows their original function, purpose, and order. Thus, for the archivist, the concept of multilevel description is deeply rooted. In 1964 Oliver Wendell Holmes defined five basic levels of archival arrangement and description—Depository, Record Group and Subgroup, Series, Filing Unit, and Document.[5] And until 1986, when Max Evans effectively destroyed the concept of record groups,[6] this system of hierarchically based levels had, according to Terry Abraham in 1991, achieved the status of "dogma" in the American archival profession.[7] This dogma was based on the essentially hierarchical nature of archives from which, according to Holmes, proceeded distinct descriptive and arrangement requirements inherent in these levels.

Recognizing that any structure that did not accommodate archival hierarchies or levels was both inadequate and doomed to failure, NISTF took a harder look at the MARC

---

[2]Elaine Engst, "Standard Elements for the Description of Archives and Manuscript Collections," unpublished report delivered to the National Information Systems Task Force, 1979.

[3]H. Thomas Hickerson, "Archival Information Exchange: Developing Compatibility," in *Academic Libraries: Myths and Realities, Proceedings of the Third National Conference of the Association of College and Research Libraries*, edited by Suzanne C. Dodson and Gary L. Menges (Chicago: Association of College and Research Libraries, 1984), 64.

[4]This section is based on an earlier article: Steven L. Hensen, "The Use of Standards in the Application of the AMC Format," *American Archivist* 49 (Winter 1986): 33.

[5]Oliver W. Holmes, "Archival Arrangement—Five Different Operations at Five Different Levels," *American Archivist* 27 (January 1964): 21–41.

[6]Max Evans, "Authority Control: An Alternative to the Record Group Concept," *American Archivist* 49 (Summer 1986): 249–61.

[7]Terry Abraham, "Oliver W. Holmes Revisited: Levels of Arrangement and Description in Practice," *American Archivist* 54 (Summer 1991): 371.

formats. There, in some relatively undeveloped fields, they discovered that the structures established to accommodate library analytics (i.e., description of a part of a larger work) were not only perfectly suitable for controlling archival hierarchy but were also, in their "part-to-whole" configuration, philosophically consistent with archival levels of description. This idea, while perfectly obvious now, was an epiphany at the time and paved the way for subsequent full development of the MARC AMC format and the full integration of archival description into heretofore strictly "bibliographic" systems. In the RLIN application of the USMARC AMC format, the Research Libraries Group fully implemented these "linking" fields, and they have become the very essence of effective description of archival material (particularly government records) within RLIN, providing a means to describe materials at any appropriate level while logically associating that description with that of other hierarchically related materials.

No matter how well-suited the MARC AMC format was to archival descriptive needs, it was, however, simply an empty vessel—a "data structure standard," as we now understand these things.[8] To make MARC AMC usable inside the framework within which most MARC records were created, a companion "data content standard" was also required. Once again, the forces of serendipity were at work for archivists, when the second edition of the *Anglo-American Cataloguing Rules (AACR2)* was published in 1978.

Archives, Personal Papers, and Manuscripts

Although the publication of *AACR2* cannot be said to have had much direct impact on the archival world, the archival response to it has been of major significance. Most of the archival world took little note of *AACR2,* but this was not the case in the Manuscript Division of the Library of Congress where I was then employed as Senior Manuscript Cataloger. As the Library of Congress was one of the principal partners in the development of *AACR2,* I was more or less obliged to use it. However, a brief review revealed that the rules were written with no obvious input from anyone in the manuscripts or (even more so) archives communities.

The specific problems which rendered *AACR2* essentially unusable for archival cataloging have been described elsewhere.[9] The Manuscript Division's response was to develop an alternate set of rules consistent with sound archival principles while retaining as much as possible the overall spirit and structure of *AACR2.* These alternate rules were subjected to a thorough review within the Library of Congress, as well as by an editorial committee drawn from the American archival community and by a number of other commentators from around the country. The result was the first edition of *Archives, Personal Papers, and Manuscripts* (*APPM*).[10]

---

[8]Distinctions such as these were first identified in an archival context through the work of the Working Group on Standards for Archival Description (WGSAD). The reports of this group can be found in *American Archivist* 52 (Fall 1989): 431–537 and in *Standards for Archival Description; A Handbook* (Chicago: Society of American Archivists, 1994).

[9]See, for example, Steven L. Hensen, "The Use of Standards in the Application of the AMC Format," 31–40 (from a paper delivered at the annual meeting of the Society of American Archivists, Washington, D.C., 1984) (also reprinted in *A Sourcebook on Standards Information: Education, Access, and Development,* edited by Steven M. Spivak and Keith A. Winsell (Boston: G.K. Hall, 1991); and Steven L. Hensen, "Squaring the Circle: The Reformation of Archival Description in AACR2," *Library Trends* 36 (Winter 1988): 539–52.

[10]Steven L. Hensen, *Archives, Personal Papers, and Manuscripts: A Cataloging Manual for Archival Repositories, Historical Societies, and Manuscript Libraries* (Washington, D.C., 1983) (hereafter *"APPM"*).

This manual, now in its second edition,[11] has been widely accepted by the American archival community as the standard for the cataloging of archives and manuscripts—especially in an automated environment. It is important to understand that this is *not* a manual of general archival description, nor is it a guide for the construction of archival finding aids (though its rules and principles are based upon the existence of such finding aids and upon a general presumption of standardized data elements).

APPM's success is based, first of all, on the fundamental premise that archival cataloging is simply one facet of a larger descriptive apparatus. As noted earlier, the preparation of a variety of internal descriptive finding aids is central to the mission of most archival repositories; no archives or manuscript repository could long survive without such tools, and this manual does not in any way supplant or replace that process. *APPM* clearly states that "in such a system, a catalog record created according to these rules is usually a summary or abstract of information contained in other finding aids."[12] This approach is based upon the assumption that, however effective traditional finding aids might be for describing and controlling our holdings, they are a cumbersome way to share information in a broader information retrieval environment which also includes nonarchival materials. If archival repositories were ever going to share data with the broader research community, summary descriptions, or cataloging records, were, at the time, the most effective way to do this.

Perhaps most important, however, is the fact that *APPM* assumes the legitimacy of archival material as part of the larger universe of cultural artifacts. The introduction to the first edition states:

> A fundamental and compelling rationale for this attempt to reconcile manuscript and archival cataloging and description with the conventions of *AACR2* lies in the burgeoning national systems for automated bibliographic description. If these systems, which are largely based on the descriptive formats for books and other library materials outlined in *AACR2*, are to ever accommodate manuscripts and archives a compatible format must be established. This manual is based on the assumption that, with appropriate modifications, library-based descriptive techniques can be applied in developing this format.[13]

Underpinning this is the conviction that it is both appropriate and desirable to catalog and describe archival materials as a part of those systems which describe more traditional library materials such as books, films, serials, maps, sound recordings, graphics, etc. It is thus now axiomatic from the point of view of access to research information that there are logical, vital, and inextricable relationships among all of these materials, and that it is important to show those relationships in a bibliographic context.

Thus, the acceptance of *APPM* is based upon the ways in which it synthesizes basic archival principles into the broader framework of bibliographic description, fine tuning that framework to transform it into a vehicle for specifically *archival* cataloging. This synthesis is based on four major principles:

---

[11]Steven L. Hensen, *Archives, Personal Papers, and Manuscripts: A Cataloging Manual for Archival Repositories, Historical Societies, and Manuscript Libraries*, 2d ed. (Chicago: Society of American Archivists 1989) (hereafter *"APPM2"*).

[12]*APPM2*, 4 (Rule 0.7).

[13]*APPM*, 1.

First, *APPM* recognizes the primacy of provenance in archival description. This principle holds that the significance of archival materials is heavily dependent on the context of their creation, and that arrangement *and description* should be directly related to the materials' original purpose and function. This results in an emphasis on the use of notes, since the complexities of substance and provenance cannot be captured in the sort of brief formulaic encryption that characterizes most bibliographic description. Moreover, the expanded use of notes is consistent with archival traditions of subjective analysis as an essential part of description.

The second principle embodied in *APPM* is that most archival material exists in collectivities or groupings, and that the appropriate focus of the control of such materials is at this collective level. While the practical effect of this is to relieve the archivist of the overwhelming burden of creating literally millions of item-level catalog records, it also supports the principle of archival unity, in which the significance of individual items or file units is measured principally by their relation to the collective whole of which they are a part. A corollary of this is that the most appropriate place for component-level description and analysis is within the archival finding aid, not the catalog record.

The third principle in *APPM* is that archival materials are generally preserved for reasons different from those for which they were created. They are the unself-conscious byproduct of various human activities and consequently lack "the formally presented identifying data that characterize most published items, such as author and title statements, imprints, production and distribution information, collations, etc. Personal or corporate responsibility for the creation of archival materials (another way of saying provenance) is generally inferred from, rather than explicitly stated in the materials."[14] Such identifying data is normally created by the archivist in the course of arranging and describing the material. The principal implication for cataloging is to legitimize traditional archival descriptive systems such as finding aids, guides, and registers as sources of cataloging data, and to move the cataloging process away from the literal transcription of information that characterizes most bibliographic description.

Fourth, *APPM* recognizes that there are "a number of appropriate levels of description for any given body of archival material. These levels normally correspond to natural divisions based on provenance or physical form."[15] Thus, the rules provide a framework for multilevel description, making it possible for archival catalogers to prepare consistent records regardless of the level of description. Given the overwhelming importance of hierarchy and provenance, this has been an essential feature of *APPM*, and one which recognizes the significance of NISTF's work to embed in MARC AMC the ability to accommodate multilevel description.

The superstructure provided by MARC AMC and *APPM* for the description and control of archival and manuscript materials would have remained an untested abstraction without some concrete evidence that it actually worked. As noted earlier, many archivists in the United States were still deeply suspicious of the library origins and essentially "bibliographic" structure of MARC AMC. Fortunately, however, even before NISTF had completely finished its work, several university libraries that were members of the Research Libraries Group were urging RLG and the National Endowment for the Humanities to support a project that would truly test the viability of this new approach. This early project

[14] *APPM2*, 5 (Rule 0.11).
[15] *APPM2*, 4-5 (Rule 0.12).

involving Yale, Cornell, and Stanford quickly proved not only to the archival community, but also to a skeptical RLG and the larger library world, that MARC AMC and *APPM* could be used successfully to integrate archival materials into heretofore strictly bibliographic databases.

Early Standards and EAD

While the history of MARC AMC and *APPM* may seem to have very little to do with SGML and archival finding aids, it seems clear that the foundation provided by these events directly enabled the Berkeley Finding Aid Project by providing the impetus for more archivists to begin exploring the broader world of related standards. Most archivists had survived for years in splendid, idiosyncratic isolation and, but for their homage to a few archival principles, saw no need to standardize the way they went about their business. What the experience of MARC AMC and *APPM* showed is that there was a real benefit in being able to communicate archival information—not only among archivists, but also with the larger world of historical scholarship and research. And perhaps most importantly, that archivists were much more closely allied with other information professionals such as librarians than they had realized.

In retrospect, it seems safe to say that few of us involved in these projects in the late 1970s and early 1980s would have predicted the eventual impact of our work. The task that NISTF had designed for itself was initially very simple; to wit, heading off a potentially unpleasant jurisdictional dispute between the *National Union Catalog of Manuscript Collections* and the repository guide project of the National Historical Publications and Records Commission. The fact that MARC AMC emerged from NISTF's deliberations was a result more of fundamental pragmatism on the part of the task force than any new vision of the future of archival description: it was easier to adapt the MARC format to our needs than it was to develop an entirely new system to underpin any archival ''national information system'' that might emerge.

Similarly, my own work in recasting *AACR2* to accommodate modern manuscript and archival cataloging was undertaken with rather more modest goals than those that ultimately resulted. Like NISTF, I was simply looking for a practical solution to what seemed like a relatively small problem; there was little sense that this solution would have wider application or appeal. In addition, though I am somewhat chagrined to confess it, there was also little sense of the vital connection between the work of these two projects. It was by the sheerest coincidence that they were roughly contemporaneous. Thus it was that the combined work of these efforts was presented before the world with a distinct sense of uncertainty and unease. The message of the film *Field of Dreams* notwithstanding, there was little assurance that anybody would come, no matter *what* was built.

These concerns ultimately were groundless. The development of the MARC AMC format and *APPM* has transformed the world of manuscripts and archives—certainly in this country, but also to an increasing extent in Canada, Western Europe, and even into Russia. There are over 475,000 records in RLIN alone from hundreds of repositories in the United States and Europe for previously elusive primary resources and special collections. More significantly, the integration of these materials into heretofore primarily *bibliographic* systems is now understood to have been a logical and necessary evolutionary step.

Moreover, these systems are gradually evolving into integrated research tools in which the entire range of cultural artifacts is both accommodated and encouraged, and where information is accessible without regard to the particular physical form that it might take. The world of research and scholarship has become increasingly interdisciplinary and less concerned with whether information is to be found in traditional printed and published forms or in archives, photographs, motion pictures, videotapes, computer files, or museum registers. It is now recognized that information of all kinds is part of a seamless web, and that service to research and scholarship is optimized when there are no artificial restrictions on the particular form that information takes.

As significant as these advances have been for the world of archives and manuscripts—and I wish in no way to minimize them; they have been spectacular—they have nonetheless been constrained by the limitations of the systems in which they have operated. The MARC format is a thirty-year-old database structure that provides a functional standard through which libraries and cultural repositories can communicate descriptive information. Given the relatively short half-life of more modern database systems, one can only wonder at either the foresight of the early developers of MARC or its stubborn durability in a world not given to easy or sudden changes of direction.

Taking the Next Steps

Is there anything wrong with this picture? Some would argue that this approach has endured because it is effective and serves us well. Several years ago, Richard Pearce-Moses responded to some statements I had been making on the LCSH-AMC listserv regarding the future of bibliographic description:

> I certainly don't expect to see the baby thrown out with the bath water. But I wonder how much the fundamental paradigms of description and access will really change. The format of description may (finally) evolve away from the card catalog style; yet, that style may have remained fairly constant because it's effective in the way it telegraphs information....Even the notion of hyperlinks to full text would not necessarily dictate change to the bibliographic description. At some point all those e-documents are going to be impossible to find, as would a library of several million volumes be useless without some guide. The bib[liographic] database is an abstraction of the documents, and we will continue to need abstraction to avoid having to search the entire haystack.[16]

Pearce-Moses is correct; we will still need pointers, or "metadata," to get to the information that resides within the collections of our cultural repositories, and cataloging of some sort may still be the way to do this. However, our current cataloging systems are ill-equipped to do this on two counts.

First, as noted above, these systems are based on an approach that focuses almost exclusively on the physical characteristics and manifestation of the thing being described. In a world in which bibliographic "items" or works increasingly exist in many different forms simultaneously, this seems curiously out of step. With our users increasingly demanding and expecting more precise content- and subject-oriented retrieval, an approach that ignores these demands seems suicidal.

Second, these systems are, as also noted earlier, unidimensional in that they are based upon the assumption that there is an object in a library and there is a descriptive

[16]Richard Pearce-Moses, "AACR2000," message to LCSH-AMC listserv, 3/10/95 3:39 P.M.

surrogate for that object, the cataloging record. That is the ''system'' in its entirety. The catalog record is used to locate a particular book, and the user, armed with call numbers and library locations, goes off in search of it, hoping (often against hope) that the book will be (a) on the shelf, and (b) contain relevant content.

With the recent explosion of Internet-based information, first via Gophers, then Wide Area Information Servers (WAIS), and now the World Wide Web, the disparity between what we *have* been doing and what we *should* be doing has become all the more acute and increasingly difficult to explain. This is particularly true as libraries become less concerned with managing physical holdings and focus more on connecting users with information—wherever that information might be and in whatever form it may exist. The catalog as a purely physical inventory has little relevance in this environment.

We must therefore reexamine not only the role of cataloging, but also the relationship between cataloging and other forms of metadata. A more archival model for cataloging and description is well suited to solving information access and retrieval problems in the new electronic environment. The reasons for this are rooted, not surprisingly, in the essential principles of archival cataloging touched upon earlier.

First, archival cataloging is almost always part of a larger apparatus of description, which includes a variety of finding aids, guides, registers, calendars, etc. Further, archival cataloging is both derived *from* and points *to* finding aids. These finding aids are not only a fundamental and long-standing part of archival practice; they also provide the basis for the understanding that it is neither practical nor desirable for a catalog record to carry the entire burden of description. The archival model, with its hierarchically assembled layers of progressively more detailed information, though postulated in electronic pre-history, is highly suggestive of the architecture of modern information systems. If the catalog record is redefined as a window or gateway to other dynamically linked information resources, then the structure of that record and the access points that lead to it may become something entirely different.

Second, in an archival approach focused on the context of creation, descriptive notes illuminate the complexities of substance and content, particularly as they relate to that context. This approach shifts the burden of description towards content, rather than physical characteristics, which as noted above are increasingly irrelevant in an electronic environment. In addition, by using a system of hierarchically structured metadata that can nevertheless be linked to the catalog record (as with the archival finding aid), it becomes easier to accommodate a richer system of subjective analysis.

Third, in an archival approach more focused on collection-level control, the burden for item-level information shifts to forms of metadata beyond the catalog record, whether finding aids, databases, or even subunit-level cataloging. Such an approach can even be used for cataloging large groups or collections of printed materials.

For example, in 1994 the Special Collections Library at Duke completed a Department of Education Title II-C funded project to catalog the 65,000-item Guido Mazzoni collection of eighteenth- and nineteenth-century Italian pamphlets and monographs which had lain essentially untouched since they were acquired in 1948. While there had been previous sporadic attempts to catalog the collection, the combination of its size, the variety of languages represented, and the fact that it was mostly pamphlets had defeated all attempts to bring it under control. This was particularly awkward, and occasionally embarrassing, since the Mazzoni collection is well-known and contains one of the larger collections of *per nozze*[17] known to exist in the world.

Our solution was to treat the collection archivally. Since Mazzoni had originally organized this material into large, generally subject-based groupings, we would create a series of collection-level cataloging records based on those categories following Library of Congress guidelines on collection-level cataloging of printed materials.[18] Item-level control was then provided in a separate non-MARC SGML database that would be linked to the collection-level MARC cataloging records.

This distinctly archival approach recognizes that, however bibliographically significant individual items within the collection might be, what is *most* important is the collection itself. Mazzoni assembled the material with specific purposes and focuses in mind and, to the best of our ability, we maintained the original structure in our processing and cataloging in a bibliographic approach to *respect des fonds.* In so doing, adequate access to this collection was provided without the necessity of preparing a full cataloging record for each piece.

Some will argue that certain kinds of research needs will not be met with this approach, that some scholars will be disappointed; this is no doubt true. However, this is what we could afford, and most importantly, at long last the entire collection is accessible.

A more archival approach to cataloging, such as was done with the Mazzoni collection and indeed is done every day with a wide variety of manuscript collections, archival records series, and more traditional archival materials, takes the very practical perspective of preferring limited access to *all* of a repository's holdings rather than detailed control over only some. Or at least this was the case until new network-oriented approaches to information access started to emerge. It is becoming increasingly clear that perhaps we can have our cake and eat it too.

Internet Access to Finding Aids

In the early 1990s archivists and special collections librarians began putting finding aids on networked servers where they could be accessed via the Gopher technology that had come out of the University of Minnesota. It seems likely that MARC AMC cataloging records existed for many of these materials in RLIN and OCLC. As useful as these cataloging records were, however, these archivists and librarians knew that the focus of their descriptive efforts was still—as it always had been—in the finding aids and guides that they prepared and upon which the cataloging records presumably were based. There were, however, two essential problems with these finding aid Gophers.

First, there was no way to logically or dynamically link the finding aids to their corresponding catalog records. A potential user, looking at a repository's on-line catalog

[17]The term ''per nozze'' comes from the phrase commonly found in the publication title of these pieces, ''per le nozze di...,'' which means ''for the wedding of...'' The custom of preparing a gift of verse or prose in honor of a couple's wedding originated with the Greeks, who called these wedding compositions ''epithalamia.'' This tradition continued to develop as a social custom and literary genre in modern times only in Italy, with the exception of a few known examples in France, Germany, and Russia. In Italy, the custom of dedicating verse or prose as a wedding gift began in the late fifteenth century among the nobility, and reached its peak in the nineteenth century, when it was very much in vogue among not only the nobility, but the bourgeoisie as well. See <http://scriptorium.lib.duke.edu/mazzoni/nozze.html>.

[18]''Collection-Level Cataloging at the Library of Congress,'' *Library of Congress Information Bulletin* (9 September 1991) and *Cataloging Service Bulletin,* No. 53 (Summer 1991).

(often via a telnet connection) would have to exit the catalog and then log onto the Gopher site to see if a finding aid was there.

Second, the Gophers consisted principally of lengthy text files that were very awkward (and occasionally impossible) to search in any meaningful or structured manner. If the file was accessible via WAIS software, there might be a marginally more robust searching engine, but overall, Gophers were scant improvement over writing to a repository and requesting a photocopy of a finding aid.

Daniel Pitti recognized the essential inadequacy of this Gopher/WAIS-oriented approach to archival metadata when he embarked upon the Berkeley Finding Aid Project, the results of which fit smoothly with and build upon the archival standards and information systems developed in earlier years.

In the early days of RLIN's MARC AMC database there were some interesting attempts to enter entire finding aids into the system, but it didn't take long to realize that not only was MARC ill-suited to the level of detail traditionally found in those finding aids, but also that these huge "pseudo-cataloging" records were totally out of proportion to other records in the system and constituted a somewhat intimidating, if not irritating, presence. The records failed to reflect cataloging's purpose as "summary description."[19] Other institutions entered their entire finding aids into the system on a piecemeal basis, adding a separate record for each item; this approach usually fails to comprehend the "significance of the whole."[20] Neither technique reflects the essentials of archival description or cataloging.

To archivists' credit, however, these attempts do reflect our fundamental impulse to make more detailed information on archival holdings more widely accessible. That the MARC format is not particularly effective in accommodating this need helped spawn the impulse on which Pitti's project was based.

It seems useful to note that there are rough parallels between the work of the Berkeley Finding Aid Project in defining an SGML Document Type Definition (DTD) for archival finding aids and the work that Elaine Engst began in the survey of archival descriptive practice that led to the NISTF data elements dictionary. In NISTF's case, that data dictionary became the foundation for constructing the elements of the MARC AMC format. EAD, however, defines the larger universe of finding aid data elements that are at the very heart of archival description.

If this were the only point of Pitti's project, there would have been no need to invoke the power and complexity of SGML. Where NISTF separately developed the data dictionary and MARC AMC and then waited to see whether these instruments could or would be used, the EAD project is combining all these processes together. Document definition, structure (according to an already established standard), and navigational tools are all inherently part of the SGML encoding protocols.

The EAD project has had the benefit of learning from NISTF's experience but has also had the advantage of actually defining itself using the very essence of archival hierarchy: the organic hierarchy of the materials themselves as reflected in the finding aids that describe them. Beyond this, however, EAD has the potential to provide for an unprecedented level of structural hierarchy within the overall descriptive apparatus. By this I mean that it is now possible to fully realize the entirety of that apparatus within our

[19] *APPM2*, 4 (rule 0.7).
[20] *APPM2*, 5 (rule 0.10).

evolving electronic information systems so that the unbroken hierarchy of information is accessible from a single point: from the most general access point in a system, to MARC catalog records, to finding aids, to details within those finding aids, and ultimately—if desired—to linked files of digital images of actual collection materials. The catalog records are already available and, as MARC field 856[21] evolves, so too does the capacity to link those catalog records with related information resources on the Internet. What was most critically and obviously missing in this structure is precisely that which EAD provides: a way to encode those layers of metadata (i.e., the finding aids) that have traditionally existed between description at its most summary and general level and the archival material itself. In addition to providing a mechanism for this linkage, this encoding makes possible a level of navigation that was heretofore unimaginable.

Conclusion

As noted earlier, those involved in the early days of archival standards development had little conception of the eventual impact of that work. A process that started with NISTF defining a set of descriptive elements and mapping those elements into a bibliographic information communications format has now culminated in a project that has further refined and defined those elements, taking the entire apparatus onto a higher plane. The principal difference between then and now is in our expectations. Because of recent advances in technology and the evident direction of those advances, we now have a much clearer sense of the possible. More than that, however, we now have the confidence and courage to project beyond the possible and to realize that our dreams of a truly "seamless web" of information can be realized. It is particularly gratifying to realize that this model appears to have broader applicability to the larger world of cultural repositories and libraries.

Those of us in the archives and manuscripts field have only recently and belatedly come to a fuller understanding of our role in this larger world—especially in the new networked electronic environment. While some of this understanding has come from within our profession, we have also relied on the perspective, goodwill, and assistance of those in the library, museum, and computer systems fields. From RLG's willingness to accommodate the unique needs of archival description in order to develop a more complete cultural information system, to the Library of Congress' assistance in the development of *APPM* and the MARC AMC format, there is a recent history of important furtherance from outside organizations and individuals that have contributed significantly towards our professional evolution. The development of Encoded Archival Description is the most recent example of such assistance and may well be regarded by future generations as one of the most important.

[21]USMARC field 856, "Electronic Location and Access," is designed to provide an electronic address (e.g., a URL or ftp address) for a digital representation of the material or item described in the catalog record or to additional information about the material or item. "The information identifies the electronic location containing the resource or from which it is available. It also contains information to retrieve the resource by the access method identified in the first indicator position. . . . The information contained in this field is sufficient to allow for the electronic transfer of a file, subscription to an electronic journal, or logon to an electronic resource" <http://lcweb.loc.gov/marc/bibliographic/ecbdhold.html#mcrb856>.

CHAPTER 3

Navigation, Access, and Control Using Structured Information

STEVEN J. DeROSE

Introduction

WHEN THIS CHAPTER WAS originally prepared as a paper for presentation at the Berkeley Finding Aid Conference, held on April 4–6, 1995, only a few hardy souls were experimenting with encoding archival finding aids into SGML (Standard Generalized Markup Language[1]). This work used a preliminary Document Type Definition then known as the "FindAid" DTD. Since then, archivists have developed a polished tool, Encoded Archival Description (EAD). This SGML application is seeing rapidly growing use for encoding finding aids and making them available in electronic form. The author counts it a privilege to have been invited to help in some of this work (and to have been so kindly received as an immigrant to the field). The chapter presented here has been updated to address more recent events such as the completion of the EAD DTD and the appearance of XML, but otherwise it is much as it was in 1995.

What is Structure, Anyway?

Structured information is information that is *analyzed.* Not in the sense that a Sherlock Holmes should peer at it and discern hidden truth (although for some information such as ancient texts, something much like that may happen), but rather in the sense that the information is divided into component parts, which in turn have components, and so on. Only when information has been divided up by such an analysis, and the parts and relationships have been identified, can computers process it in useful ways. The choices made during this analysis are crucial; the most crucial point to be emphasized is that *how you divide up your data does matter.*

There are many models of analysis. Among the most trivial, and in my opinion least useful, is this: "a document is a list of pages." Moving in both directions from this attitude, utility increases. The domain of most concern in the context of EAD is of larger scope, involving the division and organization of recorded knowledge. Without such or-

---

N.B. "Navigation, Access, and Control Using Structured Information," by Steven J. DeRose, co-published simultaneously in the *American Archivist* (The Society of American Archivists) vol. 60, no. 3, pp. 298–309; and *Encoded Archival Description: Context, Theory, and Case Studies* (ed.: Jackie M. Dooley) The Society of American Archivists, 1998.

[1]International Organization for Standardization, ISO 8879: 1986(E). *Information Processing—Text and Office Information Systems—Standard Generalized Markup Language.*

ganization, our libraries and archives would become mere collections, inaccessible, and in the end, unusable. If we move downward in scope, a similar phenomenon occurs: As progressively finer levels of analysis are made conscious, explicit, and accessible, the range of a document's uses increases.

This is what is meant by "structured documents" and "structured information": information whose parts identify themselves, making them accessible to human and computer processing.

Form vs. Content

One can choose which parts of a document to identify based on many possible conceptual models.[2] Perhaps the first important choice is whether the goal is to represent the *form* of some data or information, or some particular "meta-" information *about* the content, or the *content* itself. This choice is fundamental and has radical consequences for what can be done with the resulting information.

On paper, form and content are partly intertwined (or as Ted Nelson has said, "intertwingled"[3]). The typographic conventions of our culture, added to our knowledge of the natural language of documents (sometimes properly linguistic, sometimes graphical or otherwise semiotic), permit us to identify the content parts of books explicitly, with consequent advantages.[4] Computer tools are notoriously bad at identifying content parts when given only form, while being superb at the opposite transformation. For example, it is trivial for a computer to render both book titles and emphasis using italics; this makes for no conflict and requires no artificial intelligence. On the other hand, given two italic portions of a text, computers will fail miserably in distinguishing a book title from emphasis.

Because of this inherent asymmetry, moving into a world of computerized information requires that we undertake the work of making content structures explicit. Without this step, we have not, in fact, moved the information to a new medium; we have merely made an electronic photocopy. Photocopiers are immensely useful, of course, but my point is this: one can do no more with a photocopy than with the original. Certain important gains can be made, such as increasing access while preserving the original from excessive handling, or creating multiple copies for security, or even providing disposable copies for special uses. "Electronic photocopies" add the advantage of inexpensive distribution via networks. But, as I stated, once someone obtains a copy, they can do no more with it than with the original.

In our move to the future, we must make it possible to do *more* with our documents. Only by representing the structure of the content, not merely the form of its expression in a prior medium, can we achieve the level of function necessary if we are to manage the exponential growth of information effectively.

---

[2]For further analysis of document representation models and their characteristics, see Steven J. DeRose, David G. Durand, Elli Mylonas, and Allen H. Renear, "What is Text, Really?" *Journal of Computing in Higher Education* 1, no. 2 (1990): 3–26.

[3]Ted Nelson, *Computer Lib*, rev. ed. (Redmond, Wash.: Tempus Books of Microsoft Press, 1987).

[4]James H. Coombs, Allen H. Renear, and Steven J. DeRose, "Markup Systems and the Future of Scholarly Text Processing," *Communications of the Association for Computing Machinery* 30 (November 1987): 933–47.

Identifying Component Parts and Relationships

Information professionals have names for the many parts that make up document and other information structures. For example, a quick examination of the *Chicago Manual of Style*[5] reveals many such names, since its purpose is to explain how to represent the components of structured content using typographic form.

When creating new information, it is relatively easy to identify the types of content objects. Authors can state authoritatively what their intent is as they place a given content object such as a paragraph, a quotation, a line of poetry, or an axiom. Indeed, they must identify the objects at least implicitly before they can choose a word-processor action to express it. At times authors may be unconscious of these choices, and that is fine—literary works are often held, in retrospect, to be most significant and meaningful at levels their authors may never have consciously considered. Nevertheless, authors' choices of structure are our key source of information about their work, and this holds at all levels, from the phonological and grammatical to the treatment of chapters, indexes, and the like.

When dealing with preexisting information, we do not have the luxury of being its author: we can only do our best to discern structure and meaning from what we have. We can look for clues to structure in typography (these are often very clear), but we may also wish to find structures that are completely implicit or that are obscured by neutralization. For example, when the *Oxford English Dictionary* was converted into a structured electronic document, researchers found roughly twenty distinct uses for italics;[6] only by the painstaking task of teasing etymologies apart from Latin cognates apart from literary examples, and so on, was the result made truly useful. At a subtler level, one may wish to explicate structures that are hypotheses: a literary critic may claim that some passage constitutes an allusion to *Paradise Lost.* The validity of such a claim normally remains debatable, but explicit structure is a way to express the claim itself.

The key innovation required to move forward is that we must choose truly useful structures and make them explicit. The structure will be there anyway, but using it must remain a purely manual task unless it is made explicit through document markup.

Why Do We Need Structure?

Structure is Really There

Structure is in our documents. We cannot avoid it, though we can choose what kind to use in any situation. Authors think in terms of linguistic discourse and other structures while writing, though much of this activity becomes automatic with practice. We also use structure constantly in navigating the information we have. Finding aids have a great deal of structure, which is created by archivists through careful design.

We often make use of structure unconsciously. Examine any document and structure leaps off the page: lists, figures, footnotes and the like are pervasive. As documents grow larger, explicit structure-aware tools start to appear: indexes reflect the thematic or topical structure, tables of contents reflect the broad-stroke discourse or organizational structure, and bibliographies reveal something of the referential or link structure. In reference works,

---

[5]University of Chicago Press, *The Chicago Manual of Style*, 13th ed., 1982.

[6]Frank W. Tompa, "What is (tagged) text?" *Dictionaries in the Electronic Age: Proceedings of the Fifth Annual Conference of the UW Centre for the New Oxford English Dictionary* (Waterloo, Ont.: University of Waterloo Centre for the New OED, 1989), 81–93.

such as those of particular interest in the context of archival finding aids, structure is even more important. Without carefully designed subject categories, levels of organization and description, and other structural techniques, navigation in large information spaces bogs down.

Structure Provides a Way to Name Things

Raising the component parts of information to the level of explicit representation often leads to giving them names. As Ursula LeGuin reminds us, "the name is the thing, and the true name is the true thing. To speak the name is to control the thing."[7] Nowhere is this truer than in the realm of information.

Navigation requires naming, as does access whether by database, catalog, finding aid, or hypertext link. Choosing the right names for information units is perhaps the most crucial issue facing the electronic document community today. We have spoken already of type-names, which identify what manner of thing a thing is. Let us now turn to instance-names, which identify specific individuals: not X is *a* book or quotation or word or link, but X is *that* book, or *that* quotation, or *that* word, or *that* link.

Imagine for a moment that we lacked such names for information units: what if there were no chapter, section, or even page divisions for authors to reference? This is almost inconceivable at the level of whole documents: a book without a title will be given one or will die a quiet death. But what of internal components? Ancient texts lacked internal names, and the important works have been forced to acquire them. One can hardly find a modern Bible printed without chapter and verse divisions, and the same is true for scholarly editions of most classical works. Manuscripts often lack such internal cues, making the texts before us that much more complex.

For recent works we resort to page numbers for cross-reference; for example, "see page 37 of Smith (1995)." This is possible because the number of copies whose pagination matches is very high; many books never achieve a second edition, or even a second printing. But for those that do, the use of page numbers poses a problem that brings us back to structure: *page numbers break.* This is obvious, but easily forgotten:

- A large-print edition cannot be published without either making the pages physically huge and unwieldy or making the page numbers inconsistent and therefore useless for edition-independent reference. This is inherent with pre-formatted data, and is easily seen in most word processors: one cannot narrow the window without clipping off the end of every line.
- Even a tiny change to the content may break all later page numbers, and such effects are cumulative.

Why do these things happen? It is simply because pages are not structural units in literature. They are certainly structural units in the far different domain of typography, but typography is not our context of interest. A book is "the same" if reprinted from quarto to octavo and from Garamond 24 to Times 12 in all but a few senses.

Precisely the same issue affects reference tools such as finding aids. What if the only names for things were chosen from a space that itself had little structure? For example, imagine a library organized and accessed solely by ISBN or acquisition number, or a

[7]Ursula LeGuin, "The Rule of Names," in *A Treasury of Fantasy: Heroic Adventures in Imaginary Lands* (New York: Avenal Books, 1981), 495–504.

finding aid lacking levels of organization. While the presence of names would enable minimal access, a radical loss in functionality would be inevitable.

Structure vs. the Alternatives

The careful choice and use of structural elements, together with the careful assignment of systematic element names, provide the tools required to navigate the vast information-spaces that are just around the corner.

Many proposals have been made to utilize only the notion of pages in the electronic world. The most naive form may be ''Just scan everything in LC and drop it on the net.'' A few years ago one heard the same theory, but suggesting optical disk jukeboxes, and before that, microfilm. Such approaches, even ignoring obvious feasibility problems, would not truly achieve the benefits expected of a new medium. Unstructured data forms such as the bitmap are merely new kinds of papyrus on which to make copies: highly useful but purely a quantitative, incremental change. This path can never lead to the new world of navigable, accessible information space that we hope to attain. It carries over most weaknesses of the paper medium, while failing to retain paper's compensating strengths.

This is because a scanned image does not contain explicit structural information that can be used to support computer processing that could add value. For example, one could build an ''electronic catalog'' by simply scanning three by five cards and then saving the bitmaps without performing optical character recognition. Such a catalog could be ''on-line'' and would have the advantage of being easily copied, backed up, and transported. But imagine using it!

The next step up from mere pictures of information was once very popular: the ''plain ASCII text file'' sings the Siren song of portability and is indeed more amenable to machine processing than a bitmapped page. It can be word-searched or mailed around, and nearly any software can at least display it. But to put the seeming advantages into perspective, one must also consider the costs. For example, many important information structures cannot be represented in ''plain ASCII,'' including:

- *Foreign languages*: Any characters not in the very restricted set used by English, such as French accented vowels, not to mention the deeper difficulties of Greek, Hebrew, and Japanese.
- *Footnotes*: Where do you put them, in-line, or at the bottom of the page, or at the end of the book? How are they identified as footnotes in the first place?
- *Running headers* and any other constructs where information recurs, or appears without being part of the ''actual'' text, or appears out of order.
- *Graphics*, charts, and other nontextual information.

Beyond these obvious limitations lies a subtler problem: ''plain ASCII'' files often use idiosyncratic conventions to represent information about structure. For example, block quotes may be indented by adding spaces before each line, or titles may be indicated by adding enough spaces to ''center'' them. Such conventions can add potential for more useful functionality, but such a file is no longer ''plain ASCII.'' Some of the characters are no longer just characters: they have become markup, or ''metadata,'' giving information *about* the text. The main difference between such conventions and true markup is that the conventions are inconsistent and undocumented. Many interesting and desirable electronic texts are freely available in ''plain ASCII,'' but a closer look sometimes reveals that these texts are not all they claim to be.

- *Gaps* are often present, such as a missing chapter (possibly due to copyright problems, but that is another set of issues).
- *The source edition* often is not identified (after all, it's not "part of the text"). Identifying the source text can be a formidable task in documenting archival materials, and so it is essential that provenance information be retained (and marked up) when it *does* exist.
- *Footnotes*, graphics, accented characters, sidebars, and other display elements are often missing or misplaced.
- *Page and other references* are lost with no provision of a substitute, so important tools such as indexes, tables of contents, and cross-references are either deleted or useless.
- *Typographic nuances* such as emphasis are lost, even though they may be crucial to understanding the text. For example, I recently read a magazine article on world hunger which included the sentence "World hunger is not *a* problem" with the "a" in italics. The point, of course, was that hunger is a complex of many problems, from the biological to the political. Keep the "a" and delete the italics as "plain ASCII" must do, and the meaning changes radically: "World hunger is not a problem."
- *The lowly spacebar* attempts to carry the full load of representation, leading to insoluble ambiguity such as a title that happens to be long enough that "centering" it indents it exactly as if it were a paragraph. How do you tell what you've got?

Pity the scholar who analyzes such a text, or the cataloger who tries to identify it. *The names we need are missing.* In LeGuin's terms, we do not know the true name and so cannot control the thing. And if, as in her story, we should magically learn the true name, we find to our pain that the thing we name is not what we thought—not an unassuming local wizard, but a dragon in disguise.

Structure Provides Handles for Searching

My final point about the need for structure is that structure facilitates searching. Only if component parts are explicitly identified can we search for information *in some particular part.* This is why a database of personnel records is better than a list typed into a word processor. In a database, one can search for "Jones" as a name but not a street, or for "401" as an area code but not a street number. Likewise, no one could sell a personnel database where a search for numbers ">10" could not specify whether this refers to a "salary" or "month of hire." And in my favorite example from one on-line library catalog, it is painful to search for the journal titled simply *Linguistics* if you cannot avoid all the materials indexed under "Linguistics" as a subject. Such cases are so obvious that we may hardly think of them as "structure," but as full-text documents are put on-line, the same issues and tradeoffs apply. If we do not represent structure within documents, we cannot do the kinds of processing we increasingly want to do.

Many finding aids occupy a typological middle ground between databases at one end (especially simple flat-form databases, or the more complex and heterogeneous databases such as MARC) and typical documents at the other. This makes finding aids even more complex and in need of careful design than many other data structures. This continuum from simple flat-form databases to highly structured document bases raises the issue of what kinds of structure to represent. As we move from catalogs and abstracts toward finding aids and eventually to full content, correlating the levels of information and using levels and structure to increase ease of use will continue to grow in importance.

What Kinds of Structure Are Needed?

Basic Kinds of Data

I would like to suggest a few basic kinds of structured information, ranging from *forms* at one extreme to *documents* at the other, and then to argue that certain reference materials ranging from MARC records to finding aids fall along the continuum in between. I do not think that finding aids fall cleanly into either extreme: I think that because of their intermediate nature, they have both advantages and difficulties not present at either extreme. First, let us consider forms, such as those we all fill out from time to time on a sheet of paper with little boxes or in a relational database (RDB). Form or tabular data has these central characteristics:

1. *Many instances* of the same group of information items—that is, many copies of the same form. Particular instances of a form may have some items left blank, but if there are many such items we suspect a bad form, because not all instances are comparable. Likewise, explanatory notes about such variations are considered signs of a bad form.
2. *Order is not important* to the meaning, although the information on a form is inevitably presented in some order. The order of the instances of a form is also irrelevant. For example, the order in which employment applications appear in a paper or computer file is generally irrelevant. Perhaps "who filled out the form first" matters, but that is quite a different issue.
3. A form's *context is not part of its meaning.* More concretely, taking one instance of a form out from among its fellows does not change its meaning. This is crucial to the way in which form databases work: a report or the result of a search is a list of form instances isolated from their fellows; each makes full sense independently of the others.
4. Forms also involve a subtle notion of the *identity of information.* If two forms are filled out exactly the same, they are indistinguishable for all processing purposes: they are *the same.* This is why companies assign customer and order numbers, and why it is so troublesome when the same number is accidentally assigned twice.
5. Items on a form have *little hierarchy,* which is to say that there tend to be few item/subitem relationships. A person may have both home and business addresses, each with several parts, and it would be wrong to mix the street address of one's home with the zip code of one's business, but such examples are few and are provided explicitly. Forms cannot have unbounded repetitions of structured subparts.

Documents, at the other extreme, have quite a different pattern regarding the same central characteristics:

1. *Few instances* of a given sequence of pieces of information; for example, it is pure coincidence if two books have the same number of chapters and sections. It is odd to think of a book or article leaving certain structural elements blank, such as chapter one—even a nonstructural unit such as a page is amusing if it is "intentionally left blank" on paper, and is absurd on-line. Likewise, "explanatory notes" such as footnotes, sidebars, and digressions are the norm in documents.
2. Unlike information stored as forms, the *serial order* of most information in a document matters to the meaning. It matters greatly which paragraph comes

first,[8] and this poses a deep performance problem in the relational database model so useful for other kinds of data. An RDB would typically store each paragraph (or section, or other unit of text) as a record, and records are by definition unordered. To produce the correct order, serial numbers must be added. The RDB must select records with serial numbers in a certain range (likely a slow operation) and then *sort* them. This is wasted effort if, as with documents, a single basic order is almost always needed, yet must be reconstructed over and over. A database model that *preserves* order saves all this work.

3. *Context* matters regarding information in documents. While for form data, taking one instance out from among its fellows does not change its meaning, the opposite is clearly true for document data. This too is crucial to the way in which document bases work: The result of a search is not a list of small components isolated from their fellows, but a component *in its context.* Some time ago a document query language was proposed that lacked this key feature. In it, a query for all occurrences of the word ''sower'' would get sower, sower, sower, etc. What one must have is the list of where ''sower'' occurs, so as to navigate to those places and examine the context.
4. Unlike forms, two *identical objects* in a document are not necessarily the same. It is possible for a word, a sentence, or even a paragraph to be repeated in a document, and if this happens, the repetition matters. These repeated instances do not duplicate each other.
5. Finally, while forms have little *hierarchy*, layers upon layers of substructure are a hallmark of documents. This characteristic is even more pronounced in finding aids than in most other documents.

Forms and documents differ radically on all these fundamental axes. My conclusion is that different tools and methods must be applied in the two domains, and indeed the history of document processing systems has (with some digressions) followed this course.

Where do finding aids fit in? I believe they share some characteristics of both categories, and this may make them particularly complex. A finding aid must include a great deal of information about content, since that is what one is trying to find. Some meta-information in finding aids can be reduced to something resembling forms; in one sense, a finding aid is similar to a MARC record: a large though typically sparse list of fields. But there is more going on. MARC fields do have interdependencies, they do have levels (a colleague working on the John Carter Brown Library's bibliography of European Americans ended up dividing author names into something like twenty subcomponents and three or four levels). But finding aids have a much more detailed and complex hierarchy, and so presumably must go even further.

A finding aid must provide access based not only on demographic information—author, title, subjects, added entries, and a host of other fields—in addition, it must make

[8]Information order is central to hypertext theory, though Ted Nelson's definition of hypertext as ''non-sequential writing'' seems to contradict this. I take Nelson's definition to mean writing that is not *strictly* sequential: not locked into a single sequence as imposed by the paper or film medium. Authors instead give their readers many choices—this is precisely where poor hypertext systems and documents most frequently fail. Yet even the most labyrinthine hypertext is highly sequential. Even Faulkner must make some passages prerequisite to others. So while hypertext goes radically beyond the idea of a *single* sequence or even a small number, it does not overcome time, language, and cognition. This is why authors carefully craft hypertext links, rather than merely having a computer draw and quarter the texts.

use of characteristics of the content itself. What is this collection or group of records about? What school of thought from the discipline does it represent? What does it relate to in other disciplines?

There is especial benefit in being able to determine relationships as yet unnoticed or unremarked. Markup that identifies relevant content and structure facilitates such a discovery process by making explicit many of the basic facts upon which conclusions about relationships are based. One approach to this is the preparation of abstracts, and this has proven very useful. Another is the application of statistical methods to vocabularies and word frequencies, now well understood. But the ultimate answer, I believe, comes from making whole documents available with as much structure as possible explicitly represented. This is the true information, labeled by true names, from which abstracts and statistics come.

Particulars of Document Structure

How then do we represent useful structure? Many parts are obvious, and, within the hard constraints of time and budgets, we should represent as many of them as possible.

First, almost all documents include various *generic component parts*: PARAGRAPH, LIST-ITEM, QUOTE, TITLE, EMPHASIS, FOREIGN, IMAGE, and the like. Even rudimentary software can help locate such parts, because they map almost one-to-one to word processor or scanner objects. Reasonably skilled yet not scholarly workers can identify them quite reliably, even when software cannot.

Second, there are various *generic aggregates*: BOOK, CHAPTER, SECTION, FRONT-MATTER, LIST, TABLE. For historical reasons, however, typical software gives no help with these. We have all suffered from word processors not knowing what a "list" is and failing to number items correctly, not keeping numbers up to date, or forcing us to reselect each list each time we add or delete an item, all because the software can't remember any unit larger than a single paragraph. We suffer the same pain when we want to move, delete, or otherwise deal with sections and chapters. Add-on outliners help, but most word processors lack structural knowledge and instead use heuristics (such as "Find the next paragraph of type HEADING-2, and assume everything between is the current SECTION") that are both slow and unreliable.

Third, each genre, from poetry to manuals to finding aids, requires *specialized objects*: STANZA, REPAIR-PROCEDURE, AXIOM, PART-NUMBER, CATALOG-CODE. Identifying the right ones for finding aids is a crucial step, requiring ongoing research. A closed set of elements cannot be established once and for all, just as the list of defined subject headings for literature cannot be defined once and for all. The Berkeley Finding Aid Project undertook this task with zeal, and the EAD tag set that has been developed based on a large corpus of finding aids promises many advances in the portability and accessibility of such information.

Fourth, there is ever-increasing need for *access tools*: these range from the ubiquitous footnote and sidebar to cross-references, bibliographies, and the like. Use of paper documents necessitated other navigation tools as well, such as indexes and tables of contents, and of course these components should be represented. Most of these access tools can be expressed on-line as one or another type of hypertext link: any such reference should be linked to its source, as should any quotation. As referenced documents change through critical editing or a rewrite by a living author, the user may wish quotations to be dynamically updated. HTML and the Web have made one very basic type of hypertext link and one kind of name (the URL) ubiquitous, yet there remain many other and more powerful types of linking and locating, now coming into mainstream use through efforts such as the Extensible Linking Language (XLL), part of the Web Consortium's XML effort.[9]

Some phenomen a evident in printed texts are not structural units that need to be identified for most purposes. Line breaks, discretionary hyphens, font and other typographic choices, and the like usually are not structural except insofar as they may serve to communicate some other structures. This is precisely why electronic delivery methods that closely mimic paper have problems: they transfer ephemera and accidents of typesetting with as much primacy as they accord the very words and structure of a document, even though such accidents usually are liabilities rather than advantages in the electronic medium. The most obvious example is font size, which can safely be far smaller in print than on-line, yet must be slavishly followed in any page-fidelity-driven approach.

How to Decide What's Structure?

When planning an encoding project, two primary questions are "What structures are of interest?" and "Which are to be encoded?" *How* structures are encoded is important, but strictly less so than the *fact* that they are encoded. Any encoding project faces economic as well as intellectual decisions, and I will not address how to decide which things *not* to encode when finances are limited; this depends on the goals and usage scenarios envisioned for the data. My normal advice on the subject is that within the constraints of budget, encode anything likely to be of independent use later. Here are a few specific diagnostic questions to ask about a component under consideration for structural markup:

- Does it survive reformatting the document?
- Is it useful for multiple purposes?
- Would an author or reader have a name for it?
- Might someone want to search for it specifically, or constrain text searches to it alone?
- Does it surround, fill, or associate with other particular units?

This list clearly is biased toward conceptual units at the expense of the merely typographic, in keeping with the state of the art in document encoding. Deciding which structures to encode is, fortunately, not an embryonic field, nor is the use of particular structural representations such as SGML and its offspring XML. There is much good work to build upon, such as that of the Text Encoding Initiative (TEI),[10] Encoded Archival Description, and many other projects in varied domains.

How Does SGML Fit the Bill?

SGML is the best choice for encoding conceptual structural units in documents. It has two crucial advantages: First, SGML imposes no fixed set of component types. You can define the structures as appropriate for the task at hand. At the Center for Electronic Texts in the Humanities (CETH) *Workshop on Documenting Electronic Texts* held in 1994, one of the speakers expressed some doubt as to whether SGML was flexible enough to provide a complete equivalent to MARC (that is, an alternative representation of all the

[9]For more information on XML see <http://www.w3.org/TR/WD-xml>.

[10]C. Michael Sperberg-McQueen and Lou Burnard, eds., *Guidelines for Electronic Text Encoding and Interchange* (Chicago, Oxford: Text Encoding Initiative, 1994). Also available on-line from ftp://ftp-tei.uic.edu/pub/tei and many other places, most of which are pointed to from http://www.sil.org/sgml/acadapps.html#tei (part of Robin Cover's extensive SGML information guide).

same data). By the next coffee break, three of the SGML experts present had drafted DTDs (hardly polished of course, but sufficient proofs of concept).[11]

Second, SGML is a public, nonproprietary standard that will not change with each new release of a company's software. Software vendors conform to SGML, rather than SGML and an individual's data having to conform to particular software vendors. This is what justifies confidence that SGML data will survive for the long term, beyond any current software used to process it.

Third, SGML provides a very direct representation of data. As with HTML, other SGML can be read even with *no* specialized software; there is no binary hash, interpretable only by intermediary software. This contributes greatly to data longevity, even though it slightly complicates SGML's means of representing nonhierarchical structures such as links. So are there any downsides to SGML? Only a few. To some it may seem problematic that SGML requires more thought about the data. OCR and proofreading are no longer the end of the data integrity story, but the work must continue into making sometimes difficult decisions about the nature of your data. I consider this an upside: it does require extra effort, but the effort generally pays off.

The main downside to SGML is that it provides too many options: alternative syntax, abbreviation conventions, and the like. Few people bother to learn them all. Fortunately, such options are just that—options. Many do not add functionality or capability, merely alternative methods, and so any project can simply choose to avoid them. Thus most SGML experts have adopted what has come to be called a "monastic" approach—"just say no" to any features you don't need.

This is precisely the strategy that the Extensible Markup Language (XML) uses. XML has all the extensibility and representative power of SGML, but without the syntactic complexity. For example, implementing an XML parser requires roughly a week's work, rather than a year's; this allows the focus to shift from technical implementation details to data analysis, which has more value in the long term. The other "X*L" standards, XLL and XSL, achieve similar grand simplifications of existing standards for hypermedia linking and for stylesheets.

Summary

Great progress has been made in the last decade in shifting electronic information from purely format-driven forms to more processable, flexible, structure-driven forms. Processable finding aids are one of the next logical steps as archivists strive to progress from information about the *form* of documents toward treating documents themselves as sophisticated information objects. At each stage, what the computer can do with data depends most importantly on the model applied to the data. A simple facsimile of a manuscript or other object is useful but it does not enable qualitatively new processing, just as a microfilm copy of a card catalog is useful but not revolutionary.

In designing new models for electronic data, it is important to consider where traditional models such as the relational database do and do not fit. In examining several basic properties of relational data versus documents in general, it becomes clear that the "fit" is questionable. Newer technologies are needed, and new design questions need to

[11]Lisa R. Horowitz, *CETH Workshop on Documenting Electronic Texts, May 16–18,* 1994, *Radisson Hotel, Somerset, N.J.*, Technical Report #2 (New Brunswick, N.J.: Center for Electronic Texts in the Humanities, 1994).

be researched and solved. It is also increasingly important to create, manage, search, and maintain ''metadata'' (information about other data). Metadata comes in many forms, from PICS ratings of Web page appropriateness, to cataloging information, to critical reviews and commentaries. Standards for representing such metadata for Internet use are a very recent and interesting development.

SGML provides a generic way of representing document structure models, and of representing documents and other data given those models. Because SGML is a formal standard and has achieved widespread and diverse use, it is a safe long-term vessel for important data. As with many standards, a streamlined approach to SGML, such as XML, enhances portability, durability, and interoperability by attaining the freedom of simplicity.

CHAPTER 4

Encoded Archival Description: A Structural Overview

JANICE E. RUTH

Introduction

AFTER DEVELOPING HIS FIRST Document Type Definition (DTD) for archival finding aids, Daniel Pitti bravely assembled a group of seven archivists and one expert in Standard Generalized Markup Language (SGML) in July 1995 to critique and revise his data content model.[1] Most members of the group had little or no experience with SGML or its derivative, HyperText Markup Language (HTML), but they did possess a strong knowledge of archival descriptive practices and were especially familiar with that particular class of documents (or "document type") known as archival finding aids. The group shared a common understanding of how and why finding aids are constructed, the kinds of information they contain (or should contain), and the uses to which they have been put. This knowledge and appreciation of traditional paper-based finding aids, coupled with ideas for electronic enhancements, influenced the group's review and redesign of Pitti's original model and inspired the development of a new DTD named Encoded Archival Description (EAD).

Other chapters in this section examine the value of SGML and discuss EAD's development as a potential international standard. Those same themes also surface in this chapter, but the focus here is on a two-part structural analysis of EAD. The first part begins by examining SGML's role in structuring documents and then proceeds to explore EAD's theoretical underpinnings by reviewing the development team's deliberations, especially its early formulation of design principles and goals. The second part leads readers

---

N.B. "Encoded Archival Description: A Structural Overview," by Janice E. Ruth, co-published simultaneously in the *American Archivist* (The Society of American Archivists) vol. 60, no. 3, pp. 310–29; and *Encoded Archival Description: Context, Theory, and Case Studies* (ed.: Jackie M. Dooley) The Society of American Archivists, 1998.

[1]The group gathered for a week in Ann Arbor, Michigan, in July 1995, to review and revise Pitti's FindAid DTD under the auspices of the Research Fellowship for Study of Modern Archives, a program supported by the Andrew W. Mellon Foundation, the Division of Preservation and Access of the National Endowment for the Humanities, and the Bentley Historical Library, University of Michigan. The participants were Steven J. DeRose, Jackie M. Dooley, Michael J. Fox, Steven L. Hensen, Kris Kiesling, Daniel V. Pitti, Janice E. Ruth, Sharon Gibbs Thibodeau, and Helena Zinkham. This article draws heavily from the work done by the original design team at that meeting, and by them and Anne J. Gilliland-Swetland, Thomas A. LaPorte, Deborah Lapeyre, and others during the subsequent three years. It incorporates definitions, element descriptions, and other language contributed by this author and other team members to previously issued group documents.

systematically through EAD's high-level elements and suggests how the design considerations described in part one influenced the current DTD structure.

Understanding SGML Document Type Definitions

As a registered international standard, SGML is a public, nonproprietary technique for defining and expressing the logical structure of documents. It is the language used to write Document Type Definitions (DTDs), which are sets of rules for marking up or encoding classes of documents so that the text therein may be searched, retrieved, displayed, and exchanged in a predictable, platform-independent manner. Archivists interested in applying EAD need not become SGML experts, but an awareness of a DTD's three major functions will promote an increased understanding of the EAD structure and assist beginning encoders in interpreting the EAD tag library and other user documentation.

First, a DTD names and defines all the elements or data fields that may be used to mark up a particular type of document. In the same way that MAchine-Readable Cataloging (MARC) provides a structure for information in a catalog record, the EAD DTD designates the fields or categories of information contained in a finding aid. These data fields in a DTD are called "elements," and each one is assigned a unique name, abbreviation, and definition. Elements are represented by short alphanumeric words (or "tags") captured as simple ASCII characters that surround the text (or content) being designated. These tags, which are enclosed in angle brackets, indicate to a computer where the text of an element begins and ends. For example, in EAD, the beginning of a paragraph is marked as <p> and the end of the same paragraph as </p>. Similarly, the beginning of a scope and content note is identified with the element tag <scopecontent> and the end of that same note with the close tag </scopecontent>.

In developing the EAD DTD, the design team attempted to identify and name elements that reflected both the content and structure of traditional archival finding aids. These included features generic to most text-based products, such as paragraphs, headings, titles, abbreviations, block quotes, lists, and tables, as well as other properties such as scope and content notes, biographical notes, agency histories, and series descriptions, which may be unique to finding aids. Also identified as elements were external and internal pointers, references, and other links that would enable EAD to support hypertext and hypermedia, paving the way for finding aids to become more dynamic in an on-line environment and facilitating the capability to link electronic finding aids to digital representations of the archival materials described therein.

The second function of a DTD is to determine which elements should be further specified through the use of SGML "attributes." For example, an element called <date> was established to encode all dates except those associated with the creation of archival materials. (Creation dates are identified by the separately named element <unitdate>.) The design team quickly recognized, however, that there may be value in differentiating the many other kinds of dates (e.g., birth dates, flourish dates, publication dates) that appear in a finding aid. To accommodate the potential need to search different kinds of dates separately or to display them in a unique manner, an attribute named TYPE was created and linked to the <date> element for optional use during finding aid markup. Since it seemed impossible to predict every type of date archivists may want to specify, the value or content of the <date> TYPE attribute was not limited to a predetermined list of choices but instead was set to accept any character string the encoder enters. Thus if the intention is to identify a birth date within a finding aid, the DTD permits the general designation <date>1922</date> or the more precise tagging <date TYPE="birth">1922 </date>.

However, a DTD is more than a listing of elements and associated attributes. Its third and perhaps most important function is to specify where and in what sequence elements may be used. For example, a DTD may permit a Title <title> element to be used within a Paragraph <p> element, but it probably would not permit a <p> element to be used within a <title> element. One article has suggested that archivists are well suited to writing DTDs because the process is similar to organizing a collection of papers or group of records.[2] In arranging or processing a collection, the archivist analyzes the material, identifies its parts, and determines its logical structure. This process involves recognizing or defining hierarchical arrangements and then developing methodologies to implement those arrangements. Building a DTD also involves analyzing a set of documents (such as finding aids, in the case of EAD), determining how the parts relate to one another, identifying the major structural units, and then subdividing those larger parts into smaller and smaller units or subelements.

Document Analysis and the Ann Arbor Accords

In identifying the elements of a finding aid and determining where and in what sequence they should appear, the EAD developers were guided by certain fundamental observations about finding aids and several overriding principles and goals, which the design team articulated at its first meeting in Ann Arbor, Michigan. Named for the meeting site, these principles or accords stated the group's philosophy and outlined the DTD's intent, parameters, and structural features.[3] Responding first to confusion over the meaning and scope of the term "finding aid," the group decided to limit its focus to that class or genre of documents known specifically as archival inventories and registers. This decision narrowed a larger universe of finding aids that typically includes bibliographies, subject guides, repository handbooks, and other descriptive tools, and permitted the developers to optimize the DTD's design for guides to individual collections, record groups, fonds, etc., regardless of the guide's length or the type of materials described therein.

Within this finding aid subset, the group determined that the DTD must handle both the creation of new finding aids and the conversion of existing ones. This requirement posed a slight problem during the development phase, because although a single DTD might be used for many purposes, such as data conversion, interchange, authoring, etc., it could be optimized for only one function.[4] The design team was not prepared to abandon the community's "legacy data" (all those filing cabinets and shelves full of useful finding aids), nor did it want to discard traditional finding aid designs, which were both familiar and functional. Simultaneously, however, the team sought greater structural uniformity across finding aids in the belief that adherence to a consistent data model increased the potential for union databases and document interchange among repositories. Since efforts to ensure structural uniformity meant possible roadblocks to conversion, a compromise had to be reached.

---

[2]"Linking the Encoded Archival Description and the TEI," *CETH Newsletter* 4 (Spring 1996): 4–6.

[3]"Ann Arbor Accords: Principles and Criteria for an SGML Document Type Definition (DTD) for Finding Aids," *Archival Outlook* (January 1996): 12.

[4]SGML expert Deborah Lapeyre, who had been retained by the Library of Congress National Digital Library Program to assist with EAD development, alerted the EAD design team of the conflicting requirements in the Ann Arbor Accords at the group's 1–3 November 1995 meetings.

Team members decided that the DTD should not be expected to accommodate all existing practices; they also acknowledged that converting current finding aids to an ideal EAD markup would likely necessitate shifting some text or adding data to conform to the DTD's sequencing of elements and the consignment of certain elements to specific settings. An attempt was made, however, to minimize conversion difficulties by creating a special element called Other Descriptive Data <odd> to encode information, principally in existing finding aids, that may not fit easily into EAD's otherwise distinct categories. The <odd> element could be used when information did not correspond to another element's definition; when the information was of such mixed content as to make a single classification difficult; and when shifting the information to permit more specific content designation would be too costly or burdensome. Despite making the <odd> element widely available throughout the DTD, the team acknowledged that <odd> should be used with restraint and only after carefully considering the consequences that unspecified content designation poses for searching, retrieving, and displaying information in a networked environment.

Having limited the document class to both new and existing registers and inventories, the design team then confined itself to developing an archetypal data structure, resisting efforts to specify or prescribe the intellectual content that would reside inside that structure. The task was not to develop a data content standard, but to create instead a content designation or encoding standard. The group felt that subsequent content guidelines should be developed to address questions of "best practice" and to do for finding aids what the *Anglo-American Cataloguing Rules*, 2d edition (*AACR2*) and *Archives, Personal Papers, and Manuscripts (APPM)* accomplished for catalog records.

In deciding which elements and attributes to include within the DTD, the group recognized that "while there are certain elements that ought to appear in any finding aid, various intellectual and economic factors influence the depth and detail of analysis employed."[5] Concerned that it not create an overly enforcing, prescriptive, or burdensome DTD, the team created few required elements and allowed for both the nesting and reuse of elements to capture "progressively more detailed and specific levels of description as desired."[6] For example, the DTD contains an element called Administrative Information <admininfo>, which is used to provide descriptive background information concerning an institution's acquisition, processing, and management of a body of archival materials. The <admininfo> element designates facts about acquisition, access and reproduction restrictions, availability of microform and digital surrogates, preferred form of citation, and other descriptive details that help readers of the finding aid know how to approach the archival materials and make use of the information they find. All the specific pieces of information captured in <admininfo> have their own corresponding elements in the DTD—with tag names such as <custodhist>, <accruals>, <acqinfo>, <accessrestrict>, <appraisal>, <userestrict>, <altformavail>, <prefercite>, and <processinfo>—which may be applied individually if desired. Should such specificity not be needed, however, the archivist may elect to tag the entire body of information at the parent level <admininfo>, and not to encode separately the text relating to each nested subelement.

The design group was cautious about adding to the DTD every element that a team member could identify. Each proposed element was expected to support one of the fol-

[5] "Ann Arbor Accords," 12.
[6] "Ann Arbor Accords," 12.

lowing functions: description, control, navigation, indexing, or on-line and print presentation. For each element, the team assessed whether staff or researchers would want to search for that particular piece of encoded information, display or print it in a unique way, or take some other specific, definable action on it. If none of these situations was anticipated, then the element was not adopted. If the element passed the "functionality test," it was added to the DTD, often under a language-neutral name designed to enhance broad international application of EAD. Terms such as collection, personal papers, archives, series, fonds, and record group were avoided in favor of "generic terms like unit and component that are not specific to any individual setting or institution."[7]

Hierarchy, Formatting, and Other Design Considerations

Although not specifically enumerated in the Ann Arbor Accords, several other important observations about paper-based finding aids played a crucial role in the development of EAD. Foremost was the recognition that many archival inventories and registers describe a unit of records or papers at several different, but related, levels of detail. Within these hierarchical, multilevel views, information about the archival materials is both repeated and inherited. For example, many archival inventories and registers begin by presenting information about the entire body of records or papers described in the finding aid. This information may be conveyed in a provenance statement, a scope and content note, or by means of some other narrative device that describes the unit of materials in its entirety. Certain specific pieces of information about the unit, such as its title, creator, span dates, identification number, extent, location, scope, content, and arrangement, may (and should) be captured in these high-level descriptions, which are intended to give a broad overview of the whole unit. The design team created the Archival Description <archdesc> element to identify this description of the whole.

Within the <archdesc> element, other more detailed descriptions of the subordinate parts may be presented, which the EAD designers designated by the element Description of Subordinate Components <dsc>. For example, an archivist may elect to describe separately and in greater detail all the series within a manuscript collection. This description of the series presents another view of the entire unit, this time in terms of its major components. Similarly, the archivist may elect to prepare lists of files or items within each series. Again, these contents lists are views of the entire collection, but they usually contain an even greater level of detail than was captured in either the first collection-level description or the second series-level description. The EAD design team recognized that successive levels of description inherit information from the preceding component- or unit-level summary, and that every level repeats or reuses some of the same basic data elements, such as title, creator, span dates, identification number, extent, location, scope, content, and arrangement. This recursive, repeatable character of finding aids is reflected in the EAD structure.

Also noted by the design team, but perhaps less elegantly resolved, was the problem that although SGML permits almost complete separation of format from content, archival finding aids do not. The tabular formatting of finding aids is a mechanism for imparting information about the organization and arrangement of the materials being described. Archival inventories and registers often contain parallel structures—one that conveys the

[7] "Ann Arbor Accords," 12.

intellectual arrangement of the materials, and the other representing the physical arrangement. In many paper-based finding aids, these dual structures are presented through the use of columns: The intellectual hierarchy runs down one side of the page, and a listing of container numbers or microfilm locations runs down the other side. Often these dual structures shift or break at different points. Since SGML does not simultaneously accommodate dual structures effectively, the design team had to choose which structure it would optimize the DTD to handle.

It was agreed that the intellectual arrangement of the archival materials was more important and more permanent than the physical order, and the DTD was designed accordingly. The team also decided that the DTD need not slavishly recreate the exact appearance of every finding aid; in other words, fidelity to the printed page would not be supported. Nevertheless, the designers sought to enable DTD users to replicate columnar layouts in two ways. First, SGML stylesheets may be used to manipulate intellectual content elements for basic columnar output. Secondly, for more precise columnar layouts, including greater control of indentations, encoders may overlay the intellectual markup with a special set of tabular display elements, Table Specification <tspec>, Display Row <drow>, and Display Entry <dentry>, created specifically for EAD. The tabular elements serve as outer wrappers when manipulating groupings of intellectual content elements in order to achieve desired on-line and print presentations. Utilizing EAD's special tabular superstructure has been problematic, however, and many early implementers have achieved satisfactory display results without it. Reacting to early implementers' general lack of interest in the display elements, and concerned about the confusion those elements have caused for some archivists just beginning to learn the DTD structure, the design team decided during version 1.0 development to reduce the presence of the display elements within the DTD. Under version 1.0, if encoders wish to use the tabular display elements, they must first make a minor modification to their copies of the DTD in order to access the elements.

A final consideration in designing EAD was the DTD's relationship to other standards, especially the USMARC Archival and Manuscripts Control (AMC) format and the General International Standard Archival Description (ISAD(G)). After much discussion on the degree to which MARC-formatted data should be extractable from an EAD-compliant finding aid, the group decided that it would not design EAD for exporting MARC fields down to the indicator and subfield levels. The team acknowledged that finding aids are the chief source of information for creating cataloging records in the MARC AMC format but felt that it would be burdensome and unwieldy for EAD to be structured so that a complete MARC record could be harvested automatically from the SGML markup. A compromise was reached: With the exception of the Controlled Access Headings <controlaccess> element (discussed in part two of this chapter), no elements were added to the DTD simply for the sake of providing a corresponding data structure to MARC, but for those MARC-like elements already represented in EAD, the team added an optional ENCODINGANALOG attribute, which permits the designation of the applicable MARC field or subfield together with the authoritative form of the data. By using these ENCODINGANALOG attributes, archivists can generate skeletal MARC records automatically from EAD finding aids.

Although EAD began its development in the United States based on archival descriptive practices used in this country, its progress has been closely followed by members of the international archival community. From the beginning, the EAD design team was hopeful of creating a model with worldwide appeal, and the international community was represented on the team by a longtime member of the International Council on Archives

(ICA) Ad Hoc Commission on Descriptive Standards, which developed the ISAD(G).[8] As mentioned earlier, the EAD design team adopted neutral language throughout the DTD as a means of facilitating global acceptance, and as the EAD structure evolved, a separate special effort was made to test its international applicability by comparing it to the ISAD(G), which had been approved by the ICA in 1994.

Issued as a guideline to be followed in the preparation of archival finding aids, the ISAD(G) consists of two major segments: 1) a segment that provides rules for systematic, multilevel presentation in a single finding aid of descriptive information about a whole unit of records or papers and its component parts or divisions; and 2) a segment that specifies the individual elements that may be presented about the whole archival unit or any component part in accordance with the multilevel rules.[9] Like EAD, the ISAD(G) assumes the following three things: 1) a finding aid consists of hierarchically organized information describing a unit of records or papers along with its component parts; 2) information in the finding aid is inherited from one descriptive level to another; and 3) descriptions of both the whole and the parts each comprise essential data elements. A direct comparison of EAD with ISAD(G)[10] conducted by an EAD team member found that EAD can accommodate a finding aid that complies with ISAD(G). The EAD DTD provides for the tagging of all the essential elements specified in the ISAD(G), and the direct parallels can be indicated by invoking the same optional ENCODINGANALOG attribute used for MARC comparisons. This compatibility between EAD and the ISAD(G) affirms the validity of the EAD structure and suggests a role for EAD in fostering the international exchange of archival descriptions.

Overview of the EAD Data Model

Through an examination of a DTD's major functions, a description of the Ann Arbor Accords, and a look at other design considerations, the first part of this chapter attempted to highlight aspects of EAD's theoretical framework preparatory to exploring the DTD's high-level elements in greater detail. The intent of the second part of this chapter is not to describe every element and the circumstances surrounding its use (a tag library and application guidelines[11] are designed for that task), but instead to provide a general over-

---

[8]EAD team member Sharon Gibbs Thibodeau served on the ICA's Ad Hoc Commission on Descriptive Standards from its inception in 1990 until 1997. The author is grateful to her for providing a summary of ISAD(G) for use in this article and for conducting the EAD-ISAD(G) comparison for the team.

[9]For the full text of ISAD(G), see International Council on Archives, *ISAD(G): General International Standard Archival Description, adopted by the Ad Hoc Commission on Descriptive Standards, Stockholm, Sweden, 21–23 January 1993* (Ottawa: International Council on Archives, 1994) or the ICA's homepage at http://www.archives.ca/ica/.

[10]See Sharon Gibbs Thibodeau, "A Mapping of EAD Tags to the Elements of Description Incorporated in the International Standard Archival Description, ISAD(G)," in "Encoded Archival Description Document Type Definition (DTD) Applications Guidelines," by Anne J. Gilliland-Swetland, edited by Thomas A. LaPorte, unpublished draft disseminated electronically, December 1996, 70–73 at <http://scriptorium.lib.duke.edu/findaids/ead/guidelines/index.html>.

[11][Deborah Lapeyre and Janice E. Ruth, eds.], "Draft Tag Library for EAD Alpha DTDs," unpublished draft distributed in limited paper copies and disseminated electronically, February 1996; Anne J. Gilliland-Swetland and Thomas A. LaPorte, eds., "Encoded Archival Description Document Type Definition (DTD) Beta Version, Tag Library," unpublished draft disseminated electronically, October 1996; and Gilliland-Swetland and LaPorte, "Encoded Archival Description Document Type Definition (DTD) Applications Guidelines." The URL for both the beta tag library and applications guidelines is http://scriptorium.lib.duke.edu/findaids/ead/guidelines/index.html. A version 1.0 tag library will be published by SAA at roughly the same time that the revised DTD is released in summer 1998.

view of some of the major elements and their relationship both to one another and to the design considerations previously discussed. Since EAD is an ongoing project, changes to the version 1.0 DTD structure outlined here are inevitable, and readers are advised to monitor new developments by subscribing to the EAD listserv and consulting the official EAD website maintained by the Network Development and MARC Standards Office of the Library of Congress, where the most recent version of the DTD and related documentation are posted.[12] Since some readers of this chapter may have been familiar with the beta version of the DTD, footnotes provide commentary about significant changes between that version and version 1.0, scheduled for release in summer 1998.

Designating Bibliographic Information About Finding Aids

Although not universally employed, title pages, prefaces, and use instructions are often the first pieces of information found in archival inventories and registers. Observing this fact led the EAD design team to deduce that at the most basic level, archival finding aids consist of two segments: 1) a segment that provides information about the finding aid itself (its title, compiler, compilation date, etc.); and 2) a segment that provides information about a body of archival materials (a collection, a record group, a fonds, or a series).[13] As shown in Figure 1, the EAD DTD splits the first segment into two high-level elements known as EAD Header <eadheader> and Front Matter <frontmatter>. The second segment, consisting of information about the archival materials, is contained within the third high-level element named Archival Description <archdesc>.[14] All three of these high-level elements are contained within the outermost element named Encoded Archival Description <ead>. The beginning <ead> and closing </ead> tags wrap around the entire document.

The <eadheader>, outlined in Figure 2, is modeled on the header element in the Text Encoding Initiative (TEI), an international humanities-based effort to develop a suite of DTDs for encoding literary texts or other objects of study. In an attempt to encourage as much uniformity as possible in the provision of metadata across document types, the design team elected to use a TEI-like header to capture information about the creation, revision, publication, and distribution of finding aid instances. The resulting <eadheader> consists of four subelements, some of which are further subdivided: EAD Identifier <eadid> provides a unique identification number or code for the finding aid and can indicate the location, source, and type of the identifier. File Description <filedesc> contains much of the bibliographic information about the finding aid, including the name of the author, title, subtitle, and sponsor (all contained in the Title Statement <titlestmt> element), as well as the edition, publisher, series, and related notes encoded separately. Profile Description <profiledesc> is used to record the language of the finding aid and

---

[12]Version 1.0 of the DTD is scheduled for release in summer 1998. The URL for the official EAD website maintained by Library of Congress, Network Development and MARC Standards Office is http://lcweb.loc.gov/ead. The site contains information on subscribing to the EAD listserv.

[13]"Encoding Standard for Electronic Aids: A Report by the Bentley Team for Encoded Archival Description Development," *Archival Outlook* (January 1996): 10.

[14]Those familiar with the beta version of the DTD should note that the <findaid> element no longer exists. In response to input from early implementers, the Adjunct Descriptive Data <add> element was made available directly within <archdesc>, eliminating any need for the <findaid> element, which had served as a wrapper for the <archdesc> and <add> elements. For a fuller discussion of the change to <add>, see footnote 20.

Figure 1. Overview of the Encoded Archival Description (EAD) DTD, Version 1.0

Only high-level elements are listed below. Lower-level elements as well as formatting, cross-reference, and linking elements are not given. Elements that appear at the same level share the same indentation. Subelements are indented under the element that contains them and are listed in alphabetical order unless a different sequence is required by the DTD.

```
<ead>
        <eadheader>  (See Figure 2)
        <frontmatter>
        <archdesc>
                <did>
                        <abstract>
                        <container>
                        <dao> and <daogrp>
                        <note>
                        <origination>
                        <physdesc>
                        <physloc>
                        <repository>
                        <unitdate>
                        <unitid>
                        <unittitle>
                <add>
                        <bibliography>
                        <fileplan>
                        <index>
                        <note>
                        <otherfindaid>
                        <p>
                        <relatedmaterial>
                        <separatedmaterial>
                <admininfo>
                        <accessrestrict>
                        <accruals>
                        <acqinfo>
                        <altformavail>
                        <appraisal>
                        <custodhist>
                        <note>
                        <p>
                        <prefercite>
                        <processinfo>
                        <userestrict>
                <arrangement>
```

information about who created the encoded version of the document, and when. Revision Description <revisiondesc> summarizes any revisions made to the EAD document.[15]

[15]The beta version of the DTD also included a <footer> element in the <eadheader>. In version 1.0, the <footer> element became the <runner> element, which is available only within <archdesc>, immediately

Figure 1. Continued

```
<ead> (continued)
        <archdesc> (continued)
                <bioghist>
                <controlaccess>
                        <corpname>
                        <famname>
                        <function>
                        <genreform>
                        <geogname>
                        <name>
                        <occupation>
                        <persname>
                        <subject>
                        <title>
                <dao> and <daogrp>
                <note>
                <odd>
                <organization>
                <scopecontent>
                <dsc>  (See Figures 3-5)
                        <c01>
                                <did>
                                <add>
                                <admininfo>
                                <arrangement>
                                <bioghist>
                                <controlaccess>
                                <dao> and <daogrp>
                                <note>
                                <odd>
                                <organization>
                                <scopecontent>
                                <c02>
                                        <did>
                                        (and so forth)
```

The sequence of elements and subelements in the <eadheader> is specified by the DTD, with the expectation that searches across repositories will be more predictable if the

before <did>. The <runner> element provides for a header, footer, or digital watermark to appear on every page of the finding aid.

Figure 2. Model for EAD Header <eadheader> Element

```
<eadheader>
        <eadid>
        <filedesc>
                <titlestmt>
                        <titleproper>
                        <subtitle>
                        <author>
                        <sponsor>
                <editionstmt>
                <publicationstmt>
                        <address>
                        <date>
                        <num>
                        <p>
                        <publisher>
                <seriesstmt>
                <notestmt>
        <profiledesc>
                <creation>
                <langusage>
        <revisiondesc>
```

elements are uniformly ordered. Such searches may help filter large bodies of machine-readable finding aids by specific categories, such as title, date, repository, language, etc. Required use of the <eadheader> compels archivists to include essential information about their machine-readable finding aids that often went unrecorded in paper form. In addition, elements in the <eadheader> may be used to generate electronic and printed title pages for finding aids.

Because the elements within the <eadheader> must follow a prescribed order to ensure uniformity across finding aids, the team also created an optional <frontmatter> element, which can be used to generate a title page that follows local preferences for the sequencing of information. The Title Page <titlepage> subelement within <frontmatter> reuses many of the same subelements designated in <filedesc>. The <frontmatter> element also can be used to encode structures such as prefaces, dedications, or other text concerning the creation, publication, or use of the finding aid. The design team did not create a specific element for each of these structures, opting instead for a single generic Text Division <div> element.

Encoding the Heart of the Finding Aid

As noted in Figure 1, the third high-level element in <ead> is Archival Description <archdesc>, which consists of information about a body of archival materials. Within this element is found hierarchically organized information that describes a unit of records or papers along with its component parts or divisions. It includes information about the content, context, and extent of the archival materials as well as optional supplemental information that facilitates their use by researchers.[16]

When most of us think about archival finding aids, we envision the kinds of hierarchical, multilevel descriptions discussed earlier. Those descriptions form the heart of archival inventories and registers, which generally describe a unit of records or papers at several different, but related, levels of detail. As noted in the design team's first progress report, <archdesc> encompasses these unfolding, hierarchical levels by first allowing for a descriptive overview of the whole, followed by more detailed views of the parts, designated by the element Description of Subordinate Components <dsc>. Data elements available at the <archdesc> or unit level are repeated at the various component levels within <dsc>, and information is inherited from one hierarchical level to the next. As further explained in a set of remarks first prepared for the EAD alpha tag library, <archdesc> not only serves as a wrapper for all the descriptive information about an entire body of archival materials, it also, through a LEVEL attribute, identifies the highest tier of the materials being described.[17]

Imagine a typical scenario: An archivist begins encoding a finding aid by first opening the <ead> element and creating the required <eadheader>. He or she may then add some optional <frontmatter> before opening the <archdesc> element and setting its required LEVEL attribute to the value "collection," "record group," "fonds," or "series," depending on which term best reflects the character of the whole unit being described in the finding aid. What then follows are data elements that describe that whole unit, including a special subset of core data elements that are gathered together under a parent element called Descriptive Identification <did>. These <did> subelements are among the most important for ensuring a good basic description of an archival unit or component. Grouping these elements together serves several purposes. It insures that the same data elements and structure are available at every level of description within the EAD hierarchy. It facilitates the retrieval or other output of a cohesive body of elements for resource discovery and recognition. And, because the elements appear together in the tag library and on software menus and templates, it helps to remind encoders to capture descriptive information that they may otherwise overlook.

As Figure 1 shows, the <did> element may contain, in any order, one or more of the following descriptive subelements, which are familiar mainstays of archival cataloging: Container <container>, identifying the number of the carton, box, folder, or other holding unit in which the archival materials are arranged and stored;[18] Origination <origination>, denoting the individuals or organizations responsible for the creation or assembly of the

[16]"Encoding Standard for Electronic Aids: A Report by the Bentley Team for Encoded Archival Description Development," 11.

[17]Janice E. Ruth, "Introductory Remarks About High-Level Elements," in [Lapeyre and Ruth, eds.], "Draft Tag Library for EAD Alpha DTDs," 11–12; reproduced in Gilliland-Swetland and LaPorte, eds., "Encoded Archival Description Document Type Definition (DTD) Beta Version, Tag Library," 6–7.

[18]The <container> and <physloc> elements are new to version 1.0 of the DTD. In the beta version, they were attributes on the <unitloc> element, which no longer exists.

archival materials; Physical Description <physdesc>, identifying the extent, dimensions, genre, form, and other physical characteristics; Physical Location <physloc>, identifying the stack number, shelf designation, or other storage location; Repository <repository>, designating the institution responsible for providing intellectual access; Date of the Unit <unitdate>, designating the creation dates of the archival materials; Identification of the Unit <unitid>, containing an accession number, classification number, lot number, or other such unique and permanent identifier; and Title of the Unit <unittitle>, containing the title of the archival materials at whatever level they are being described, such as collection title, series title, subseries title, file title, or item title. The <did> element also provides for the use of both an Abstract <abstract> and a general Note <note> element, as well as for Digital Archival Object <dao> and Digital Archival Object Group <daogrp> elements, which may link to digital surrogates of the material being described in the finding aid. Attributes also are available for all <did> subelements to specify their content further.

Having used the <did> elements to capture a basic description at the <archdesc> level, the archivist may proceed directly to a description of the unit's component parts. More likely, however, the finding aid creator will provide additional narrative information about the content, context, or extent of the whole unit. This description usually appears in prose form within elements with tag names such as <admininfo>, <bioghist>, <scopecontent>, <organization>, and <arrangement>, which are suggestive of the categories of information typically present in traditional paper-based finding aids.[19] For each of these categories of information, the encoder may use the Heading <head> element to provide a heading based on local preferences, which may or may not correspond to the element name. For example, the DTD permits encoders to identify a biographical note or agency history by any heading they choose (e.g., Biographical Summary, Biography, Jane Doe's Key Dates) as long as the content is correctly tagged as <bioghist>. Structurally, from an SGML perspective, the content models for these narrative-based elements are "heads" and "text," with the latter generally composed of paragraphs or various types of List(s) <list>, including the specially created Chronology List <chronlist>, consisting of Chronology List Item(s) <chronitem> that pair a <date> with its corresponding <event> to enable linking and tabular display. By comparison, the information within the <did> subelements is often presented as a short labeled phrase, or several subelements are pieced together to form a simple uniform data string.

Once an archivist has completed the description of the records or papers at the highest (or unit) level, the <dsc> element may be opened, and the focus shifts to describing one or more of the unit's component parts. As explained in the tag library, the <dsc> can assume several different forms, which are identified by the element's TYPE attribute. The TYPE attribute can be set to a value of analytic overview ("analyticover"), to identify a series or subseries description; "in-depth," to identify a listing of containers or folders, a calendar, or a listing of items; "combined," to identify instances in which the description of each series is followed immediately by a listing of containers or folders for that series; and "othertype," to identify models that do not follow any of the above-mentioned formats.

[19]The discussion in this and the following paragraphs is based on Ruth, "Introductory Remarks About High-Level Elements."

After the form of the <dsc> has been selected, the archival components are identified, and a LEVEL attribute may be assigned. For example, as shown in Figure 3, an archivist who wishes to provide a summary listing of all the series in a collection may open a <dsc>, set the TYPE attribute to "analyticover," open a Component <c> or <c01> (components may be numbered <c01> through <c12> to keep better track of the hierarchical levels), set the LEVEL attribute to "series," and proceed to describe the first series-level component by utilizing the same extensive set of elements that previously were available for describing the whole unit at the <archdesc> level. The same procedure would be followed again for the second and all subsequent series-level components, after which point the <dsc> element would be closed. In general, certain <did> subelements, such as <repository> and <origination>, are unlikely to be used within a <c> because the information they contain has been encoded at the <archdesc> level and inherited by the <c>. Other <did> subelements, such as <container>, <unitdate>, and <unittitle>, will frequently be used within a <c> to encode new information or more detailed descriptions at a lower hierarchical level.

As Figure 4 shows, a second <dsc> might then be opened with a TYPE attribute set to "in-depth" so that a container list can be presented. Each series, subseries, file, or item represented in the container list would be tagged as recursive, nested components, possibly with optional LEVEL attributes set to identify their hierarchical order within the collection or record group. As in the series description, information about each component <c> may be identified, if desired, by utilizing the full complement of descriptive elements. It is also possible to use within each <c> the <drow> <dentry> display elements mentioned earlier in this chapter. This structure of endlessly nested components inside a <dsc>, and further, inside <archdesc>, addresses the design team's desire to provide for descriptive information that is inherited from one level to another and that shares or repeats the same essential data elements.

The approach described in the previous paragraph may be termed the "two-<dsc>" model. An alternative to encoding a <dsc TYPE = "analyticover"> followed by a <dsc TYPE = "in-depth" would be to simply use the <dsc TYPE = "combined">. This may be referred to as the "combined" model. As Figure 5 shows, the combined model is perhaps a purer manifestation of an unfolding hierarchical description, in that the first component <c01> (in this case, a series) is encoded only once, followed immediately by a fuller description of its nested parts (subseries, files, and items). The combined model avoids the potential confusion of machine-processing identical information that has been encoded twice in the same document, a situation that occurs in the two-<dsc> approach. Depending on the sophistication of a system's searching and processing capabilities, the two-<dsc> approach may hamper the ability to show a relationship between the description of the <c01> and the description of its parts. On the other hand, using the two-<dsc> approach not only readily accommodates a legacy data structure found in many existing finding aids, it also replicates the functionality which that structure provided. For example, many archivists have found it extremely helpful to assemble in one spot all the first-level component descriptions to provide researchers with a quick overview of the archival unit's content and organization and to permit ready comparisons between components. Flipping through a long paper guide or scrolling and jumping through an electronic finding aid to locate all the first-level summaries is a drawback of the combined model, a problem which an on-line delivery system would need to address.

Figure 3. Tagged Example of <dsc type = ''analyticover''> (Analytic Overview Model)

Description of Series

Container Nos.	*Series*
1	Diary and Diary Notes, 1932-34, n.d. A high-school diary and an undated, single-page diary fragment kept by Jackson. Arranged chronologically.
2	Family Papers, 1938-65, n.d. Letters received, notes, and cards. Organized alphabetically by family member and arranged chronologically therein.
3-12	Correspondence, 1936-70, n.d. Letters received and occasional copies of letters sent, telegrams, postcards, and miscellaneous enclosures. Organized alphabetically by correspondent and arranged chronologically therein.
13-19	Literary File, 1943-70, n.d. Correspondence, manuscript drafts, royalty statements, printed matter, notes, outlines, research material, screenplays, and miscellaneous items and enclosures relating to books and short stories by Jackson. Organized alphabetically by type of material and arranged alphabetically by title or topic therein. Publication dates of books are given in parentheses.

Tagged Example

<dsc type="analyticover"><head>**Description of Series**</head><thead><row valign="top"> <entry colname="1">**Container Nos.**</entry><entry colname="2">**Series**</entry></row> </thead>

<c01 level="series"><did><container>**1**</container><unittitle>**Diary and Diary Notes,** <unitdate>**1932-34, n.d.**</unitdate></unittitle></did><scopecontent><p>**A high-school diary and an undated, single-page diary fragment kept by Jackson.**</p><arrangement> <p>**Arranged chronologically.**</p></arrangement></scopecontent></c01>

<c01 level="series"><did><container>**2**</container><unittitle>**Family Papers,** <unitdate> **1938-65, n.d.**</unitdate></unittitle></did><scopecontent><p>**Letters received, notes, and cards.**</p><arrangement><p>**Organized alphabetically by family member and arranged chronologically therein.**</p></arrangement></scopecontent></c01>

<c01 level="series"><did><container>**3-12**</container><unittitle> **Correspondence,** <unitdate> **1936-70, n.d.**</unitdate></unittitle></did><scopecontent> <p>**Letters received and occasional copies of letters sent, telegrams, postcards, and miscellaneous enclosures.**</p><arrangement><p>**Organized alphabetically by correspondent and arranged chronologically therein.**</p></arrangement></scopecontent></c01>

<c01 level="series"><did><container>**13-19**</container><unittitle>**Literary File,** <unitdate>**1943-70, n.d.**</unitdate></unittitle></did><scopecontent><p>**Correspondence, manuscript drafts, royalty statements, printed matter, notes, outlines, research material, screenplays, and miscellaneous items and enclosures relating to books and short stories by Jackson.**</p><arrangement><p>**Organized alphabetically by type of material and arranged alphabetically by title or topic therein. Publication dates of books are given in parentheses.**</p></arrangement></scopecontent></c01></dsc>

Adjunct Descriptive Data <add>

In addition to providing information about the content, context, and extent of the archival materials, the <archdesc> element also includes optional supplemental information that facilitates use of the materials by researchers. This supplemental information, bundled within the Adjunct Descriptive Data <add> element, includes additional access

Figure 4. Tagged Example of <dsc type = ''in depth''> (In-depth Model)

Container List

Container Nos.	*Contents*
LITERARY FILE, 1943-70, n.d.	
46	Bibliographies and publishing lists, 1951-66
	Books
	Raising Demons (1957)
	Reviews, 1956-57, n.d.
	Royalty statements, 1956-69
47	*The Road Through the Wall* (1948), 1947-70, n.d.
	Short stories and other writings
	"The Lottery"
	Dramatic adaptations
	Correspondence, 1949-53, 1967-70
	Scripts and screenplays, n.d.
	Royalty statements, 1950-53, 1964-70
	"Lover's Meeting," n.d.

Tagged Example

```
<dsc type="in-depth"><head>Container List</head><thead><row valign="top"><entry
colname="1">Container Nos.</entry><entry colname="2">Contents</entry></row></thead>

<c01 level="series"><did><unittitle>LITERARY FILE, <unitdate type="inclusive">1943-70,
   n.d.</unitdate></unittitle></did>
      <c02><did><container>46</container><unittitle>Bibliographies and publishing lists,
         1951-66</unittitle></did></c02>
      <c02><did><unittitle>Books</unittitle></did>
         <c03><did><unittitle><title render="italic">Raising Demons</title> (1957) </unittitle></did>
               <c04><did><unittitle>Reviews, 1956-57, n.d.</unittitle></did></c04>
               <c04><did><unittitle>Royalty statements, 1956-69</unittitle></did> </c04></c03>
         <c03><did><container>47</container><unittitle><title render="italic">The Road Through the
           Wall</title> (1948), 1947-70, n.d.</unittitle></did></c03></c02>
      <c02><did><unittitle>Short stories and other writings</unittitle></did>
         <c03><did><unittitle><title render="quoted">The Lottery</title></unittitle> </did>
            <c04><did><unittitle>Dramatic adaptations</unittitle></did>
                  <c05><did><unittitle>Correspondence, 1949-53, 1967-70</unittitle> </did></c05>
                  <c05><did><unittitle>Scripts and screenplays, n.d.</unittitle> </did></c05></c04>
            <c04><did><unittitle>Royalty statements, 1950-53, 1964-70</unittitle> </did></c04></c03>
         <c03><did><unittitle><title render="quoted">Lover's Meeting,</title> n.d.
         </unittitle></did></c03></c02></c01> . . . </dsc>
```

tools to the materials, such as indexes, file plans, and other finding aids, as well as descriptions or lists of materials separated from or related to those described in the finding aid. The <add> element reflects one of the design principles mentioned earlier in this chapter in connection with the <admininfo> element, namely that EAD accommodates both detailed and ''lite'' approaches to tagging. Archivists may elect to tag all the adjunct information simply as an <add> containing a series of paragraphs <p>, or they may open the <add> element and encode each piece of information with its specific corresponding tag, such as <bibliography>, <fileplan>, <index>, <otherfindaid>, <rela-

Figure 5. Tagged Example of <dsc type = "combined"> (Combined Model)

Container List

Container Nos.	*Contents*
	LITERARY FILE, 1943-70, n.d.
	Correspondence, manuscript drafts, royalty statements, printed matter, notes, outlines, research material, screenplays, and miscellaneous items and enclosures relating to books and short stories by Jackson. Organized alphabetically by type of material and arranged alphabetically by title or topic therein. Publication dates of books are given in parentheses.
46	Bibliographies and publishing lists, 1951-66
	Books
	Raising Demons (1957)
	Reviews, 1956-57, n.d.
	Royalty statements, 1956-69
47	*The Road Through the Wall* (1948), 1947-70, n.d.
	Short stories and other writings
	"The Lottery"
	Dramatic adaptations
	Correspondence, 1949-53, 1967-70
	Scripts and screenplays, n.d.
	Royalty statements, 1950-53, 1964-70
	"Lover's Meeting," n.d.

Tagged Example

<dsc type="combined"><head>**Container List**</head><thead><row valign="top"><entry colname="1">**Container Nos.**</entry><entry colname="2">**Contents**</entry></row></thead>

<c01 level="series"><did><unittitle>**Literary File,** <unitdate>**1943-70, n.d.**</unitdate></unittitle></did>
<scopecontent><p>**Correspondence, manuscript drafts, royalty statements, printed matter, notes, outlines, research material, screenplays, and miscellaneous items and enclosures relating to books and short stories by Jackson.**</p><arrangement><p>**Organized alphabetically by type of material and arranged alphabetically by title or topic therein. Publication dates of books are given in parentheses.**</p></arrangement></scopecontent>

<c02><did><container>**46**</container><unittitle>**Bibliographies and publishing lists, 1951-66**</unittitle></did></c02>
<c02><did><unittitle>**Books**</unittitle></did>
<c03><did><unittitle><title render="italic">**Raising Demons**</title> **(1957)** </unittitle></did>
<c04><did><unittitle>**Reviews, 1956-57, n.d.**</unittitle></did></c04>
<c04><did><unittitle>**Royalty statements, 1956-69**</unittitle></did> </c04></c03>
<c03><did><container>**47**</container><unittitle><title render="italic">**The Road Through the Wall**</title> **(1948), 1947-70, n.d.**</unittitle></did></c03></c02>
<c02><did><unittitle>**Short stories and other writings**</unittitle></did>
<c03><did><unittitle><title render="quoted">**The Lottery**</title></unittitle> </did>
<c04><did><unittitle>**Dramatic adaptations**</unittitle></did>
<c05><did><unittitle>**Correspondence, 1949-53, 1967-70**</unittitle> </did></c05>
<c05><did><unittitle>**Scripts and screenplays, n.d.**</unittitle> </did></c05></c04>
<c04><did><unittitle>**Royalty statements, 1950-53, 1964-70**</unittitle> </did></c04></c03>
<c03><did><unittitle><title render="quoted">**Lover's Meeting,**</title> **n.d.** </unittitle></did></c03></c02></c01> . . . </dsc>

tedmaterial>, and <separatedmaterial>. As a subelement of both <archdesc> and <c>, <add> may appear throughout a finding aid in whatever information sequence best suits the repository's needs. For many encoders, the best sequence will likely be to group all the <add> information together near the end of the finding aid.[20]

Enhanced Searching Capability Through Access Terms

Aside from encoding the major structural parts of a finding aid and designating the core descriptive data about the unit and its components, users of EAD also have the option of identifying character strings throughout the finding aid that are likely to be the objects of searches, such as personal, corporate, family, and geographic names; occupations; functions; form and genre terms; subjects; and titles. All of these elements (<persname>, <corpname>, <famname>, <geogname>, <name>, <occupation>, <function>, <genreform>, <subject>, and <title>) permit, through the use of attributes, the designation of encoding analogs and authorized forms as mentioned in the earlier discussion of MARC and ISAD(G). Additional optional attributes allow for specifying the role or relationship of persons and corporate bodies (e.g., author, editor, photographer) and the source of the controlled vocabulary terms used (e.g., *AACR2, Library of Congress Subject Headings, Library of Congress Name Authority Files, Art and Architecture Thesaurus, Dictionary of Occupational Titles*). Although the DTD permits liberal access to these elements throughout the finding aid, especially within the <p> and <unittitle> elements, special mention should be made of the ability to bundle them together under the parent element Controlled Access Headings <controlaccess>.

The design team created <controlaccess> specifically to enable authority-controlled searching across finding aids on a computer network. The developers envisioned that users may approach on-line finding aids via a variety of avenues. Some may search a repository's on-line catalog, locate relevant entries, and follow links from those entries to on-line versions of finding aids. Others may start by searching the finding aids directly, bypassing the catalog and losing the advantage of the authority-controlled search terms contained therein. The <controlaccess> element is designed to replicate in a finding aid the collection-level search terms found in the 1xx, 6xx, and 7xx fields of MARC catalog records. Finding aid searches limited to the <controlaccess> element will improve the likelihood of locating strong sources of information on a desired subject, because access terms will have been entered in a consistent and authorized form across finding aids, and also because only the most significant terms are likely to have been selected for encoding.

[20]In response to input from early implementers, the EAD developers decided for version 1.0 of the DTD to make the <add> element part of the <archdesc> element rather than maintaining its separate existence under <findaid>. Early implementers of EAD, especially those familiar with using ISAD(G), demonstrated that adjunct descriptive data is not always supplemental "appended" data, as originally conceived by the EAD developers, but instead may be necessary information that is inseparable from other elements of description in a finding aid. Attempting to tease apart, for example, information about related or separated materials from information about the materials featured in the finding aid may not always be possible or desirable. Similarly, finding aid creators may determine that their researchers are better served if a file plan or bibliography relating to a specific unit or component of material appears with other elements of description for that unit or component as opposed to surfacing elsewhere in the finding aid, such as in an appendix. By subsuming <add> as a subelement under <archdesc>, the DTD may become more flexible in handling legacy data and more accommodating of European finding aid practices. The <add> element is now available at various places within <archdesc> to enable finding aid creators to select an information sequence that best suits their needs. The change does not preclude EAD users from following the beta model of gathering at the end of the finding aid all adjunct descriptive data; such users would simply insert the <add> just before the close </archdesc> tag rather than immediately after </archdesc> as was done under the beta DTD. With the change to subsume <add> under <archdesc>, there was no longer any need for the <findaid> element to serve the function of wrapping the <archdesc> and <add> elements. Consequently, <findaid> was eliminated from the DTD.

Summary

Although EAD has been under development for more than three years and has been significantly improved during that time by feedback from early implementers and by new insights from the design team, much of the DTD's basic structure and approach remains unchanged from the blueprint created during the team's first meeting in July 1995. At the week-long gathering in Ann Arbor, the EAD developers acquired a working knowledge of SGML, articulated their ideas about finding aids, established a set of guiding principles and goals, and created a rudimentary high-level model. Led by the team members most knowledgeable about SGML, the group began tackling three of the most important steps in building a DTD: naming and defining the elements; naming and defining the attributes; and determining where and in what sequence elements may appear. To accomplish these tasks, group members analyzed the structure and functionality of traditional finding aids and made a series of choices about the scope and purpose of their endeavor.

They agreed to create a DTD optimized for authoring new archival inventories and registers, which are a subset of all finding aids, but they also sought to make the structure flexible enough to accommodate existing legacy data. They created only those elements that served a function, and they nested and repeated the elements in an order that reflected the hierarchical, recursive structure of finding aids. The resulting DTD successfully addressed other design goals as well, such as enabling both ''lite'' and detailed levels of tagging, giving preference to intellectual order over physical arrangement, preserving tabular display features, and accommodating the ISAD(G) and MARC standards.

The model that emerged from the first week's deliberations underwent extensive fine-tuning during the next fourteen months before culminating in the release of a beta version of EAD in September 1996. More than a year of beta testing followed, after which proposals for change were considered by SAA's EAD Working Group, which had been charged with intellectual maintenance of the DTD. The working group will issue version 1.0 of the DTD by late summer 1998. Like earlier versions, it separates information about the finding aid from information about the body of archival materials being described. It encodes the rich, hierarchical descriptions we most closely associate with inventories and registers, while also accommodating the markup of optional supplemental access tools and lists. The DTD's recursive structure allows for multilevel descriptions that begin with a summary of the whole unit and proceed to description of the component parts. Essential descriptive elements are repeated at each level, and linking, display, and search term elements are widely available.

Whether the version 1.0 DTD structure will withstand the test of time is not yet known. After both the alpha and beta test periods, important changes were made to the DTD, and additional revisions are still likely as more archivists, situated in a greater variety of settings, begin to work with version 1.0 of the DTD and contribute to shared or linked databases of finding aids. Only through the continued input and assistance of the entire archival community can EAD develop into a dynamic new tool for accessing and exchanging the wealth of information contained in archival finding aids.

CHAPTER 5

Implementing Encoded Archival Description: An Overview of Administrative and Technical Considerations

MICHAEL FOX

ENCODED ARCHIVAL DESCRIPTION (EAD) is a tool for making archival finding aids such as inventories and registers available for search and display in an electronic format. The process of implementing EAD is not fundamentally different from the launching of any new program or initiative. Many of the programmatic and administrative issues presented here will be familiar from other contexts, with the added complications inherent in the adoption of any new technology.

Is EAD right for your archives? This chapter identifies the ingredients necessary for successful implementation of this technology as a way of helping archivists and managers answer that question. It first addresses programmatic and administrative concerns, followed by an overview of technical issues, including a description of several methods for "publishing" electronic finding aids. The structure of this review may also serve as a framework for considering the six case studies in Part II in this publication.

Programmatic Issues

Implementing EAD is a more complex undertaking than simply buying computer software and sitting down to mark up finding aids.[1] To ensure success, an archives must first address the fundamental issues raised by the following questions: Does EAD meet our institutional mission, goals, and strategies? What resources will be required? How will we manage and carry out the work?

Mission, Goals, and Strategies

It is axiomatic that an archival institution should undertake no new initiative without first carefully considering whether it conforms to the organization's larger mission, goals,

N.B. "Implementing Encoded Archival Description: An Overview of Administrative and Technical Considerations," by Michael Fox, co-published simultaneously in the *American Archivist* (The Society of American Archivists) vol. 60, no. 3, pp. 330–343; and *Encoded Archival Description: Context, Theory, and Case Studies* (ed.: Jackie M. Dooley) The Society of American Archivists, 1998.

[1]This chapter uses interchangeably the expressions finding aids, inventories, and registers.

and strategies. EAD implementation is surely no exception; the use of EAD makes sense only if the actual benefits correspond to institutional objectives. What then, does EAD offer? Your assessment might focus on the following characteristics and merits. EAD is:

- A descriptive standard for finding aids that enables multiple uses of the information they contain, their interchange, and their long-term accessibility;
- A communication format for finding aids that enables archives to deliver them electronically to distant users;
- A technology that is standards based, computer platform independent, and employs powerful tools for the searching, retrieval, display, and navigation of finding aids.

Answers to some pointed questions about your clientele, and the ways in which your inventories are now used and their current condition, will help frame your response.[2] Candor is required. Is the digital delivery of both metadata and collection materials themselves an important goal for your institution? How might the delivery of searchable, electronic inventories fit into that objective? Are off-site users a target audience? Who uses your inventories? How often and in what ways are they used (to identify box numbers, to make copies for researchers)? How many finding aids do you have? Are you confident about their quality and completeness? If they are less than optimal, would you be willing to share them in their present condition? If not, how much revision would be required? In what physical format are they? In light of your answers, are the long-term benefits of EAD worth the effort involved?

For many institutions, adherence to standards is a key strategic goal when deploying new technology. It is seen as insurance that protects one's investment in technology by making it possible to take advantage of a broader and more diversified marketplace, while also enhancing one's ability to migrate data to future systems. For decision makers such as library and archives directors who have adopted this strategy, the standards-based, community development aspects of EAD will provide a convincing rationale for its adoption.

Priorities and Resources

Simply assessing the benefits is not enough; even highly desirable projects must be weighed against other useful activities as one sets priorities and allocates limited resources. Such planning decisions are subject to an array of local variables that are beyond the scope of this chapter, but the relative costs of a project typically are one significant factor. The major costs for EAD will be the purchase of the technology (hardware and software) and staffing.

Staffing

It probably will come as no surprise that personnel costs will be by far the largest expense, though hard figures are difficult to come by for several reasons. The pool of archives with EAD experience is relatively small. Personnel costs are very institution-specific (for example, colleges and universities may have access to a talented but relatively inexpensive student labor pool). EAD work absorbed by current staff may appear to be "free."

---

[2]The author wishes to acknowledge the "EAD Implementation Checklist" developed by Helena Zinkham and others at the Library of Congress as a source of many useful recommendations incorporated into this chapter. This checklist is available within the FAQ section of Anne Gilliland-Swetland, "Encoded Archival Description Document Type Definition (DTD) Application Guidelines," unpublished draft disseminated electronically, December 1996. Available at <http:/scriptorium.lib.duke.edu/findaids/ead/guidelines/index.html>.

To help in calculating staff costs, I will describe the principal tasks that may be necessary for implementing EAD. The full recitation of these activities may seem overwhelming—even discouraging at first and perhaps beyond the reach of many archives. However, this overview lays out many options, only a subset of which will actually have to be acted upon. The experience of the Special Collections Department of the library at the University of Vermont, as told by Elizabeth Dow in another chapter of this publication, illustrates how much a small archives can do.

Prior planning is vital if costly missteps are to be avoided. Many issues must be resolved before the first finding aid is mounted on a computer. All of the case studies in this book speak forcefully about the need to plan. A thoughtful review of the status quo will be a good beginning. What is the role of finding aids in your institution's reference and access system? Do the catalog and inventories work together in an integrated search process? Where does their content overlap? Are they created in the most efficient manner, given their interrelationship? Dennis Meissner's chapter describes how the Minnesota Historical Society spent considerable time rethinking the structure and presentation of its finding aids before beginning markup. This included asking fundamental questions about the purpose of inventories, their relation to collection-level descriptions in MARC, and their physical appearance. These were evaluated in terms of the informational content of the finding aids, how users in the reading room perceived them, and how remote access might affect their use.

Staff must evaluate hardware and software requirements and then select, acquire, and install the tools. As we shall see later, there are multiple options for creating EAD-encoded finding aids and making them electronically available to users. Archives will have to assemble their own systems from a mixture of components as there are no real turnkey systems available at this time. It will take staff time to evaluate these choices and reach decisions. As always with technology, this process is complicated by rapid evolution in the computer marketplace, which tends to cloud choices. If EAD implementation occurs as part of a multiple-repository effort or other consortial project, one must factor in the overhead attendant on resolving these issues in a collaborative context.

Once implementation is underway, the project must be appropriately managed. The work of purchasing equipment, contracting for services, negotiating with partners, and hiring and supervising staff is not a trivial matter. Ongoing operations require personnel to mark up, proof, and test the finding aids; load and manage files on computer servers; and handle any associated image files. Quality control will be important for any work that is contracted out. If the finding aids are to be electronically linked to the on-line catalog, the relevant MARC records must be edited to add the necessary pointers. As will be discussed later, one might also wish to supply an HTML version of each EAD finding aid for users with older Web browsers that do not support SGML or XML. If so, a process for converting the EAD files into HTML must be developed and implemented, as Nicole Bouché describes Yale's implementation of EAD in a later chapter in this book. Many early implementers of EAD are offering explanatory materials on their websites that describe what finding aids are, how they are used, and methods for access.[3] This text must be prepared, encoded, and loaded.

Technology-based programs are always dynamic, subject to continuous evolution and revision. Depending on the options chosen, as described later, the level of technical

[3]For examples, see the Yale EAD site at <http://webtext.library.yale.edu>.

expertise required to deliver finding aids electronically will range from modest to substantial. Archivists are resourceful people, and many of the early implementers of EAD have undertaken their projects with existing staff who have acquired new computer skills. Repositories that have access to in-house technical support staff, perhaps from a parent organization, may be able to tap into those resources. Purchase of support services is always a possibility, especially where it involves standard computer activities such as setting up desktop computers and servers or installing and configuring common tools such as Web servers. SGML database search engines may be less familiar to contract personnel, and so such services may be more difficult to locate or more expensive to acquire.

Training

Staff education and training needs are easy to overlook. Besides acquiring a working knowledge of the structure and content of the EAD standard, those who will work with EAD must master specific software packages for creating, converting, and editing finding aids. The Yale, Harvard, and Library of Congress implementation case studies in this book describe a process of collaborative self-education. The technical computer skills required will be described in greater detail in the technology section of this chapter. As usual, training options range from reading the software manuals to enrolling in formal classes or workshops.

Outsourcing

Contracting for services is a popular approach to special projects and may be appropriate for some aspects of EAD implementation. The choice between performing work in-house and contracting it out is usually one of trading time for money. Doing the work oneself usually involves less out-of-pocket expense but consumes precious staff resources. In some institutions, it may be easier to obtain funds such as grants, gifts, or extraordinary budget allocations for ''special projects'' such as implementing EAD than it is to hire additional regular staff. Some tasks, such as text markup, database installation and administration, and Web server maintenance are obvious choices for outsourcing.

Some level of involvement by regular staff is inevitable, however. Planning and operational oversight are difficult, if not impossible, to contract out. Moreover, the contracting process itself generates administrative overhead. Certain staff skills are required: a knowledge of the issues involved; the ability to articulate institutional objectives and convert them into clearly measurable vendor deliverables; familiarity with contract negotiations; and an understanding of the dynamics of contract supervision, especially where quality control is an issue. A successful vendor-customer relationship requires both parties to have a clear and detailed agreement on their objectives and requirements. This would be particularly important, for example, in outsourcing EAD encoding services, given the wide range of choices that EAD provides for marking up finding aids. The options exercised in this area will directly and perhaps significantly affect the time required to encode an inventory, and with that the cost of conversion.

Cooperative Ventures

Early implementers of EAD, institutions large and small, have found direction, support, and funding in consortial undertakings, joint projects, and other shared ventures. These include cross-campus cooperation at Harvard and Yale, as well as multi-institution projects such as the American Heritage Virtual Archive Project (Berkeley, Duke, Stanford, and Virginia) and the University of California EAD Project (nine campuses). While the view of these repositories may be that they are large and well staffed, Leslie Morris's chapter reveals that they are often just a loose federation of smaller operations (one to three persons) whose staff are as thinly spread across multiple responsibilities as in any small archives. The ways in which they have been able to work together to plan for, educate themselves about, and implement EAD suggests a cooperative model that others may beneficially replicate. This approach will be particularly useful for planning, procurement, and technical support.

Workflow

One hallmark of success for any new project is its ability to incorporate new activities into existing operations without significantly adding to daily workloads. While the planning and managerial activities previously described are significant, they largely represent an initial investment of time that need not be repeated, or at least continued at the same level of intensity, in the future. Ongoing operations, chiefly the encoding of inventories and the maintenance of the computer infrastructure, are where the real increase in effort is likely to occur. The most efficient implementation, therefore, will be one in which those activities can be closely integrated into, or simply replace, existing tasks on a one-for-one basis. Most archives today create printed inventories with a word processor. If one can continue to create finding aids in the same way and convert them afterwards into EAD (as Yale and the Minnesota Historical Society do), or substitute an SGML editor for the word processor (as Harvard does), the impact on workflow may be minimal. Indeed, the net effect of such changes may actually be greater efficiency and less work. Meissner reports on the use of standard word processing templates at the Minnesota Historical Society, where their use appears initially to have reduced the time needed for keying container lists and the subsequent cleanup of data entry errors.

Conversion of existing finding aids raises another group of prioritization and workflow issues. Encoding newly processed collections will be relatively straightforward and ''clean;'' new work, new methods. Marking up preexisting finding aids is more complex, raising at least three sets of issues: priorities, techniques, and editorial and stylistic revision. Realizing that the conversion of older inventories may go on for an extended period, how does one set priorities? Technically, what is the best method of converting existing finding aids, both those already in word processing format and those available only in paper form? How much editing to match current institutional practices is feasible? These issues will be familiar to repositories that have implemented MARC cataloging and undertaken the associated retrospective conversion of their catalogs.

Whether one converts all or only some existing inventories, it is necessary to select those to be done first. Early implementers of EAD have taken several approaches to this matter. Selection criteria may focus on materials relating to a particular topic, activity, or group; for example, the Minnesota Historical Society has begun to convert collections documenting environmental and natural resources issues. One might emphasize the ''significance'' of collections for research. Focusing on the potential for enhancing access is another possibility. The ability to perform text searches of the contents of an inventory will yield greater rewards for some finding aids than for others. For example, searching a container list that consists chiefly of an enumeration of box numbers, volume titles and span dates, as one often encounters in certain types of government and organizational records, may not significantly enhance subject access. The availability of an existing electronic version of the text could be another determining factor, as David Seaman's chapter reports was the case at the University of Virginia.

The level of tagging to be used is also an important workflow consideration, one discussed extensively in the Library of Congress, Harvard and Yale case studies. Protocols developed range from minimal content designation to experiments with richer markup, such as tagging each instance of personal and geographic names wherever they appear in the inventory. These decisions affect current encoding costs and, at least potentially, future retrievability. The Library of Congress staff describe the numerous hypertext links embedded within their finding aids, a task requiring additional data entry and testing.

Technical Issues

The programmatic and planning concerns addressed thus far share many traits in common with other institutional initiatives. In addition, EAD implementation requires consideration of the full range of technical issues that surround the introduction of any new computer technology. The staffing implications of the procurement, installation, and management of systems have already been described. This section focuses on the operational side of technology: how one creates encoded documents, disseminates them to users, maintains the files, and otherwise manages the technical system that supports these activities.

The technical aspects of EAD that lie ahead (for the implementer and for the reader of this chapter) are both complex and ambiguous. They are complex because there are so many options, because the technical details may be difficult to visualize without actually seeing them (especially for those not versed in EAD), and because the terminology of converters, styles, templates, and macros may be unfamiliar to the reader. They are ambiguous because, lacking a full understanding of how electronic finding aids actually may be used, we cannot fully anticipate all the consequences of the decisions that must be made today.

Authoring EAD Documents

First, one must create encoded finding aids; multiple approaches are available. Each will be described, including a list of its strengths and weakness and its suitability for creating new inventories (for collections that are being processed for the first time or where typed inventories are being rekeyed into electronic form), as well as the method's potential for converting existing electronic files. The authoring choices fall into five categories: native SGML authoring packages, SGML-aware text processors, word processor add-ons, other text processing tools, and databases.[4]

Native SGML Authoring and Editing Software. Native SGML authoring and editing software, such as SoftQuad's Author/Editor, ArborText's ADEPT Editor, or Incontext2 from InContext Systems, may be used to key inventories as an alternative to using word processing programs such as WordPerfect or Microsoft Word. While specific features vary somewhat, all SGML authoring packages include a Macintosh or Windows graphical interface for WYSIWYG[5] keying and editing of inventories. Typically, data entry begins with a user-created template on the screen that contains commonly used EAD elements, much the same way a cataloger uses a workform that displays a set of the most often used MARC tags. The text of the inventory is keyed into the appropriate tags. At each point in the inventory, the software displays a list of the currently valid elements from which the typist selects the correct tag; the software thus assists the user during the encoding

[4]This taxonomy is the author's; other writers may choose to categorize these tools in other ways.
[5]"What you see is what you get."

process by enforcing compliance with the structural syntax of EAD and the inclusion of mandatory attributes and elements. These products are also parsers; that is, they check the finished document for conformance with the DTD. This assures that a valid SGML "instance" (i.e., a finding aid document) is produced, one that can be successfully displayed, indexed, shared, and retrieved. The software prevents the typist from making encoding errors during data entry that would require subsequent adjustments (an ounce of prevention is a useful thing!). Other important features include the ability to create templates for standardized content and layout, including the insertion of "boilerplate" text, and the use of keyboard macros to avoid repetitive key strokes and to speed data entry. Documents are produced directly in SGML for permanent storage.

As with any software, there is a learning curve in mastering authoring software. The experience of archivists who have used them in EAD workshops suggests, however, that they are no more challenging than word processors and are perhaps less confusing to learn, as they have fewer bells and whistles. User-defined data templates may be employed to make the work easier for data entry operators who are not trained archivists, but some basic understanding of the hierarchical structure of container lists will be required.

Most institutions will want to create nicely formatted print copies of their inventories in addition to electronic versions. Authoring packages vary in their capabilities for producing such printing details as running headers and footers, pagination, graphics and fonts. SoftQuad, for example, offers an interface to the desktop publishing software Quark as a means of producing more sophisticated print output from its Author/Editor software. ADEPT Editor has a companion product, ADEPT Publisher, for generating print output. Incontext2 has its own style language to generate well-formatted print copy.

SGML authoring software also may be used for the conversion of existing inventories that are already in an electronic format or that can be scanned and passed through optical character recognition (OCR) software to produce readable text. Two approaches are possible. One may create a template containing empty EAD tags and cut-and-paste the existing electronic text into the appropriate tags. The other choice would be to "wrap" the preexisting text, in situ, with the proper EAD tags. While the use of keyboard macros can expedite this process, this approach requires a strong knowledge of the EAD tag set to avoid creating parsing errors in the process. Converting the container list portion of an inventory will always be the most time-consuming and relatively complex part of the work, whichever solution is employed.

SGML-aware Text Processors. SGML-aware text processors such as Framemaker+SGML from Adobe and recent versions of WordPerfect offer another alternative for authoring EAD documents. These differ from SGML authoring packages in that they are a standard desktop publisher and word processor, respectively, that have the ability to work directly with an SGML DTD such as EAD.

In many respects, WordPerfect functions very much like authoring software. Prior to creating inventories, one loads a copy of the DTD into the software so that it can intelligently manipulate files. A dialog box with a list of valid elements appears in a window, and the typist selects the appropriate tags as data entry proceeds. But WordPerfect goes one step further by applying styles to format the document simultaneously for printing. Styles are a convention employed in many word processors that define how certain parts of a document appear on a printed page or the screen. For example, the style assigned to an individual paragraph can govern the size and type of the font employed, line and paragraph spacing, tab setting, indenting, and other display characteristics. In WordPerfect the user may create a "layout file" that defines an appropriate display style for each EAD element. In this manner, one creates an EAD SGML file and, at the same time, a properly formatted WordPerfect document.

This method has three distinct advantages. There are the synergy and time savings of an integrated solution. The use of familiar tools may reduce start-up costs for software and training, enhance staff acceptance of new processes, and integrate easily into existing workflow. These packages also have the built-in ability to generate nicely printed output. The downside is that they require more work for initial set up. Someone on staff will have to learn features of the software such as styles, templates, and other conventions. As no standard templates exist for inventories at this time, each institution will need to create its own initial mappings. While most word processors have the capability to create templates and styles, an informal (and admittedly less than scientific) poll of participants in EAD workshops reveals that few archives have made use of these features in the past.

Word Processor Add-ons. The third method for producing EAD documents is a variation on the former approach, one that might be characterized as the use of post-authoring converters. Microsoft's SGML Author for Word and Microstar's Near and Far Author enable one to convert documents produced using the Windows versions of the popular Microsoft Word word processor.

It may be easiest to imagine this scenario as the reverse of the previous. With WordPerfect, one encodes a document in EAD and associates the SGML elements with particular display styles. Using Word add-ons, one creates a document using the styles feature of Word and then maps the styles to EAD elements. A Word template is created that defines a separate style for each part of the inventory that corresponds to a particular EAD tag. For example, one might create a style called "C01Title." That style would then be assigned to the text of the finding aid that would later be encoded as <c01><did> <unittitle>. The text converter is then programmed, through an interactive editor, to associate particular Word styles with corresponding EAD tags. For instance, one would instruct the software that the text in style C01Title should be encoded as the element string <c01><did><unittitle>, and so forth throughout the document. As the finding aid is typed in Word, one assigns the proper style to each section of text. When done, one simply saves the file as SGML and the converter program outputs a correctly tagged EAD instance using an association file to map Word styles to the appropriate EAD elements. The Microsoft Word converters and the SGML-aware text processors also can convert existing SGML files into their native Word, WordPerfect, or Framemaker format respectively.

This class of software also can be used for the conversion of existing finding aids. One imports an existing document, applies the appropriate styles to each section of text, and runs the conversion program. The Minnesota Historical Society experience suggests that while this process requires manual intervention and some sense of the EAD hierarchical structure, it requires only a basic knowledge of the tag set. Where lengthy container lists contain simple folder listings, whole blocks of text may be highlighted and converted to an appropriate style in one step.

Other Text Processing Tools. The fourth authoring scenario involves the use of other text processing tools and techniques. The simplest way (and least expensive in terms of software cost) to mark up documents is to use a basic text editor like Notepad (which comes with every copy of Windows), to type EAD text, beginning with "<ead><eadheader><eadid>MHS75-0005798</eadid></eadheader>. . .", etc. This is a perfectly possible but complex, exacting, and time-consuming solution; one that requires a detailed knowledge of EAD to create parsable documents. A number of freeware parsers are available for the technically adventurous who wish to use this approach.

Other possibilities exist as well. For example, University of California library staff have created a tool using "perl" (a text manipulation computer programming language) that generates finding aids through the use of a fill-in-the-boxes screen template. A program written in perl does the rest of the work, generating an EAD document.[6] One might call this "markup for dummies," as it requires little knowledge of EAD structures, but writing perl "scripts" is a fairly sophisticated programming exercise that will be beyond the skill or training level of most archivists. The perl programming language also has proven useful for converting text already in electronic form into EAD. Other text manipulation programs may be used as well. At least one institution has achieved the same effect using the macro language of Microsoft Word to convert word processing documents into EAD. The Minnesota Historical Society uses this tool to translate SGML documents into HTML format. Bouché describes how Yale relies on the use of the macro language in WordPerfect and Edix/Wordix for conversion of existing text. The 8.0 version of WordPerfect also includes extensions to its macro language to make it more SGML-aware. There are also commercial text manipulation programs such as DynaTag from Inso Corporation and OmniMark from OmniMark Technologies that can perform this same function. They are powerful and efficient, particularly because they are SGML-aware and understand the basic concepts of wrapping text and nesting elements that are fundamental to SGML structures such as EAD.

These text manipulation solutions typically utilize "visual" clues such as the formatting of text, punctuation, and the use and location of tabs, paragraph markers, and line breaks to make "educated guesses" about the content and structure of a document in order to convert it into SGML. The more consistently one's inventories have been physically laid out on the page, the more successful these techniques will be across a corpus of existing finding aids, as described in Bouché's report of the Beinecke Library's conversion experience.

Databases. The last option is the use of databases to generate EAD files, creating documents in a proprietary database format and converting them to EAD when exported into a text file. Two commercially developed products fall into this category: Gencat from Eloquent Systems and Internet Archivist from Interface Electronics. There are substantial differences between the two products. Gencat is a proprietary database package that can be used for the creation, storage, searching, and delivery of descriptive information about archives at a variety of levels, from collection- or fond-level descriptions to container lists. As such, Gencat is a full-fledged authoring and publication system. As an additional feature, it can export this data in different formats, including MARC and EAD, though its ability to do the latter has not yet been fully demonstrated. Internet Archivist, now in the final stages of development, is strictly an authoring tool that stores the EAD finding aid in its own database structure for convenience but exports the file as an SGML document. From the user's point of view, the software functions just like the native SGML authoring or text processing tools that feature a fill-in-the-boxes interface. Its strength lies in the fact that it is the closest thing to a turnkey authoring package available, as it was designed to work specifically with EAD; as such, it will be simple to install and operate. The developer has announced its intention to produce additional modules that will provide data import and conversion services and the capability to search across finding aids. The ability of these two packages to export data in a standard format such as EAD will certainly offset

[6]The templates generated for the University of California EAD Project may be viewed at <http://sunsite.berkeley.edu/FindingAids/uc-ead/templates/>.

some of the concerns about the long-term viability of storing one's data in a proprietary database structure.

Some further words of caution about databases are in order. They are powerful tools for data management, but they do have limitations. Archivists who like to develop their own databases are cautioned against assuming that they will be able to incorporate the hierarchical structure of EAD easily and cheaply into an application built with off-the-shelf database management software such FileMaker Pro or Microsoft Access. This is not to say that it cannot be done, but the effort would be significant.

Publishing Inventories

''Publishing,'' or the electronic delivery of finding aids to users, is the second technical aspect of EAD implementation. There currently are at least three ways, described here as scenarios, of accomplishing this; they are not mutually exclusive.

Publication of EAD-encoded finding aids does not necessarily require use of the World Wide Web. After all, SGML products preceded the appearance of the Web, and other distribution methods such as CD-ROM are possible. However, the ubiquitous presence of the Web and the widespread use of browser software for the dissemination of information suggest that we should focus on these tools. One important forthcoming development that will have considerable impact on making EAD accessible over the Internet is Extensible Markup Language (XML). A simplified ''dialect'' of SGML, XML can be thought of as SGML-Lite for the Web. XML will have an impact on the authoring and electronic publishing of EAD finding aids in two ways. First, additional authoring tools will certainly emerge. Second, and more importantly, Web browsers such as Netscape's Navigator and Microsoft's Internet Explorer will be able to read EAD files in SGML/XML directly without requiring that they first be ''dumbed down'' to HTML. Even so, there will still be a transitional period when some Web users have XML-aware browsers, while others have not yet upgraded to the newer software.

Since these browsers currently cannot read full SGML files, archivists who wish to use the Internet must adopt other solutions in the interim. Either the SGML files must be converted into the simpler HTML tags that current browsers can read, or the user must load and configure a software helper application such as Panorama Pro or MultiDoc Pro. Several options for the former are described in the following scenarios.

Scenario One: Access Through A Website. Many archives have access to an Internet website, either their own or that of a parent organization. In this scenario, the Internet-searching patron locates a page on the archives' website that lists those collections for which an electronic finding aid is available, clicking on a collection name to display a copy of the inventory in the user's browser. The archives may choose to provide an SGML/XML or an HTML version, or to offer the reader a choice of formats as Yale University, the Library of Congress, and the University of Vermont do.[7] Alternatives to a simple alphabetical listing of collections are possible, including groupings by time period, locality, or subject focus. Links to finding aids might also be embedded in an on-line bibliography or topical collection guide.

This scenario is the simplest and least expensive option to implement, but it also offers the lowest level of searching access. Users must either browse the finding aids or

[7]For examples, see their websites at <http://webtext.library.yale.edu>, <http://lcweb.loc.gov/rr/ead/eadhome.html>, and <http://sageunix.uvm.edu>.

know from other sources which collections are appropriate to their needs; searching is limited to the text of only one individual finding aid at a time.

Requirements:
Encoded finding aids.
- Location on a website containing a listing of collections.
- Storage space for the finding aid files on a hard drive accessible by the Web server that serves that website.
- A process for converting EAD files to HTML, if that display option is offered.
- Stylesheet and navigator files to support the display of SGML/XML documents.

Scenario Two: Access from a Web-based On-line Catalog. Many on-line library and archives catalogs now have public interfaces that use a Web browser to access their MARC-based holdings. These are generally available to all Internet users. MARC field 856 permits a cataloger to embed a link in the catalog record, in the form of a uniform resource locator (URL) address that points to another electronic document such as an EAD finding aid.[8] In this scenario, the patron searches the MARC descriptions of archival collections in the on-line catalog using the searching capabilities of the catalog software. When the entry for a relevant collection is displayed, the reference to the electronic version of the finding aid appears as a highlighted browser hyperlink; clicking on that link loads the finding aid into the user's browser. The archives may chose to supply the finding aid in either SGML/XML or HTML format.

This scenario continues the two-step discovery process patrons have used for years in many repositories. First, relevant collections are identified by a search of the catalog, then an inventory that contains greater detail than the catalog record is consulted to narrow the search and select appropriate files. In this scenario, these two steps now occur on-line, possibly far from one's reading room.

For institutions with Web-accessible catalogs, this option offers substantial benefits. Prior investment in a familiar tool, the MARC catalog, is leveraged to provide public access to finding aids. The summary descriptive information in the MARC records offers access by topics, provenance, and other criteria and serves as a useful search filter. Some developers are concerned that the results of a search across the full text of multiple finding aids would produce overwhelming results—a little like trying to take a sip from a fire hydrant. This viewpoint is reinforced for many by their experiences with Web search engines. Providing access to electronic finding aids via an on-line catalog minimizes this concern. For those with a Web-based catalog, costs will be modest.

Requirements:
- Encoded finding aids.
- Web-based on-line catalog with MARC records for archival holdings.
- Ability to update catalog records to provide appropriate hyperlinks.
- Storage space for the finding aid files on a hard drive accessible by the Web server that serves that website.
- A process for converting EAD files to HTML, if that display option is offered.
- Stylesheet and navigator files to support the display of SGML/XML documents.

---

[8]For examples of links from on-line catalogs, search records in these collections at <http://webpac.library.yale.edu> or <http://scriptorium.lib.duke.edu>.

Scenario Three: Access Through Finding Aid Databases on the Internet. There are several software ''search engines'' that index and distribute text documents, such as SGML finding aids, via the Internet. Users can search them with a standard Web browser. A single query of such a ''database'' searches the full text of multiple finding aids simultaneously and returns to the user a list of relevant collections. This activity mirrors what happens when one queries a library catalog that then displays a list of all the titles that match the search. Such a finding aid ''database'' may contain all the inventories of a single archives or function as a ''union database'' for multiple institutions. The files need not reside on a single server. At least one product simply stores a central index to multiple finding aids that are themselves physically located on servers at other institutions and which are retrieved only in response to a particular search request. This eliminates the need for each archives to continually transfer new or updated finding aids to the central server.

This approach affords detailed searching of all the richness of the finding aids themselves, across collections and institutions, to a depth of detail never before possible.[9] Four products of this type are in current use: PAT and LiveLink from OpenText, DynaWeb from Inso Corporation, and Site Search from OCLC. All vary in significant details such as ease of configuration and hardware requirements, as well as in the details of ''publication'' such as the use of stylesheets and the dynamic conversion of files to HTML. DynaWeb, for example, converts SGML files to HTML ''on the fly'' so that users do not require any special software beyond the customary Web browser. These products are not inexpensive; expect hardware and software costs to begin at $20,000, though Inso does make ''grants'' of free software (DynaWeb) to ''educational'' institutions. Elizabeth Dow reports how the University of Vermont received one such grant in her chapter.

Other options are feasible, though it is unclear which archives, if any, are currently using them. Text search engines that are not ''SGML-aware'' might be used, including products such as Folio and Star, that could import and translate SGML files into their proprietary formats, and provide a Web-based search interface to the files, although they will undoubtedly lose the hierarchical structure of EAD in the conversion. If the archives converts the SGML files into HTML format, a locally mounted Web-based search and retrieval engine such as AltaVista could provide indexing and display.

Various public interfaces for searching are under development at individual archives and at the Research Libraries Group as institutions test the various ways in which users might wish to query finding aid databases. For better or worse, user interaction with online catalogs is better known, if less than optimal, for archives patrons. We are only beginning to understand how researchers will react to these new searching opportunities.

Requirements:

- Search engine software and hardware.
- Encoded finding aids.
- Stylesheets for the display of SGML/XML files.
- Web server that can access the search engine.
- Conversion routines for translating SGML files into HTML.

[9]For examples, see the following websites: <http://scriptorium.lib.duke.edu:8000/dweb_help/dweb_searching.html> and <http://hul.harvard.edu/dfap>.

Possible Future Scenario. The Z39.50 standard facilitates computer-to-computer communication. Its most widespread application is facilitating the searching of multiple databases, such as library and archives catalogs, without having to use the particular search syntax of each. Work may begin shortly on the development of a Z39.50 ''profile'' for EAD that would add finding aids to the list of data types that could be handled directly by Z39.50 databases and browsers.

Conclusions

The issues raised in this chapter may seem daunting, even insurmountable. The need to describe many options may leave a misimpression that there are thousands of decisions to be made, which is not the case. There are three large decisions to be reached: Shall we do it? How will we create electronic finding aids? How will we distribute them? Choices will become clearer as more institutions begin implementation, as consortia of archives develop support systems, and as the tools and underlying SGML/XML applications move more prominently into the Internet mainstream.

The adoption of EAD is in an initial phase. Perhaps it is still most appropriate for the technically adventurous archives, large or small. Some institutions may wish to defer full implementation until issues surrounding the technical infrastructure for creating and publishing EAD files are more clearly defined, or until professional support systems such as cooperative projects are in place to provide direction and succor. But is not too soon for any archives to begin to understand EAD and the implications for standardized practices that it suggests, to begin to evaluate local practices in advance of later adoption of EAD, and certainly not too soon to contribute to the community discussion of what our users need in electronic information systems. EAD implementation is a function of the entire archival community, as well as a programmatic decision of individual archives.

CHAPTER 6

EAD as an Archival Descriptive Standard

KRIS KIESLING

"THE MARC ARCHIVAL AND MANUSCRIPTS CONTROL (AMC) format has the potential to change the lives of archivists forever," wrote Steve Hensen at the beginning of a paper on the use of standards in the application of the AMC format.[1] Twelve years later the same could easily be said of Encoded Archival Description, the next logical step in the evolution of archival descriptive standards and the answer to MARC for finding aids. Just as the MARC format was the mechanism that provided a consistent structure for archival catalog records and set archivists on a course toward acceptance of a host of bibliographic standards, so EAD will now be the impetus that leads us toward standardizing the structure and possibly the content of finding aids, and it may well unite the international archival community in the process.

Developing a standard for finding aids is hardly a new idea. Archivists have sought mechanisms to standardize archival description for over a century,[2] but the most recent efforts to standardize and automate began with SPINDEX II in the late 1960s. This was followed a decade or so later by the National Information Systems Task Force (NISTF) and the creation of the "Data Elements Dictionary"[3] that formed the basis of the MARC AMC format. In 1978 the publication of *AACR2* caused the Library of Congress to draft an alternate cataloging code for archives and manuscript materials, and in 1983 the first edition of *Archives, Personal Papers, and Manuscripts (APPM)* was published.[4] The revised edition of *APPM* (1989) fully merged the data structure to the data content by supplying extensive MARC examples for the cataloging rules. Throughout these two dec-

N.B. "EAD as an Archival Descriptive Standard," by Kris Kiesling, co-published simultaneously in the *American Archivist* (The Society of American Archivists) vol. 60, no. 3, pp. 344–54; and *Encoded Archival Description: Context, Theory, and Case Studies* (ed.: Jackie M. Dooley) The Society of American Archivists, 1998.

[1]Steven L. Hensen, "The Use of Standards in the Application of the AMC Format," *American Archivist* 49 (Winter 1986): 31.

[2]For a concise history, see the "Chronology of Key Developments in the Evolution of Standards for Archival Description" presented as part of the "Report of the Working Group on Standards for Archival Description," *American Archivist* 52 (Fall 1989): 441–50.

[3]"Data Elements Used in Archives, Manuscripts, and Records Repository Information Systems: A Dictionary of Standard Terminology," in Nancy Sahli, *MARC for Archives and Manuscripts: The AMC Format* (Chicago: Society of American Archivists, 1985) (now out of print).

[4]Steven L. Hensen, *Archives, Personal Papers, and Manuscripts: A Cataloging Manual for Archival Repositories, Historical Societies, and Manuscript Libraries* (Washington, D.C.: Library of Congress, 1983); second edition published by the Society of American Archivists in 1989.

ades, many archivists regarded standards for finding aids as an impossibility, arguing that variations in the nature of holdings and the needs of users dictated basic differences in approach. Along with a general resistance to "library practices," these same arguments were made against the development and adoption of MARC. Yet there were efforts afoot in the Society of American Archivists, the National Archives, and the Library of Congress to create descriptive standards,[5] and by the early 1980s archivists were using word processing programs and databases at the local level in an effort to control the structure of their finding aids.

At about the same time, the Canadian archival community also was working diligently on descriptive standards. The Bureau of Canadian Archivists published *Toward Descriptive Standards: Report and Recommendations of the Canadian Working Group on Archival Descriptive Standards* in 1985.[6] As a direct result of the recommendations articulated by the Canadian Working Group in its report, *Rules for Archival Description (RAD)* was issued over a period of several years beginning in 1990.[7] While the Canadians chose to focus on descriptive theory and content rather than on data output, and even though *RAD* follows very closely the structure of *AACR2*, implementation of *RAD* to this point in time has focused primarily on finding aids, not catalog records.

In the late 1980s the Working Group on Standards for Archival Description (WGSAD) was formed to devise "the tools and procedures for evaluating, adopting, and maintaining description standards for the profession."[8] The working group's recommendations resulted in the establishment of a standards board within SAA, publication of a handbook on standards related to archival description,[9] and the Society's participation in the National Information Standards Organization (NISO), which is the principal U.S. standards-developing body for libraries and publishers. In describing the evolution of archival description, the report of the working group states, "The strong consensus that now exists on the need for and desirability of standards for archival description has emerged only recently and, when viewed against opinions widely held only a decade or two ago, is just short of revolutionary."[10] Why then, has it taken archivists nearly another decade to begin to implement a standard for finding aids?

EAD in the Larger Standards Setting

In one sense, EAD is already a standard, since its Document Type Definition (DTD) is compliant with the International Standards Organization (ISO) 8879 Standard Generalized Markup Language (SGML), a metalanguage for constructing markup languages.

[5]Implementation of standardization was at least partly responsible for LC's efforts to develop the Master Record file (1964–70), the National Archives' use of SPINDEX to produce an index to the *Papers of the Continental Congress* (early 1970s) and NHPRC's use of SPINDEX as the basis for the *Directory of Archives and Manuscript Repositories in the United States* (1974–78), and the publication of *Inventories and Registers: A Handbook of Techniques and Examples* (1976) by SAA's Committee on Finding Aids.

[6]*Toward Descriptive Standards: Report and Recommendations of the Canadian Working Group on Archival Descriptive Standards* (Ottawa: Bureau of Canadian Archivists, 1985).

[7]*Rules for Archival Description* (Ottawa: Bureau of Canadian Archivists, 1990).

[8]Lawrence Dowler, "Introduction" to "Archival Description Standards: Establishing a Process for Their Development and Implementation: Report of the Working Group on Standards for Archival Description," *American Archivist* 52 (Fall 1989): 432.

[9]*Standards for Archival Description: A Handbook*, compiled by Victoria Irons Walch (Chicago: Society of American Archivists, 1994).

[10]"Report of the Working Group on Standards for Archival Description," *American Archivist* 52 (Fall 1989): 443.

EAD also utilizes and is compatible with other technical and descriptive standards, including the ISO character sets, graphic notations such as TIFF and GIF, and the International Standard Archival Description General (ISAD(G)). Version 1.0 of EAD also will be compatible with XML (Extensible Markup Language), which may replace HTML as the standard for the presentation of documents on the World Wide Web. More importantly, however, in order to achieve the status of a descriptive standard within SAA, EAD must be embraced by the archival community as the most appropriate mechanism for the long-term electronic storage of finding aids and for their presentation over the Internet. Through the acceptance and use of EAD as the standard for the *structure* of archival finding aids, the archival community also can work toward establishing a standard for their *content.*

The library community began to standardize the descriptions of books and other traditional library materials for a very compelling reason—to share the burden of cataloging those materials. Archivists have equally compelling reasons to standardize the descriptions of the unique materials in their holdings. Aside from the pragmatism of making our finding aids intelligible to researchers not only within an institution, but also among repositories, by presenting consistent types of information in a relatively uniform paper format, we now live in a technological world that demands further standardization to facilitate the sharing and retrieval of data. The general clamor for some form of indexing and control of the vast array of Internet resources should be proof enough of that fact. Finding aids generally are not transitory documents; barring the acquisition of additional materials for a collection, a finding aid can serve generations of researchers. The need to migrate data over time and across platforms is therefore an important aspect of standardization, as well as a strong rationale for the use of EAD to encode this data.

EAD was created *by* archivists *for* archivists, which gives it several advantages over other data structures that archivists might employ. First, we are not reliant on any software vendor or other outside organization to set or maintain this standard for us. Anyone who has tried to migrate data over several versions of HTML, of a database program, or even of a word processing program, understands how frustrating data migration can be. Some archivists tried to shoehorn entire inventories into the MARC AMC format soon after its development; their lack of success is an excellent illustration of the critical need for a good fit between the data and the data structure. The hierarchical nature of SGML's nesting capabilities and the hierarchical structure of finding aids is a good fit. Second, EAD has very broad appeal. Currently the museum community, the medieval manuscripts community, and the archival communities in several countries are considering EAD as an encoding standard for their collection descriptions. Third, EAD is very flexible; while it was designed to accommodate the types of finding aids typically referred to as inventories and registers,[11] it is adaptable enough to be generated as output from relational databases or word processing programs. This flexibility and adaptability results from the fact that EAD is solidly based on the content of finding aids rather than their presentation format. The EAD development team made a conscious effort to accommodate existing archival descriptive practices while looking toward a future that embraces standardization.

Any discussion of Encoded Archival Description as a standard must consider multiple aspects of standardization: the standards process within SAA; the creation of formal documentation to support the standard; the broad acceptance of EAD by the archival

[11]See "Ann Arbor Accords: Principles and Criteria for an SGML Document Type Definition (DTD) for Finding Aids," *Archival Outlook* (January 1996): 12–13.

community; and the suitability of EAD as a data structure standard and as the basis for a data content standard. Accomplishing this last aspect will require a close examination of current finding aids, exploration of the optimal level of markup for display and retrieval, and the establishment of best practices.

The Standards Process in SAA and Beyond

The Society of American Archivists controls the intellectual component of EAD, which means that suggestions for additional elements, elimination of elements, modifications of attributes, and any other changes to the Document Type Definition (DTD) will originate from archivists, be reviewed by archivists, and be implemented by archivists. Suggestions for changes to the DTD will be funneled, at least for the time being, through the Committee on Archival Information Exchange's EAD Working Group. The working group currently comprises the original Bentley Library development team (whose contributions to EAD development are described in Janice Ruth's chapter in this book, as well as representatives from RLG and OCLC, from Canada and the United Kingdom, and from several other institutions in the United States.[12] The Society of American Archivists should eventually establish a permanent body, perhaps modeled on the American Library Association's MARBI (Machine-Readable Bibliographic Information) Committee or the US-MARC Advisory Committee of the Library of Congress (though perhaps on a smaller scale), to continue the development and maintenance of the DTD.[13] The Library of Congress[14] has agreed to work closely with the Society to maintain and distribute the DTD and other documentation, including EAD Technical Document #2 (the Tag Library) and Technical Document #3 (the Application Guidelines).

Maintenance and support for EAD will be a new type of endeavor for SAA. It is one thing to review standards developed by other organizations and endorse them for use by the archival community; maintaining an internally developed standard, on the other hand, requires a stable infrastructure and ongoing financial support. We can learn from the model provided by MARBI and its strong working relationship with the Library of Congress. The members of the EAD maintenance body within SAA must have a thorough knowledge of EAD structure and its application. The financial backing for the development and maintenance of EAD up to this point has come from a variety of sources, including the federal government and private foundations who have responded favorably when fund-

[12]As of September 1997, the Working Group included Randall Barry (LC Network Development/MARC Standards Office), Jackie Dooley (UC Irvine), Ricky Erway (RLG), Michael Fox (Minnesota Historical Society), Anne Gilliland-Swetland (UCLA), Steve Hensen (Duke University), Kris Kiesling (University of Texas, chair), Eric Miller (OCLC), Chris Petter (University of Victoria, Canada), Daniel Pitti (University of Virginia), Janice Ruth (LC Manuscript Division), Rob Spindler (Arizona State University), Meg Sweet (Public Record Office, UK), Rich Szary (Yale University), Sharon Thibodeau (NARA), and Helena Zinkham (LC Prints and Photographs Division).

[13]In accordance with the recommendations of the Task Force on Organizational Effectiveness and with approval of SAA Council (June 1998), the Committee on Archival Information Exchange will evolve into a technical subcommittee on descriptive standards under the new Standards Committee. It is not clear at the time of this writing whether the EAD Working Group will continue as a component of this new subcommittee, or if a separate subcommittee within the Standards Committee will be responsible for the continued revision and maintenance of EAD.

[14]LC's Network Development/MARC Standards Office also maintains the documentation for the US-MARC format. While LC also has considerable decision-making authority regarding the intellectual structure of MARC, that will not be the case with EAD.

ing was requested for a specific purpose.[15] For EAD to become a robust and viable standard, however, this piecemeal funding scenario cannot continue.

Before EAD can be endorsed as a formal SAA standard, it must pass through a fairly rigorous review process. The SAA Standards Board is concerned primarily with the process of standards development, review, and approval for standards created both within and outside the Society. The Standards Board "recognizes the central importance of consensus to the development of strong standards. However, consensus on a specific standard may not always equate with unanimous and unqualified approval by all concerned, for in most cases that will be difficult to achieve."[16] To achieve as much consensus as possible, the standards review process involves activities ranging from the establishment of the need for the standard, publication of notices in *Archival Outlook* regarding the initiation and development of the standard, distribution of the full text of the proposed standard in SAA publications and elsewhere, and formal invitation to representatives within SAA and from appropriate outside organizations to participate in the development and/or review of drafts. These latter groups, in turn, are expected to seek input from a wide audience. If the reviewing bodies support approval, the Standards Board makes a recommendation to SAA's Council. The final step in the process is endorsement of the proposed standard by the Council.

Beyond the SAA standards sphere, the National Information Standards Organization has more than once invited the Society of American Archivists to submit EAD for NISO approval. It was felt that submission during beta testing was inappropriate, but version 1.0 may be sent forward. The development of EAD also is being closely monitored, and its effectiveness tested, in archival repositories in Canada, in the United Kingdom and various European countries, and in Australia and New Zealand. Kent Haworth, one of the principal architects of *RAD,* has characterized EAD in the following way:

> One of the reasons why I am so taken with the EAD is that it accommodates multi-level description, which is so vital to the application of RAD....The development of the EAD is a very positive development for the archival community, not only here in Canada and in the United States, but also internationally. Some very exciting projects are underway in the U.K., for example. I think that pilot projects need to be undertaken, in much the same way as the Berkeley Project was developed; to test, experiment, and enhance our methods for making available information in our archives. Most importantly, we need to advance our knowledge and understanding of these developments and as much as possible avoid taking easy roads out that in the end will lead us to dead ends.[17]

[15]Between 1993 and 1997, the EAD effort received funding from the Department of Education, the Commission on Preservation and Access, the Council on Library Resources, the National Endowment for the Humanities, the National Digital Library, the Mellon Foundation, and the Delmas Foundation.

[16]"Standards Development and Review in the Society of American Archivists: Introduction and Procedures for Review and Approval of an SAA-Developed Standard," developed by the Standards Board and approved by SAA Council, June 1995, 2.

[17]E-mail message from Kent Haworth to ARCAN-L, the Canadian archives listserv, 12 September 1997. The discussion involved the implementation of the Canadian Archival Information Network (used with permission).

EAD Documentation

Descriptive standards require formal documentation. The EAD documentation will comprise four technical documents: the DTD, the tag library, application guidelines, and possibly a compendium of practice.

Technical Document #1 will be the DTD itself, the ''rules'' that must be followed in creating a valid EAD ''instance,'' which is to say, a validly encoded finding aid. As the maintenance agency for EAD documentation, the Library of Congress will make the current version of the DTD available electronically. The DTD can be downloaded and used by anyone who wishes to do so. The EAD development team has received queries from repositories and individuals requesting permission to ''adapt'' EAD for their own particular uses. Adaptation is possible, of course, but then the DTD would no longer be Encoded Archival Description, and the entire purpose of standardization would have been abandoned. Naturally, EAD will evolve over time, but only within a conscientious standards review process.

Technical Document #2 is the EAD Tag Library, the EAD equivalent of the *USMARC Format for Bibliographic Data.* The Tag Library lists, in alphabetical order by their generic identifiers (tag names), all of the data elements that comprise EAD. Each element entry contains a brief description of the element's purpose and a list of attributes that can be used to modify the element. To provide the hierarchical context for the use of a specific element, each element entry also lists other elements within which the element may occur (May Occur Within), as well as other elements that may be used within the element (May Contain). Finally, most elements in the Tag Library include one or more examples illustrating use of the element.

In an effort to keep the number of elements to a minimum, EAD makes extensive use of an SGML feature known as ''attributes.'' Attributes are used to modify elements, making it possible to restrict the universe of elements to the most significant structural aspects of finding aids. For example, the use of attributes enabled the development team to focus on the structure of finding aids without being concerned about whether the highest level of description was a collection, a record group, or a series. The same element, Component <c>, is used to encode every level of description after the highest one in a given finding aid, but a ''level'' attribute is used to define each level by modifying the meaning of the <c> element. The list of options for the level attribute includes such intellectual groupings as collection, fonds, record group, series, and item. The DTD requires that a level be specified for the highest level of description in the finding aid, but the attribute is optional thereafter. The alternative approach to the use of attributes would have been the creation of separate elements for collection, record group, series, and so on. This technique of making elements do multiple duty through the use of attributes also enabled the development team to avoid the use of certain ambiguous archival terms when creating the element names; it would have been quite controversial, for example, to attempt to define what a ''series'' is.

Technical Document #3, the EAD Application Guidelines, articulates recommended practice for the use of the most basic and important EAD fields. For example, Date of the Unit, the <unitdate> element is to be used only for single, inclusive, or bulk dates for the archival materials being described. The Date <date> element, on the other hand, is to be used for other types of dates, such as a date of publication or the date of creation of the finding aid. The Digital Archival Object <dao> element should be used only for links to digitized surrogates of archival materials described in the finding aid, while other types of pointers and links apply to nonarchival documents and images. Elements grouped within the Control Access Headings <controlaccess> element should be used for controlled vocabulary, such as personal names from the *LC Name Authority File* or genre headings from the *Art and Architecture Thesaurus*. The Application Guidelines can be viewed as an initial step toward establishing a content standard for EAD.[18]

The Application Guidelines also address a repository's management of EAD in the form of FAQs (Frequently Asked Questions). Particularly useful for those wondering about implementing EAD in their institutions are FAQs that address "Do we still need to do MARC cataloging?" and "Where do we start?" The guidelines also contain a number of appendices, such as the "Ann Arbor Accords" (the design principles that were followed by the Bentley development team), a bibliography, and a glossary.

A compendium of practice is under consideration by the EAD Working Group as Technical Document #4. The compendium would include finding aids from a variety of repositories representing various types of collections; it would provide guidance on tagging issues and establish parameters for an appropriate level of markup. The compendium would serve the same purpose as did *MARC for Archives and Manuscripts: A Compendium of Practice*, which introduced archivists to desirable styles of practice for creating MARC AMC records.

EAD as a Data Structure Standard

Janice Ruth's chapter in Part I of this publication outlines the structure of EAD, which was formulated by the development team over the course of a week at the Bentley Library in July 1995, working from the Berkeley Finding Aid Project's FindAid DTD. Since the EAD structure was created, it has remained quite stable through alpha and beta testing. The beta DTD was subjected to fairly rigorous testing by a number of institutions in the United States and abroad for a period of one year; it was then opened to comments and suggestions for change in the summer of 1997.[19] No major structural changes were suggested by any of the repositories who responded to the call for comments.

The high-level structure of EAD is such that most archivists readily recognize within it components of the finding aids that they routinely create in their descriptions of fonds, collections, record groups, and series. The structure is broadly applicable to all types of materials and is useable by any type of repository, whether the collecting focus is primarily textual or object-oriented, government or organizational records, private papers or historical manuscripts, photographs or museum objects, or a combination of all of these. Through the course of numerous EAD workshops, which have been attended by individuals from repositories large and small, not a single participant has said that EAD's structure does not make sense or that it cannot be applied to the finding aids at their repository. Given the results of institutional testing and the feedback received from workshop participants, it would seem that EAD is a viable data structure standard for finding aids that can be readily accepted by the archival community.

---

[18]A draft set of Application Guidelines, prepared by Anne Gilliland-Swetland and Thomas A. LaPorte, is available at <http://scriptorium.lib.duke.edu/findaids/ead/guidelines/index.html>. The EAD Working Group will begin work on the final version of these guidelines after EAD version 1.0 and the final EAD Tag Library are issued in late summer 1998.

[19]SAA's EAD Working Group sent out a formal request for comments via the EAD listserv (ead@loc.gov), the official venue for discussion about EAD, on 23 June 1997, and collected comments from the list until 22 August 1997.

EAD has already formed the basis for a number of cooperative projects. RLG's digital collections project, "Studies in Scarlet,"[20] has encoded finding aids for materials at seven institutions relating to marriage and sexuality in the United States and the United Kingdom from 1815 to 1914, linking them to collection-level records in RLIN and to digital surrogates of collection materials. The University of California system has a project underway to encode finding aids in the repositories of all nine UC campuses, in which the campuses that have the resources to mark up finding aids are assisting the campuses that lack those resources.[21] The goals of the UC project are to develop an implementation toolkit for conversion of existing finding aids and encoding new ones and to create a prototype union database of finding aids. The American Heritage Virtual Archive Project, an NEH-funded cooperative endeavor between Stanford University, the University of California at Berkeley, Duke University, and the University of Virginia, will develop a "demonstration system, which will provide a test bed to evaluate both the effectiveness of the prototype's 'virtual archive' in providing access to distributed digital library resources, and the feasibility of the decentralized 'real world' production methods that the project will use to create it."[22] The project will also establish, as Daniel Pitti has aptly put it, "an acceptable range of uniform practice" among these four institutions.

Archivists in small repositories (especially those that are not part of a larger institution) lacking the resources to implement EAD have expressed frustration at not being able to "keep up." It may serve as a useful parallel to note that not all repositories have been able or willing to implement MARC in an on-line system. Some have chosen to use MARC-compatible systems such as Minaret or MicroMARC, and others have chosen not to create catalog records at all, even in a manual system. Similarly, archivists can approach use of EAD in whichever way best suits their particular situations. If the resources exist, this can be a full encoding and publishing implementation, enabling the repository to reap the benefit of the stable long-term storage for electronic finding aids that SGML provides, as well as make the finding aids available via the World Wide Web. If resources are limited, a phased approach, in which the finding aids are marked up in EAD but not immediately made available on the institution's own server, might be an option. If no resources are available, repositories can at least take advantage of the establishment of the standard data structure that EAD provides by using it to model their paper-based finding aids, as Dennis Meissner describes in his case study of EAD implementation at the Minnesota Historical Society.

EAD as the Basis for a Content Standard

In fall 1996, I presented a seminar on EAD to David Gracy's archives class at the University of Texas. As we were leaving the session, Gracy voiced his concern that repositories would use EAD in the same way that they are using HTML to make finding aids available on the Web—just marking up whatever they currently have in paper format and putting it on a server for anyone who might stumble across it. A valid concern! In their eagerness to put finding aids on the Web, some repositories are doing just that, with little regard as to whether the finding aids are "good" or complete descriptions of the

[20]For a description of the "Studies in Scarlet" project, see <http://www.rlg.org/rlgnews/news40.html>.

[21]The UC project grant proposal is available at <http://sunsite.berkeley.edu/FindingAids/uc-ead/grant.html>.

[22]See the American Heritage project's website at <http://sunsite.berkeley.edu/amher/>.

materials, whether they provide the appropriate contextual information needed to understand the materials, and without thinking through the transition from a paper-based to an electronic presentation format, let alone considering the kind of background information that remote users need in order to make sense of what a finding aid is in the absence of a reference archivist to interpret it for them.

Some institutions, such as the Minnesota Historical Society, are taking the time to reengineer their finding aids—to ensure that the information is provided in a logical progression, that the finding aid provides contextual as well as content information, and that there is some explanatory text or help for users embedded in each finding aid. Like many repositories, the Harry Ransom Humanities Research Center at the University of Texas has experienced an increase in user expectations as a result of putting our finding aids on the Web in HTML. Several researchers have contacted us, asking why they couldn't simply click on a folder title to see that folder's contents. We will be adding some explanatory text to the finding aids stating that we have not scanned the collection materials to make them available on-line—information that certainly is not needed when researchers use the finding aids in our reading room.

After more than a dozen years of experience with the USMARC format, archivists readily recognize the advantage of using controlled vocabularies and standard data elements in a bibliographic database. Applying content standards to finding aids, however, may be a new concept to many. While EAD does not, for the most part, require that elements be presented in a given order, it does support a logical progression of information that is already present in many finding aids. As is true of MARC, many EAD elements are repeatable and can be applied at any level of description, from the collection or fonds level down to the item level. And, like MARC, only a handful of elements are required to produce a valid EAD document instance. Employing only the required elements does not mean, however, that the MARC record or the encoded finding aid are good or even adequate representations of the collection. It is perfectly possible to have a parsable EAD-encoded document that contains nothing but empty elements; the SGML authoring software can detect only that the required elements are present and that certain elements are in the correct order. There are no MARC police, as the saying goes, and there won't be any EAD police either. Each repository will be responsible for ensuring that the elements are used appropriately in their encoded finding aids; for example, that the Biography or History <bioghist> element actually contains contextual information such as a biographical sketch or agency history, rather than text that is more appropriately coded as Administrative Information <admininfo> or Scope and Content <scopecontent>.

The absence of a data content standard for finding aids made the formulation of EAD as a data structure much more difficult than it might have been if a content standard had been in place. While EAD had to be designed to accommodate existing archival descriptive practices in order to encourage archivists to understand and implement it, the development team also intended to foster a data content standard for finding aids. Through examination and markup of some two hundred finding aids, the Berkeley Project reaffirmed what archivists already knew but were unwilling (or unable) to admit: that common practices existed and were being followed by the participating repositories. Many of the same structural and intellectual elements are present across these finding aids—biographical sketches and organizational histories, scope and content notes, series descriptions, and container lists—regardless of what the elements are called or the order in which they are presented. In many ways, the structure of finding aids reflects their content; EAD elements focus as much on that intellectual content as they do on structure.

Each repository has been and will continue to be responsible for establishing its own level of markup. In an on-line environment, however, the issue of retrievability across finding aids from single or multiple repositories will dictate some common practices. EAD will support as minimal or as extensive a level of markup as archivists wish to apply. We need to decide as a community what the optimal level of markup will be; this decision must be informed by a solid familiarity with how the markup affects display and retrieval. A basic question that has yet to be answered is how cost effective or necessary it will be to mark up occurrences of dates of collection materials or of an individual's name every time they appear in a finding aid. The repositories that have been testing EAD at Yale University, for example, are taking a very minimal approach to markup for their initial effort, as Nicole Bouché reports in her case study. Their feeling is that if researchers and staff learn that a more extensive level of markup is required, they can revisit the files and encode more of the text to support more sophisticated retrieval needs. An optimal level of markup can be identified only through experience with encoded finding aids in a variety of on-line environments.

Wide variation in institutional tagging practice has already been seen in various implementations of EAD, pointing to the critical need for a content standard. The element definitions in the tag library must be clear and leave little room for misinterpretation if a content standard is to be engendered. Efforts to establish common practices are occurring at Harvard University, where eight of the forty-nine archival repositories are working together;[23] the American Heritage Project has created a set of conversion guidelines,[24] which also has been adopted for use in the University of California project; and the Research Libraries Group is working on a set of guidelines for its members. As more cooperative EAD projects are initiated and as more repositories get some experience with EAD, best practice will eventually be established.

Conclusion

Data structure and data content standards provide us with sets of rules through which we as archivists can readily communicate and comprehend each other's collection descriptions; even more importantly, they enable users to recognize and interpret similar types of information as they conduct their research from institution to institution. Michael Fox has stated in many of the Research Libraries Group's FAST (Finding Aids SGML Training) workshops that if EAD were to go away tomorrow, it would still have been worth the effort just to focus on the structure and content of finding aids. Perhaps the greatest and most enduring benefit of the entire EAD development process will have nothing to do with technology, but instead will be that we ultimately become convinced that there are common structural and intellectual elements in all types of archival finding aids and that a single data structure can support them. Perhaps all we needed was a catalyst that was more compelling than any we had yet encountered.

[23]The Houghton/Radcliffe guidelines are available at the Harvard Digital Finding Aid Project website, <http://hul.harvard.edu/dfap/>.

[24]The "EAD Retrospective Conversion Guidelines" for the American Heritage Project are available at <http://sunsite.berkeley.edu/amher/upguide.html>.

Part II

CASE STUDIES

CHAPTER 7

First Things First: Reengineering Finding Aids for Implementation of EAD

DENNIS MEISSNER

Introduction

IT IS SAID THAT GOD protects drunkards and fools, and we certainly do seem to be granted a few shots at stupidity without it necessarily ruining our lives...but that does not mean that we should go around making a habit of it. An important case in point is that before we try to convert our finding aids into EAD-encoded documents we ought to make certain that those finding aids are as well thought out as possible in terms of both their structure and their content.

When the Minnesota Historical Society (MHS) began attempting to implement EAD, we started at what seemed the obvious jumping off point: we took a couple of existing finding aids and started marking them up with SGML codes. The results were not good. As we marched through a finding aid, coding each data element we came to, we found numerous situations in which the relevant EAD element could not appropriately be used at that point in the structure of the finding aid. For example, we have always positioned the accession numbers associated with a collection as a string of numbers immediately following the end of the biographical or historical sketch. The EAD structure did not want them there, which made coding these numbers awkward, if not impossible. Similar situations abounded throughout the inventories. The EAD Document Type Definition (DTD) seemed to expect particular packets of information to be associated with other packets, and to find them at particular points in the finding aid.

Our initial reaction was largely anger at what we self-righteously believed to be the wrongheaded, inflexible, and poorly conceived structure and rules of EAD. We *knew* our finding aids to be lucid and well-organized tools that had served our users well for years. Therefore, the problems we were having had to be the fault of EAD; clearly, this was a DTD that had left the drawing board a little early and was not likely to serve the needs of any repository.

N.B. ''First Things First: Reengineering Finding Aids for Implementation of EAD,'' by Dennis Meissner, co-published simultaneously in the *American Archivist* (The Society of American Archivists) vol. 60, no. 4, pp. 372–87; and *Encoded Archival Description: Context, Theory, and Case Studies* (ed.: Jackie M. Dooley) The Society of American Archivists, 1998.

After we cooled down a little and started discussing our experiences in a calmer frame of mind, however, we began opening our minds to a novel idea. What if EAD *had* been carefully conceived and its data elements organized for a purpose? What if, instead, problems with the traditional structure and presentation of our finding aids were causing our encoding difficulties? This possibility launched us into a several-month-long task of picking apart the informational elements and presentation structure of our finding aids and comparing them with other institutions' finding aids, especially those that had already been successfully converted into EAD-encoded documents.

The Reengineering Process

We realized almost from the start that we were not interested in doing minor tinkering simply for the purpose of making our finding aids fit more comfortably into the structure imposed by EAD; that might have been accomplished by simply changing the order of a few elements. We were, in fact, interested in seriously rethinking the structure and presentation of the information in our finding aids to turn them into more valuable and intuitive tools for all of our customers. We were interested not in minor revising, but in complete reengineering.

Technology consultant Michael Hammer has written that ''at the heart of reengineering is the notion of discontinuous thinking—of recognizing and breaking away from the outdated rules and fundamental assumptions that underlie operations.''[1] This was our strategy as our task group began reconsidering the composition of our finding aids. We made every attempt to start with a blank piece of paper—to forget as much as possible the comfortable look and feel of our collection descriptions and to try to think from scratch about the purpose of each information element in the finding aid, and whether each, in fact, succeeded in its purpose. As we tore apart the existing finding aid model, we simultaneously began to build a new model that would more optimally structure and present the descriptive information.

It is important to note that while we were trying not to be influenced by our existing practices, we also were making an attempt not to be swayed by EAD. We were not trying to reshape our practices simply to accommodate the predilections of the EAD designers. Our desire was, rather, to engineer a new finding aid model (or models) that would be easier for our customers to navigate and to interpret, thereby making our collection materials more accessible. The one new wrinkle here was that we were broadening the definition of our customer base to include distance users who would be led to our finding aids over the World Wide Web, rather than in our reading rooms and with the ready assistance of our reference staff.

Since all of us in the reengineering task group also serve two hours each week on MHS reference desks, we came to the table with some fairly good impressions of the more typical sorts of problems that our customers have with our finding aids. In the past, we had tended to see customer education as the way to deal with these problems; in other words, we had not perceived a need to change the finding aids, but rather a need to provide better education to users in understanding and navigating archival finding aids. Furthermore, we saw this customer education as a normal part of the process of working with our users, especially novice users, in the reference rooms. But we now began to see this

[1]Michael Hammer, ''Reengineering Work: Don't Automate, Obliterate,'' *Harvard Business Review* 68 (July/August 1990): 107.

constant process of explaining the structure and content of the finding aids as a drain on our reference resources that was probably unnecessary to a large degree. Even more significant was the fact that in delivering these finding aids to users over the Internet, we would not be able to bundle this reference support into the delivered product. It therefore became quite obvious early on in our sessions that we had to redesign the finding aid model to create a document whose purpose, structure, and content would be as transparent to the user as we could possibly make it.

In order to make this happen, our task group[2] began meeting regularly to critique our current finding aid model. We looked at each discrete informational element that we could identify, considered its particular role in informing the user about the collection or series, assessed how well it performed that function (without explanation by an archivist), and also evaluated the relative juxtaposition of these elements in the finding aid. Our methodology was to meet several times as a self-contained group, bringing an increasingly revised model to the table with each consecutive meeting. When we felt that we had developed a new model that dealt with the problems we had identified, we opened it up to a feedback group consisting of all the processing archivists at MHS. We revised the model again, based on their critique, and then expanded the feedback group to include non-processing archivists, all of MHS's reference professionals, and both internal and external customers. It was only after our model had survived all this criticism that we considered how well it would work as an EAD document. That evaluation brought some further fine-tuning, resulting in what is now the reengineered and accepted model for archival finding aids at MHS.

Problems with Existing Finding Aids

As noted already, the problems we found can be summarized by stating that our previous finding aids did not explain themselves, their purpose, or their contents well enough to permit a reasonably intelligent customer to understand and use them effectively without the intercession of an archivist. This is not to say that they were poorly written, or inaccurate, or that their descriptions of collections were incomplete. Rather, the problems lay in the way that they structured, ordered, and presented information. The effect of these problems in frustrating access to collections would be magnified tremendously when the finding aids were delivered over the Web, with no hope of explanation by a staff member. In evaluating our finding aids, we found that the problems they presented fell into four groups.

Information Elements Not Clearly Identified

This first area presented perhaps the most ubiquitous set of problems. Once we nstarted examining the individual pieces of information in a typical finding aid, we found many instances of information not sufficiently identified to be understood by most users. Consider the first page of a traditional finding aid (Figure 1). The first informational units the user encounters are several cryptic statements at the upper left corner. This is actually structured bibliographic information about the collection that has been lifted from its MARC record and which is presented in a form that imitates the organization of infor-

[2]The other members—Frank Hennessy, Monica Ralston, and Cheri Thies, all of whom are very experienced with archival description—brought a strong commitment to the redesign process and were thoughtful analysts of customer feedback.

ALPHA Franey, Edward Marx, 1899-1988.
Papers, 1940-1986 (bulk 1950-1970).
2.0 cu. ft. (2 boxes, including 1 v.).

BIOGRAPHICAL SKETCH

Edward Franey was born Aug. 10, 1899, in Eau Claire, Wisconsin. He attended both Wisconsin and Minnesota universities and began his journalism career in 1918 with the *Eau Claire Leader-Telegram*. Edward later worked as a roto editor, copy desk chief, and outdoor editor for the *Minneapolis Tribune* and *Minneapolis Daily Times*. He continued as a copy editor with the *Minneapolis Tribune* in May, 1948. He later wrote an outdoor column for the *Minneapolis Sunday Tribune* and retired in 1966. Beginning in 1947, and concurrent with his newspaper work, Edward participated as one of the original members, "Uncle Ed," of the WLOL radio and WTCN television show, "The Sportsmen's Roundtable."

Franey was a member of the Izaak Walton League for 35 years and held several offices including secretary of the South Minneapolis Chapter, Minnesota state secretary, and national director. He also edited the monthly bulletin of the South Minneapolis Chapter, *South Wind*, the official publication of the Minnesota Division, *Minnesota Waltonian*, and the *Minnesota Izaak Walton League Quarterly*. Franey worked on a number of conservation programs, most notably the "Save the Minnesota Wetlands" campaign and the Richard J. Dorer Memorial Hardwood Forest. He served as a member of the Governor's Conservation Advisory Committee during the late 1940s and early 1950s. Edward Franey died in December, 1988.

Biographical data was taken from the collection.

Frank Hennessy
July 1992

14,477
14,607

Figure 1. First page of an inventory based upon the previous MHS finding aid model, depicting the presentation of bibliographic data, biographical sketch, accession numbers, processor's name, and the date of creation.

Franey, Edward Marx
p. 2

CONTAINER LIST

Box 1. **152.F.7.5B**

National IWLA, 1958-1987. (6 folders)
National IWLA Convention, 1955, 1958, 1964-1965, 1968-1970, 1972-1974. (4 folders)
IWLA. Minnesota Division, 1946-1980, 1986. (5 folders)
IWLA. South Minneapolis Chapter, 1940, 1957-1970, 1972, 1975-1976.
South Wind, 1955-1962.
Save Minnesota Wetlands, undated and 1953-1961. (3 folders)

Box 2. **152.F.7.6F**

Fox Bounties, Tagged Fish Ban, Canadian Geese Project, and Reorganization Bill.
Boundary Waters Canoe Area, 1946-1972. (2 folders)
Memorial Hardwood Forest, 1960-1986. (3 folders)
William Voigt Correspondence, 1976-1984.
Governor's Conservation Advisory Committee, 1947-1951.
Sportsmen's Roundtable, 1947-1959.
Awards, 1963, 1983-1985.
Photographs.
Personal Correspondence, 1943, 1952-1986. (2 folders)
OWAA, Gridiron, *Minneapolis Daily Times* and *Minneapolis Tribune*.
Fishing Articles. (2 folders)
Pheasant and Cougar Articles.
Duck Hunting Articles.
Deer Hunting Articles.
Miscellaneous Articles. (2 folders)

Figure 2. Second page of an inventory based upon the previous MHS finding aid model, depicting the presentation of a container list.

Franey, Edward Marx
p. 3

DESCRIPTION OF THE PAPERS

The collection falls into two major categories: that involving Franey's career as a journalist and that dealing with his activities as a conservationist and member of the Izaak Walton League (IWLA).

Izaak Walton League and Conservation Activities. 28 folders.

National IWLA, 1958-1987. (6 folders)
Administrative records generated by the league make up the bulk of these six folders. Included are reports to the national board of directors from the executive director and various committees; minutes of national board of directors meetings (1968-1987); budget statements (1968-1973); membership reports (1964-1965, 1972); dues structure (1972, 1974); articles of incorporation and bylaws (1971) and national directors policy (1972-1973); news releases; various resolutions considered for adoption (1964-1965, 1969); and announcements of league-sponsored activities. Also included are correspondence and newspaper clippings related to the activities outlined above and issues of the League's *Activities Bulletin* (1964-1965, 1971), *National Bulletin* (1972), and *League Leaders' Digest* (undated).

National IWLA Conventions, 1955, 1958, 1964-1965, 1969-1970, 1972-1974. (4 folders)

The bulk of the material dates from 1969-1972 and consists of convention programs; reports of national officers and committees; addresses presented, including a talk delivered by Sigurd F. Olson (May 13, 1958); IWLA endowment minutes and officers' reports (1969); biographical sketches of panel members and national officers (1969-1970); copies of a daily convention newspaper titled Ham-O-Gram (1970); resolutions considered for adoption; and Edward Franey's correspondence concerning the election of national officers (1968, 1970, 1972, 1974).

Figure 3. Third page of an inventory based upon the previous MHS finding aid model, depicting the presentation of narrative descriptive information.

mation found on a traditional library catalog card. For librarians, archivists, and customers experienced in using library systems, these information elements may not require much identification, but many of our users find this information to be quite opaque. The first piece of information encountered is a catalog number, or in this case, the word "ALPHA," which simply identifies this as a collection that has no discrete catalog number. It tells the staff that the containers comprising the collection are shelved according to individual numbers identifying a particular stack shelf location rather than by a collection-based call number, and that the paper finding aid for the collection is filed alphabetically by name element along with those of the hundreds of other collections that also bear the ALPHA catalog designation. There is no way that this information can be inferred from the finding aid; it requires experience or explanation.

The next three pieces of information do a similarly poor job of identifying themselves. The first, "Franey, Edward Marx," is the name element identifying the creator and, most likely, the preeminent subject of the collection. This is followed by the title element, in this case the rather nondescript "Papers," which is in turn followed by the date element, indicating the inclusive dates of the materials, as well as the narrower range into which the bulk of them fall. The third line expresses the extent of the collection in both cubic feet and number of containers. All of this data is reasonably transparent to librarians and archivists, but most users would probably have a much more difficult time deciphering it. Would less experienced users, especially distance users, interpret the name element as being the entity around which the collection materials coalesce? Would they understand that these materials are the collected personal papers of this individual, or that the time span represents the dates of the materials in the collection? Would they necessarily infer that these are mixed materials stored in two boxes aggregating two cubic feet in volume? We archivists are so used to looking at this standard catalog-based set of expressions that we don't realize how little commonly interpretable information is being conveyed in these very stylized statements. We express a great deal of fairly standardized information about the content of our collections in what is essentially coded form, and we are not providing our current users—or a much larger number of potential users—with anything resembling a code book. The reasons for these stylized expressions are, of course, perfectly understandable and have to do with limitations imposed by tools like the catalog card, the MARC record, and the typewritten page, all of which have rewarded specific sorts of brevity in our descriptive practices. But we are now delivering finding aids as electronic documents, and brevity may certainly be sacrificed in favor of easier interpretation.

The finding aid pages in Figures 1-3 are rife with additional examples. Following the bibliographic information is a biographical sketch, but the user would probably have to read it through to understand that it is a narrative about the creator of the collection, and that its purpose is to supply context to the descriptive information that follows. The sketch is followed by the name of the archivist who processed the collection and the date the finding aid was written; the significance of these items to the uninitiated must be anything but clear. Even less intelligible are the accession numbers associated with the collection, which are printed along the lower left margin. We know how confusing this piece of information can be, since researchers in our reference room have with some frequency tried to request materials using only this number as an identifier. Finally, the container list page (Figure 2) includes the shelf locations of the containers at flush right in boldface. Nothing informs the customer that this is the single piece of information that is absolutely necessary in order to retrieve that container of manuscripts.

Just as problematic are the identification problems that we found on a much larger scale. For example, nowhere in the finding aid does it clearly identify the producing institution as the Minnesota Historical Society; a user could read every word in the document without learning this essential fact. Furthermore, the finding aid does not identify the collection as being part of the manuscript collections of MHS, an important piece of context for the user. Lastly, it does not identify the document itself as being a finding aid to the collection of materials that it describes. These missing identifiers cause occasional problems with in-house users; they would be vastly more troublesome in serving customers at a distance.

Information Elements Not Optimally Arranged

Another set of problems had to do with the arrangement of information elements throughout the finding aid. It was the difficulty of "shoehorning" some of the pieces of information in our inventories into the structure established by EAD that started us looking at whether we had arranged them sensibly. In considering the matter, it seemed to us that the units of information ought to appear in the order that would be most useful to the customer. In other words, the person studying the finding aid ought to be given bits of information in a sequence that will help determine—and quickly—whether the collection is relevant to his/her search, which parts of it he/she wants to see, and how to gain access.

In general, we decided that the finding aid should take the reader from higher levels of information to more particular levels. It would make sense to first identify the repository and the collection, then to proceed through units of information pertaining to the collection as a whole, then to administrative information about the collection, and then on to the information that describes the particular materials comprising the collection. We decided that our existing finding aid model did not follow that progression very well. Looking again at Figure 1, several such instances can be noted. First of all, had there been access or use restrictions imposed upon this collection, the word "restricted" would have appeared in bold upper-case characters at the very top of the initial page. While this is important information, it is not the first thing the user needs to see and is actually rather confusing when placed there; it really belongs with other administrative information. The same is true for the processor's name, processing date, and accession number; they are unhelpful at this point, they interrupt the flow of information about the collection, and they ought to be ported off to a later section composed of similar administrative information.

Alternating Levels of Description

This problem is similar to the preceding one in the sense that it involves information that is poorly arranged, as well as the failure of the finding aid to take the user in a predictable manner through information levels running from general to specific. This problem was highlighted early in our first experiment with encoding a couple of finding aids. It became obvious that our lengthy narrative descriptions of collection materials contained information pitched at several different levels. Some of the text described materials at the collection level, some at a series level, and some at a file level. The progression of levels sometimes changed directions several times within a narrative of several pages. This same progression of levels was then repeated in the container list that followed the narrative description. The effect of this, we came to realize, was more serious than the simple frustrations it caused in applying SGML codes. We were, in effect, forcing the reader to deal with narrative information about content at a lot of different hierarchical levels, and then to hold that information—and the hierarchical relationships—in mind while moving through similarly ordered information in the container list. This could be very frustrating indeed. It made a great deal more sense to have all information—narrative description and file listings—merge together at common levels so as to provide a single progression of information within one hierarchical structure.

User Instructions Lacking

This set of problems is closely related to those posed by poorly identified pieces of information, but the solution requires something more than improved identification. Our existing model was clearly predicated on the assumption that each user would receive an in-person orientation from an archivist before beginning research. The purpose, content, and use of the finding aids would therefore have been explained before the customer had any occasion to use one. That delivery mechanism for user instruction no longer works well, however; even in the reference rooms, the ratio of patrons to reference staff is too large to make sure that every user obtains sufficient orientation. Furthermore, it is a waste of precious time to repeat the same information about the finding aids to every customer. With distance users finding MHS collections via the Web, instruction not contained within the finding aid itself is a virtual impossibility. It therefore makes sense to build a user manual into the finding aid.

Perhaps the most notable—and egregious—example of lack of user instructions is that the inventories have not done a satisfactory job of telling customers how to request materials. The finding aids provide a lot of information about the collection materials, but they do not tell a person how to obtain them. How does a researcher request a box of collection materials? This level of information cannot be accommodated with better labeling; it necessitates putting instructions to the customer into the finding aid as standard pieces of information.

Many of the specific problems identified during our analysis are probably peculiar to the Minnesota Historical Society. There are enough similarities in finding aid construction from repository to repository, however, to suggest that while the specifics may change, the problems that other repositories can expect to encounter will fall into these four broad categories. These problem areas must be rectified if we are to produce descriptive products that are understandable and meaningful to our customers, especially the growing body of customers who find our descriptive materials from remote locations and have no immediate access to explanation by an archivist.

Revising the Model

As we deconstructed our previous finding aid model, we began building a new one that attempted to correct these problems. As I described earlier, we went through many revisions on the way to the current reengineered model. We have gone back and forth on some of the changes a number of times already, so I would expect that the new model is still to some extent a work in progress and may very well look a little different in another year. Some of the changes are significant, while others are very minor. Overall, however, the new model does represent some rather major departures from its predecessor in both look and feel, as well as in the assumptions it makes about how our customers will be using it and what sort of guidance they need. We have tried primarily to build into the model a set of wayfinding devices that we hope will help users better understand what they are viewing, the purpose the finding aid serves, how to navigate through it, and how to use it to locate collections materials relevant to their research interests.

The reengineered model is depicted in Figures 4-6, comprising three pages from the revised version of the same finding aid depicted in Figures 1-3. These pages give a fairly clear picture of how the problems were resolved.

First, let us consider the problem of poorly identified information elements. It is in this category that some of the most visually arresting changes were made, all the result of improved labeling. Figure 4 contains a logo and several headers that identify the finding aid and place it into a useful informational context. The user, especially the distance user, sees right away that this document comes from the Minnesota Historical Society, that it deals with one of MHS's manuscript collections, and that it is specifically an inventory to the papers of Edward Marx Franey. This gives the customer, especially one who stumbled onto this finding aid during a Web search, a head start in figuring out the relevance of what has been retrieved. Similarly, the group of bibliographic fields that before mimicked a catalog card are now arranged under an explanatory heading, and each element is clearly labeled. Similarly, in Figure 5, labels explain the significance of Frank Hennessy's name and the date that follows it, as well as the meaning of the disassociated accession numbers formerly positioned on page one. Perhaps a more important example is found in Figure 6: a new columnar container list layout features column headings that explain the significance of the location identifier, as well as the information found in the other columns. Furthermore, the container list has been renamed "Detailed Description of the Collection," which we think is more meaningful to a lay user than "container list."

The revised model makes several changes in the order of information elements that formerly were poorly arranged. The accession numbers, the processor's name, and the processing date all have been moved from the initial page (Figure 1) to a section created to hold administrative information about the collection (Figure 5). This has the effect of creating a more consistent and understandable arrangement of information throughout the inventory. As users progress through the finding aid, they see the following in succession: information relating to the repository, information about the collection as a whole (title, overview, biography, scope and contents, organization, related materials, and administrative information), and information about the parts of the collection (detailed description). The flow of information is more logical than had been the case with the older model, helping to make the finding aid more understandable at first glance. The several categories of data that comprise collection-level information are also more consistently ordered. First appears a terse, skeletal overview that establishes the collection's boundaries, then contextual information about the creator, a very general content summary, and finally information describing the collection's organization and arrangement. Next comes information of a purely administrative nature that *may* be useful, but probably not at this stage in the customer's perusal. The nature and content of the collection is thus presented in well-ordered stages that make it easier for users to interpret the finding aid, as well as to decide whether the collection is relevant to their needs, without having to read through the entire finding aid.

The problem of alternating levels of description was addressed partly through the changes in arrangement of elements described above, which create a smoother progression of information elements from the overarching to the particular. The principal improvement was accomplished, however, by merging most of the content narrative into the container list. As Figure 5 shows, only the narrative text that provides information at the collection level remains as a separate scope and content note. All of the more detailed narrative—those pieces that describe content at a subgroup, series, file, or even finer level—is pasted into the appropriate places in the Detailed Description section. The user is no longer forced

MINNESOTA HISTORICAL SOCIETY
Manuscript Collections

EDWARD MARX FRANEY

An Inventory of His Papers

OVERVIEW OF THE COLLECTION

Creator: Franey, Edward Marx, 1899-1988.
Title: Papers.
Date: 1940-1986 (bulk 1950-1970).
Quantity: 2.0 cu. ft. (2 boxes, including 1 volume).
Location: See Detailed Description section for box locations.

BIOGRAPHY OF EDWARD MARX FRANEY

Edward Franey was born August 10, 1899, in Eau Claire, Wisconsin. He attended both Wisconsin and Minnesota universities and began his journalism career in 1918 with the *Eau Claire Leader-Telegram*. Edward later worked as a roto editor, copy desk chief, and outdoor editor for the *Minneapolis Tribune* and *Minneapolis Daily Times*. He continued as a copy editor with the *Minneapolis Tribune* in May, 1948. He later wrote an outdoor column for the *Minneapolis Sunday Tribune* and retired in 1966. Beginning in 1947, and concurrent with his newspaper work, Edward participated as one of the original members, "Uncle Ed," of the WLOL radio and WTCN television show, "The Sportsmen's Roundtable."

Franey was a member of the Izaak Walton League for 35 years and held several offices including secretary of the South Minneapolis Chapter, Minnesota state secretary, and national director. He also edited the monthly bulletin of the South Minneapolis Chapter, *South Wind*, the official publication of the Minnesota Division, *Minnesota Waltonian*, and the *Minnesota Izaak Walton League Quarterly*. Franey worked on a number of conservation programs, most notably the "Save the Minnesota Wetlands" campaign and the Richard J. Dorer Memorial Hardwood Forest. He served as a member of the Governor's Conservation Advisory Committee during the late 1940s and early 1950s. Edward Franey died in December, 1988.

Biographical data was taken from the collection.

Figure 4. First page of the same inventory using the reengineered finding aid model.

SCOPE AND CONTENTS OF THE COLLECTION

Photographs, correspondence, telegrams, news releases, newspaper clippings, reports minutes, financial records, convention files (1955-1972), and printed material documenting Franey's career as a journalist and his activities as a conservationist and leader of the Izaak Walton League of America (IWLA).

Papers relating to Franey's journalism career describe his involvement with the WLOL Radio and WTCN Television Show "Sportmen's Roundtable" (1947-1959); the Ed Franey Outdoor Writer Award (1983-1985); his membership in the Outdoor Writers Association of America and the Twin Cities Newspaper Guild; and his work at the *Minneapolis Daily Times* and *Minneapolis Tribune*. A large number of articles written by Franey in the late 1940s are also included.

The larger portion of the collection documents Franey's 35 years as a member of the Izaak Walton League. Franey held various offices in the League and a good deal of the material relates to the South Minneapolis Chapter (1940, 1957-1969), the Minnesota Division (1946-1973), and the national IWLA (1955-1973).

The papers also document the League's and Franey's involvement in a number of conservation issues including the discontinuance of fox bounties, enactment of a ban on tagged fishing contests, the "Save Minnesota Wetlands" campaign, creation of the Richard J. Dorer Memorial Hardwood Forest, preservation of the Boundary Waters Canoe Area, and creation of the Voyageurs National Park. Correspondents related to these topics include Sigurd F. Olson, Orville Freeman, James W. Kimball and Charles Horn.

ORGANIZATION OF THE COLLECTION

The collection falls into two major categories: that involving Franey's career as a journalist and that dealing with his activities as a conservationist and member of the Izaak Walton League (IWLA).

RELATED MATERIALS

Records of the Izaak Walton League. Minnesota Division are in the Minnesota Historical Society manuscript collections.

ADMINISTRATIVE INFORMATION

Preferred Citation:

[Indicate the cited item and/or series here]. Minnesota Historical Society. See the Chicago Manual of Style for additional examples.

Accession Information:

Accession numbers: 14,477; 14,607

Processing Information:

Processed by: Frank Hennessy, July 1992

Figure 5. Second page of the same inventory using the reengineered finding aid model.

DETAILED DESCRIPTION OF THE COLLECTION

Note to Researchers: To request materials, please note both the location and box numbers shown below.

Izaak Walton League and Conservation Activities:

Location	**Box**	**Contents**
152.F.7.5B	1	National IWLA, 1958-1987. 6 folders. Included are reports to the national board of directors from the executive director and various committees; minutes of national board of directors meetings (1968-1987); budget statements (1968-1973); membership reports (1964-1965, 1972); dues structure (1972, 1974); articles of incorporation and bylaws (1971) and national directors policy (1972-1973); news releases; various resolutions considered for adoption (1964-1965, 1969); and announcements of league-sponsored activities. Also included are correspondence and newspaper clippings related to the activities outlined above and issues of the League's Activities Bulletin (1964-1965, 1971), National Bulletin (1972), and League Leaders' Digest (undated).
		National IWLA Convention, 1955, 1958, 1964-1965, 1968-1970, 1972-1974. 4 folders. The bulk of the material dates from 1969-1972 and consists of convention programs; reports of national officers and committees; addresses presented, including a talk delivered by Sigurd F. Olson (May 13, 1958); IWLA endowment minutes and officers' reports (1969); biographical sketches of panel members and national officers (1969-1970); copies of a daily convention newspaper titled "Ham-O-Gram" (1970); resolutions considered for adoption; and Edward Franey's correspondence concerning the election of national officers (1968, 1970, 1972, 1974).
		IWLA. Minnesota Division, 1946-1980, 1986. 5 folders. Included are state executive committee and board of directors minutes (1948, 1964-1973); financial statements (1957, 1968-1969); membership records (1959, 1964-1964); lists of local chapter and state officers; state officers and committee reports (1961, 1966, 1969, 1972-1973); texts of addresses given at Minnesota IWLA state conventions, including one presented by Minnesota governor Karl Rolvaag (Sept. 25, 1964); resolutions considered at state conventions (1969-1973); and newspaper clippings covering

Figure 6. Third page of the same inventory using the reengineered finding aid model.

to pull together different informational views about a particular component of the collection from multiple places in the finding aid. All information about a particular file, for example, is together in one place. The collection described in this inventory has a very flat arrangement structure; the benefits of bringing together all descriptive information about a given collection component is even more apparent in a collection that is more hierarchically complex.

Our final problem area was the lack of user instructions. While better labeling throughout the new model helps customers to understand the finding aid and navigate it more easily, the insertion of user instructions lets them know how to act on the information that they find. For local customers in our reference rooms, we anticipate that this will eliminate some unnecessary explanatory work for our reference staff, freeing them for more meaningful interactions with researchers. Distance users of the electronic finding aids will better know which components of the collection they want to use before they call or visit. The revised finding aid depicted here gives a few examples of such user instructions. Figure 4 contains a "Location" note pointing the user to the place in the inventory where the location of the collection materials is given. Figure 5 contains a "Preferred Citation" note that explains how to cite materials located in the collection. Figure 6 prefaces the container list with a note explaining the information needed to request particular containers of collection materials. These user instructions are small, few, and simple—and perhaps they seem too obvious to make a point of—but they represent an important type of wayfinding information that had been missing from our preceding finding aid model. They fairly unobtrusively convey necessary information that customers previously had to request from a reference person, and eliminating that little necessity in each finding aid adds enormous value in the aggregate. I expect that, as this new model shakes down in actual practice, we will be modifying these instructions and perhaps adding others, thereby building a reliable user manual into the finding aid itself.

Implementing the Revised Model

The reengineered finding aid model described above carries some significant overhead. All of the additional labels, boilerplate text, and formatting structures impose an additional burden on either clerical or professional staff in producing each finding aid. In fact, it seems likely that the absence of some of the wayfinding information from traditional finding aids has to do with the creation of the model during an era when the typewriter was the principal recording tool; the relative laboriousness of that method placed a justifiable premium on brevity, and we are still breaking loose from that mindset. Performing EAD coding seems to add an additional burden of labor to each inventory, but we have found ways to more fully exploit the software tools we use to produce the finding aids in the first place to actually simplify the production of these products rather than making it more complicated.

We are producing our finding aids in Microsoft Word for Windows 95 and have created a set of three templates to accommodate our basic finding aid types.[3] The archivist writing the finding aid enters text into a skeleton document, associating the various finding aid components with particular text and formatting styles. The styles comprising each

[3]The templates were created by MHS head of processing, Michael Fox. One template is used to create finding aids for collections of a single series, one for collections comprising multiple series within a single group or subgroup, and one for collections containing multiple series within more than one subgroup. The models accommodate varying degrees of hierarchical complexity within the container list.

template correspond to EAD tags. The word-processed document produces hard copies of the finding aid and also serves as the basis for enhanced versions of the electronic document; it is then converted automatically into an EAD document by processing through an SGML parser that is available as a plug-in for Word. The style codes already embedded in the electronic finding aid are translated into their SGML analogs, and an EAD document results. Since the lack of SGML browsers currently makes it is more effective to deliver the electronic finding aids as HTML documents, another parser converts the EAD document into a hypertext document for easy delivery over the Web.

Time is saved in creating the finding aid in the first place because the archivist can enter text without worrying about fonts or formatting, and without having to input many of the boilerplate elements that are found in all MHS finding aids. Creating the documents in these style sheets also saves substantial editing and clerical time farther down the production chain. The EAD document is created largely automatically, with only a small amount of manual cleanup required, as is also true with the HTML document. It therefore seems likely that we will be able to produce all three products without necessitating much additional labor.

Conclusion

Shifting to a finding aid format that facilitates use of EAD is a major step. It is therefore important to make sure that the repository's finding aids are as effective as they can be at enabling customer access to the collection materials that they describe; this is as necessary for finding aids delivered by traditional means as it is for those delivered as electronic documents. In order to ensure such effectiveness, a finding aid reengineering project is a necessary precursor to any large-scale plan for implementation of EAD. In particular, it is important to create finding aids that contain sufficient wayfinding tools to enable users to understand them and the materials they describe without the mediation of archivists. SGML markup is not the first step in delivering effective collection information to our customers; finding aid reengineering is the true first step.

CHAPTER 8

Developing a Cooperative Intra-institutional Approach to EAD Implementation: The Harvard/Radcliffe Digital Finding Aids Project

LESLIE A. MORRIS

Archives at Harvard University

TO THE WORLD OUTSIDE, the words "Harvard University" summon an image of a monolithic institution, one of the country's oldest and wealthiest universities, an organization that speaks with one voice. From the inside, the picture is somewhat different. One of the first pieces of university lore a new employee learns is the rather unlovely saying "Every tub on its own bottom." The "tubs" are the individual faculties, and they have virtually complete autonomy. The librarians for each faculty report to their respective deans, not to the university librarian. Their budgets come from the faculties as well, which means that the business and law libraries have access to more funding than the education and divinity libraries. There is, however, a "Harvard University Library." It is a department of the Central Administration, and it has a purely coordinating role. But, if one of the faculty libraries decides it does not want to be coordinated—as when the Business School decided not to participate in HOLLIS, the Harvard on-line catalog—the university library has no coercive powers.

When one refers to Harvard libraries and archives, therefore, it is important to remember this highly decentralized nature. There are not only ninety-eight separate libraries in the Harvard system, there are forty-nine separate archival repositories, including archives that are part of libraries, museums, hospitals, and a forest. Each has its own traditions, and each has its own budget. *Users* of Harvard collections, however, are almost completely unaware of this situation and how it affects their research. Since the mid-1980s, the man-

N.B. "Developing a Cooperative Intra-institutional Approach to EAD Implementation: The Harvard/Radcliffe Digital Finding Aids Project," by Leslie A. Morris, co-published simultaneously in the *American Archivist* (The Society of American Archivists) vol. 60, no. 4, pp. 388–407; and *Encoded Archival Description: Context, Theory, and Case Studies* (ed.: Jackie M. Dooley) The Society of American Archivists, 1998.

uscript and archives community at Harvard has worked very hard to ameliorate the effects of such decentralization of collections on users. The first step was the Harvard/Radcliffe Manuscript Survey and Guide Project (1984–1986), a project to make many archival and manuscript collections accessible via collection-level MARC records in HOLLIS, the then-new Harvard on-line catalog.

This was a major step forward in providing access to information about Harvard collections, but Harvard archivists still hoped for more. Easy access to the more detailed collection information available in finding aids is as important to us as is access to summary descriptions. In 1994, when Gopher sites for finding aids were all the rage, Harvard archivists received permission to set up an archives site on the central library server and received a few hours of training from the Office for Information Systems (the Harvard University Library systems office) on how to maintain it. While everyone felt the Gopher site was useful for delivering copies of individual finding aids, it was soon apparent that such unstructured text offered only clumsy and frustrating searching, particularly with large files.

While the Gopher site was under development, the university library announced that work would soon begin on the design of the next generation of the on-line catalog, known as HOLLIS II. In response to intense interest from the archives and manuscripts community (which felt that its needs largely had been ignored in HOLLIS I), the Harvard University Library Automation Planning Committee appointed a Special Collections Task Force. This group was charged to examine the automation needs of Harvard repositories that acquire and make accessible *collections* of material (as opposed to monographs). The report of that task force in November 1994[1] contained many recommendations, but the one that is key to the Harvard EAD story was the statement that the information in finding aids must be as easily available to scholars in electronic form as is the collection-level MARC record, followed by the recommendation that options for doing this should be pursued.

During the preparation of its report, the task force investigated work being done at the University of California, Berkeley, using Standard Generalized Markup Language (SGML) to encode electronic finding aids. Berkeley's work demonstrated that SGML was a powerful yet flexible tool that could address the need of the large Harvard community of archivists to produce electronic finding aids and make them available remotely in order to meet the growing expectations of our research clientele. The Automation Planning Committee agreed with the task force's recommendation and established the Digital Finding Aids Project in February 1995.

The Harvard/Radcliffe Digital Finding Aids Project (known as "DFAP") is a group with members from eight Harvard repositories: Historical Collections, Baker Library, Business School; Special Collections, Loeb Library, Design School; Manuscripts and Archives, Andover-Harvard Theological Library, Divinity School; Library of the Gray Herbarium, a special library of the Faculty of Arts and Sciences; Manuscript Department, Houghton Library, Harvard College Library; Manuscript Division, Law School Library; Schlesinger Library on the History of Women in America, Radcliffe College; and the Harvard University Archives. In addition to these collection representatives, the group includes a member from the Office for Information Systems (OIS), and the electronic texts librarian for Harvard College, whose position is in Research and Bibliographic Services.[2]

[1] <http://hul.harvard.edu/hollis2/task_groups/specialrprt.html>.

[2] A list of current members, as well as much information about Harvard's implementation of EAD, is available on DFAP's website, <http://hul.harvard.edu/dfap/>.

The group's charge is to "plan and oversee the design and deployment of a new computer application system to store, search, and retrieve digital finding aids in SGML format at Harvard/Radcliffe." Membership during this initial project phase is designed to provide broad representation of the Harvard archival and electronic systems community. Once DFAP has established standards and procedures, contributions to the finding aids database will be sought from all corners of the Harvard archival and library community.

Selection of SGML Authoring Software

DFAP's first task was to review and recommend SGML authoring software. The group wanted software that could be used by all repositories, regardless of hardware platform, thus enabling Harvard archivists to develop and share a common experience and knowledge. As "minority" members of the library community at Harvard, archivists are accustomed to depending largely on themselves and each other, rather than on understaffed computer support offices (for those who have such support available), for our specialized software needs. The authoring software had to be inexpensive, since several members of the group run single-person operations with minimal financial support. The ability of the software to import existing ASCII and word-processed files also was a factor, since the need for conversion of existing finding aids was part of the project's charge.

After investigating many SGML authoring packages, project members selected WordPerfect 6.1 SGML Edition (running under Windows 3.x) for PC platforms. Perhaps the most important reason for this was cost. Copies could be purchased for thirty dollars each under Harvard's site license with Novell (who then owned WordPerfect; it has since been sold to Corel). Also, about half of the group were already using WordPerfect for their finding aids and so felt very comfortable with the software. Two members of the group were Mac-based, and this posed a difficulty. The only package it was possible to recommend was Author/Editor—at $750, a much more expensive alternative, but still cheaper than many of the other authoring packages tested.

Since 1995, of course, the field has changed. WordPerfect now bundles its SGML module with Versions 7 and 8 (Windows95 or NT required), and many archivists obtain it "free" as standard software on local area networks. Several members of the project have recently purchased Author/Editor and are beginning to use it. The Research Libraries Group makes available to members a package including SoftQuad's Author/Editor (SGML authoring), Panorama Pro (SGML browser and style sheet editor), and HotMetal (HTML authoring) at a cost of $375 for the first copy and $600 for subsequent copies. As the DFAP project needed only one copy of Panorama Pro to write the SGML display style sheet and did not need HotMetal, the Harvard systems office negotiated a price with SoftQuad of $275/package for Author/Editor, if at least five copies are purchased at one time.

Finding Aids on the World Wide Web

The second task of the DFAP was to decide on a method for "publishing" the SGML-encoded finding aids on the Internet. After evaluating access issues, we decided that the finding aids will be available through two "gateways."

The first "gateway" is a link from the collection-level MARC record in HOLLIS, Harvard's public catalog. HOLLIS is already the database our researchers search first for information about manuscript and archival collections held at Harvard, and the project has mandated that every SGML finding aid must have a corresponding collection-level MARC record in HOLLIS. One might assume that in a place like Harvard, particularly with the Manuscript Survey and Guide Project, such records would already be in place. Not so! And Houghton (my own repository) is perhaps the worst offender. The survey project covered many, but not all, Houghton collections, and between the end of the project in 1986 and my arrival as curator in 1992, there was no one in the Manuscript Department who knew how to create a MARC record. A lack of support for MARC cataloging is still a problem for many of the smaller Harvard repositories, and this is something that Harvard will need to address programmatically. Keep this in mind if you begin your own EAD project—it will (or should) force you to think about your entire system of collection control, and there may be additional work other than EAD itself that you will need to anticipate.

The second ''gateway'' to the SGML finding aids is the search interface for a separately searchable finding aids database. It is extremely important to us to be able to do cross-finding-aid, cross-repository searching. This database will reside in HOLLIS Plus, a large group of databases outside the on-line catalog, and will be available at no cost to those outside Harvard. To implement this, an SGML search engine is necessary.

Initially, the DFAP finding aids were to serve as a test database for OCLC's SiteSearch, which the university library was considering purchasing for use with a number of Harvard databases, including the finding aids. But we found that the finding aids were simply too complicated, and too long, for SiteSearch to handle well without an enormous investment in programming time. We have now selected OpenText's LiveLink—the same package Yale is using—but do not yet (as of October 1997) have a search engine in place. The reason for the delay is that OpenText changed its pricing. Harvard needs only LiveLink Search, for which we were originally quoted a price of $7,500. Subsequently, however, OpenText said that it would not sell the search module separately; we must buy the entire suite of products for $50,000 (this includes an academic discount). While Harvard continues to negotiate with OpenText, we also are exploring other search engine options.

In the meantime, the finding aids can be viewed individually in SGML using Panorama Free, as well as in HTML. A program converts the SGML into HTML documents ''on the fly.'' Until SGML browsers are readily available—and Extensible Markup Language (XML) offers that possibility in the not-too-distant future—individual finding aids will be viewable in HTML. (The indexes used by the search engine to locate the appropriate individual finding aids will, however, be drawn from the SGML tagging.) The major drawback to viewing a finding aid in HTML is that one loses the powerful navigational features that SGML browsers such as Panorama offer. Browsing a two-hundred-page finding aid in HTML can be tedious; browser utilization of SGML markup makes going back and forth in an electronic finding aid much easier.

Doing SGML Markup with EAD

The Harvard project's third task, undertaken concurrently, was to mark up a variety of Harvard finding aids using SGML. It quickly became clear that, given the divergence of traditional practice at Harvard repositories, a Harvard standard (based, of course, on the Berkeley-developed standard, by this point in time called EAD) was needed. This standard does not so much prescribe the content of the finding aid (if you look at the Harvard guidelines on the DFAP website, almost every tag is optional), as it does the structure of the finding aid. We discovered, once we trained ourselves to think about the intellectual content of the finding aid divorced from how it ''looked'' (and this is, truthfully, the single most difficult thing to do in applying the EAD), there were not that many differences in content. Rather, what differed was the order in which information was presented and the level of descriptive detail provided.

One of the initial difficulties was how to make sense of an incredibly detailed and complex SGML Document Type Definition (DTD). I remember very clearly our first few meetings, when it was difficult to see the forest for the trees—the trees being hundreds of pointy angle brackets—and I felt very depressed at the prospect of trying to make sense of it all. This feeling passed once I realized that it was not necessary to apply *all* the EAD tags, and as I began to understand the structure of the DTD. We began the job of understanding EAD by passing around copies of what we each considered to be "typical" finding aids, and then we analyzed their various parts, trying to map them to the many EAD tags. This process will, I hope, be much simpler once formal application guidelines for EAD are available.[3]

But even with guidelines, I would urge every archivist to undertake this exercise of evaluating finding aid structure; I found it an illuminating and stimulating experience. Archivists are accustomed to doing things a certain way, not examining why or whether it is the best way, or if what we are doing is comprehensible to our user community. Learning how to apply EAD forces one to think hard about all these issues. I believe that over the next few years, finding aids will change—and not only the finding aids themselves, but also collection-level MARC records, and what information goes in which place, and how much overlap there is between them.

By analyzing and mapping the elements in each of the finding aids, we soon decided that less was more. We chose to mark the structure of the front matter of the finding aid at a fairly general, not at the most specific, level. We use optional "level" and "attribute" tags only if we feel a need to do so for indexing purposes. There are an enormous number of options available in EAD; the challenge is to use the minimum level of markup that will produce a useful electronic document. This is not to say that a Harvard repository is prohibited from doing more detailed markup; it can be as detailed as the repository deems appropriate, as long as the basic structure conforms to the Harvard guidelines. But in terms of broad access to the information in the finding aid, we reached consensus that in many instances, implementing EAD to its finest, most granular level really was not necessary.

There is greater detail, and more variety in practice, in the markup of the container listing portion of the finding aid. Here, each repository judges the level of access needed by its user community. With literary collections, for example, every correspondent's name may be an important access point. In a corporate archives, name access may not be as important, and the markup of names may be much more selective. Thus far, the participating repositories have marked up all names and all dates; many form and genre terms are also marked up. Most problematic is use of the <subject> tag, since this leads into a discussion of the usefulness of indexing uncontrolled vocabulary terms (this also is an issue with indexing names, as not all repositories do name authority work). We have not yet determined the ideal level of markup, but we continue our discussions and our experimentation. Resolution of these issues will be facilitated when a search engine is in place and we can see the results produced by different markup decisions.

[3]A draft, prepared by Anne Gilliland-Swetland and edited by Thomas LaPorte, is available at <http://scriptorium.lib.duke.edu/findaids/ead/guidelines/index.html>.

As a general principle, we mark up finding aids to a level that allows the building of useful indexes (see Appendix 1—preliminary indexing decisions). There is a school of thought that says that full-text keyword searching of finding aids, not field-specific indexing, provides adequate access. Harvard's experience with HOLLIS, with some 8 million bibliographic records, led us to favor field-specific keyword indexes, which we believe will provide more rapid and more precise retrieval of pertinent information.

In January 1997, the DFAP did a survey to attempt to quantify the scope of a possible Harvard retrospective conversion project for finding aids. Twelve of the forty-nine repositories responded. (This included all the largest collections, with the exception of the Medical School, which is undergoing renovation and reorganization.) There are more than fourteen thousand finding aids in these twelve Harvard repositories. Only 21 percent are already in electronic form, 50 percent are typed pages or cards, and the remaining 29 percent are handwritten pages and cards. We do not know exactly how many pages of data this represents, but we estimate at least five hundred thousand. In terms of numbers of alphanumeric characters, a Harvard finding aids database will be roughly equal in size to HOLLIS. Field-specific indexing will allow more precise retrieval within a very large database. Full keyword searching also will be an option, and it will be interesting to compare the uses of each approach.

In planning EAD projects, it is important to keep this question of scale in mind. For Harvard, given the potential size of a finding aids database, tagging at a level that will produce field-specific indexes is important. In the long term, if we think on a national or even international scale about access to electronic finding aids, it seems equally important. But for smaller repositories interested primarily in making finding aids available locally, detailed markup may not be seen as necessary; certainly developing a separate search engine would not be a wise use of resources. A few consortia, including RLG and SOLINET, have announced plans to provide a host site for finding aids marked up by their members; this may be the best solution for small- and medium-sized repositories who want to make their collections available to the wider research community.

The Harvard encoding guidelines have been in place (and available on the DFAP website) for more than a year, although they are frequently modified and clarified as project members gain more markup experience (see Appendix 2). Individual repositories also are working on their own implementation standards, translating the Harvard guidelines into local practice. A style sheet, which displays all Harvard finding aids in a uniform style, was developed using Panorama Pro; this work was done largely by project member Susan von Salis of the Schlesinger Library with the assistance of MacKenzie Smith of the Office for Information Systems. More than sixty finding aids had been encoded as of August 1997.

The diversity of archives at Harvard and the considerable experience of the repositories' staffs have made project meetings lively forums for informed discussion and creative problem solving. Having participated in such a collaborative approach to understanding and implementing this technology, I have intense admiration for those who have undertaken EAD projects largely on their own initiative. At Harvard, we have found it necessary to meet regularly: for the first year we met for two hours every two weeks, and more recently, while we wait impatiently for our search engine to become operational, about every two months. We need to give each other moral support, because we all work on this project in our ''spare'' time. If it were not a congenial and extremely hard-working group, none of us would have the energy to keep going, given everything else we are expected to do.

Having many people involved in the project also makes its likelihood of survival much higher. When a project is the brainchild of one person, it can atrophy or die if that person leaves the organization. At Harvard, there are now enough people involved and committed that one of us can leave (and some have), and the project will continue. I would recommend that any "lone arranger" who is considering EAD implementation try to find at least one other local archives with whom to collaborate. It is helpful to have someone with whom you can talk face to face (e-mail is good, but not really the same). As mentioned earlier, implementing EAD forces you to rethink how your finding aids are structured and what they accomplish; this takes considerable thought and energy, and it helps enormously to discuss the issues with other archivists.

Producing Houghton Finding Aids Using EAD

Over the past ten to fifteen years, Houghton finding aids were produced using a fairly standard format. In planning for the inclusion of EAD tagging in our workflow, I took the Harvard EAD guidelines, went through a typical Houghton finding aid, and created a template with SGML tags (see Appendix 3). Instead of the manuscript cataloger having to know a lot about EAD markup in order to insert the appropriate tags, the tags appear already on the screen as part of the template, and the cataloger simply "fills in the form." The template in Appendix 3 is for a collection of personal papers, which is the bulk of what we acquire, and I anticipate that a separate template will be useful for other kinds of archival records. The template can receive text as well as tags, so any repeating text also can be inserted. This reduces the amount of keying and also helps enforce which tags should and should not be used. While inevitably there is some "tweaking" of the markup that needs to be done, the bulk of it is done quickly and easily. The template works equally well in WordPerfect and Author/Editor (we are using both at the moment). One of the advantages of SGML is that data (and thus templates) can migrate between authoring packages with a minimum of fuss.

While the template approach works well for new finding aids, it is not particularly useful for Houghton's "legacy" finding aids. A finding aid created five years ago is formatted differently than one created thirty years ago. While the two contain much of the same information, the difference in the "look" makes it difficult to formulate routines for automatic conversion. This is even more the case when one looks at all the Harvard repositories over time. It will be necessary to formulate conversion guidelines not only for each repository, but for different time periods and different kinds of collection finding aids, within each repository. Conversion of existing finding aids cannot take place within each archivist's day-to-day work; outside funding and staff clearly will be needed.

The Larger Context

I will conclude with some observations about the Digital Finding Aids Project and EAD within the larger Harvard community.

My first point has to do with the "inevitability" of EAD implementation within the Harvard context. Harvard is wary of innovation, as are many other institutions. It has been critical for us to stress that EAD is an outgrowth of all the work that has gone before. Without the Manuscript Survey and Guide Project to create collection-level MARC records, without experimentation with Gopher sites, and without the recommendations of the Special Collections Task Force within the context of Harvard's preparations for a new online catalog, DFAP would not (and probably should not) have happened at Harvard.

Secondly, the long-term ''survivability'' of DFAP depends on its relevance within the overall Harvard electronic information environment. We are not solely a group of archivists. With the electronic texts librarian for Harvard College as a DFAP member, we keep in close touch with what is being planned in electronic information resources and can anticipate how our project can utilize and enhance these efforts. We obtained approval to switch the proposed search engine to LiveLink because that software was to be used for a resource much in demand by the faculty, the *Oxford English Dictionary*, and so we were able to argue that we should not stay with SiteSearch. Archives and manuscripts will continue to be a minority group within the larger electronic information system, and it is up to us to keep current with the larger context and to understand how it can serve our needs.

It also has been essential to have a good relationship with OIS, the university's library systems office, given that individual archives at Harvard will never have the staff and expertise to maintain a large and complex database over time. The university library has been very supportive of what the manuscript and archives community is attempting to accomplish. But equally, members of DFAP have put much time and effort into the project; it certainly has not been a question of archivists saying, ''We want this, please give it to us.'' The archivists in DFAP have been largely responsible for writing the style sheet (Susan von Salis, Schlesinger Library), and the SGML to HTML conversion program (MacKenzie Smith from OIS, with assistance from Kim Brookes of Radcliffe College), are maintaining the project's website (Kim Brookes) and doing all of the actual markup without external programming support, and have invested much time in developing standards. OIS is providing the programming expertise for the design and implementation of the search engine, something most archivists cannot reasonably be expected to do themselves. But our contribution has been considerable.

The archival community is in a good position to get needed support from library systems offices at the moment, because what we want to do fits in well with other projects many libraries are undertaking, or are planning to undertake. At Harvard, one member of DFAP is now the university library's digital projects librarian, four members are part of various task groups responsible for selecting the next-generation Harvard on-line catalog, and two members are part of the college library's new Digital Library Projects development team. The nationwide effort to define and develop a National Digital Library will highlight the contribution that archives and EAD can make; it also will draw needed resources into the development of fully functional electronic finding aids for all kinds of collections.

This brings me to my third point: the necessity of explaining the project to non-archivists within an institution. By making presentations to various library managers groups, we have garnered interest and support among the upper management tier, as well as potentially bringing into the project many additional finding aids from visual, microform, and audio-recording collections across the university. We regularly issue ''press releases'' on Harvard listservs and have had enthusiastic feedback, particularly from reference librarians, who are now much more aware of manuscript and archives collections when giving research advice to students and faculty. Particularly in a large and decentralized institution such as Harvard, such ''specialized'' collections can become isolated from the larger research context. Electronic finding aids, integrated into the overall information structure of the university, enable us to demonstrate that ''special collections'' are essential to the research mission of the university, not luxury items that are peripheral to the ''real'' business of research. This, to me, is the most compelling argument for implementing EAD.

Appendix 1
Harvard/Radcliffe Finding Aids Database Preliminary Indexing Decisions (February 1997)

Non-public indexes

1. <eadid> used for updating by OIS

2. <admininfo><acqinfo><corpname, famname, persname role=donor OR role=source>: to provide donor/source index

3. <processinfo><name role=processor>: to provide access to collections cataloged by a particular cataloger.
   The term "processor" is to be added to the Harvard-supplemented USMARC Code List for Relators as a standard term to be used as an attribute.

Public indexes

1. Names (keyword), including:

   <name> anywhere
   <persname> anywhere
   <corpname> anywhere
   <famname> anywhere
   <archdesc><did><origination>

   Dates and relation information found in name elements will be indexed as keywords together with the names. Names should be marked up to allow for optimal retrieval (i.e. normalized as much as possible, especially punctuation). This issue needs to be discussed further as we work on the database.

2. Repository name, to be used to limit searches

   <frontmatter><titlepage><author>

3. Call number/accession number

   <findaid><did><unitid>
   <admininfo><acqinfo><p><num>

4. Subjects (keyword) (names are not included in the subject index)

   <findaid><scopecontent>
   <findaid><bioghist>
   <occupation> anywhere

Appendix 1 — *Preliminary Indexing Decisions—Continued*

<c>...<unittitle> but not subelements within <unittitle>
<c>...<note>
<genreform> anywhere
<subject> anywhere
<geogname> anywhere

5. Geographic name index

<geogname> anywhere

6. Titles of works (as opposed to cataloger-created descriptions)

<title> anywhere

7. Dates

<c>...<unitdate>
<date> anywhere except in <frontmatter> and <admininfo>
<findaid><did><unitdate> gives inclusive dates of collection materials
<admininfo><acqinfo><date>

Dates will need to be four-digit numbers, and only those numbers will be indexed. That is, if a date field contains 1920-1930, a search for 1925 will not point to that field.

Notes

Ignore punctuation in indexing ( ) . , [ ] –

The user should probably be presented with a list of finding aids that met her/his search criteria, with each finding aid only appearing once on the list (unless we can implement weighted search results, which is unlikely). The user would then enter each finding aid at its top and be directed to do a key word search using the browser's ''find'' feature within that finding aid.

At this point, all of the indexes are envisioned as being key word indices (as opposed to exact string indexes) because of the lack of standardization in the forms of these elements and the lack of subelements (such as surname and forename) to help. If we would like phrase searching we may need to rethink how we have defined the subject index.

Appendix 2
Harvard/Radcliffe EAD Application Guidelines (for EAD version 1; March 1998)

Notes on the guidelines

Punctuation: keep punctuation together with the word(s) it modifies, inside the tags... i.e. treat it as character information that belongs with the text, not as separate white space. Punctuation, meaning the symbols such as commas, periods, quotation marks, brackets, etc. and NOT meaning whitespace (tabs and blanks and carriage returns) will be normalized out of the indexes so that users won't have to know the punctuation to retrieve documents.

If there is extra text that doesn't logically fit in the heading, or in a <c> element, like a label or a running title that was included to make the print version more readable but that has no function in the finding aid, use an <odd> element to enclose it. For example, if a box number only refers to a physical location (not the intellectual order of the material), use <odd>. If, on the other hand, the box number is uniquely identifies the material being described, tag it as a <unitid> within a <c> that begins before the box number and ends at the end of the box.

In general, do not use rendition attributes (<emph>, <lb>, etc.). Rely on the stylesheet instead.

Use a <head> element for information that helps the reader with navigation, or provides useful information, but should not be indexed, such as labels or folder summaries. For information that is there for retrieval purposes (i.e. should be indexed) use a <title> element such as the <unittitle> defined in the <c> element.

For the attribute "role," use the USMARC Code List for Relators. The term "processor" may also be used.

If the finding aid is in a language other than English you should record that fact with the LANGUAGE="en" attribute on the element. If the finding aid is in mixed languages you can't really reflect that now, so choose the predominant language and use the attribute if it's not English.

Use internal links (<ref> and <ptr>) only. Do not use external references, as these will undoubtedly change; wait until the situation is more stable.

Additional notes about our preliminary indexing decisions are also available.

Guidelines

<ead>
<eadheader>

Appendix 2 — *Harvard/Radcliffe EAD Application Guidelines—Continued*

<eadid>xxxnnnnn</eadid>
[Unique 8 character id number for the digital version of the finding aid, where xxx is the HOLLIS loc code (ex. hou for Houghton, sch for Schlesinger, or des for GSD), and nnnnn is a five digit number for the finding aid. These numbers will be used to update the union database of finding aids, so it's essential that they be unique within each repository.]

<filedesc><titlestmt><titleproper> use the same title as in the <titleproper> element from the <frontmatter> section below </titleproper></titlestmt></filedesc>

These elements are needed because the DTD requires them, but we won't be using this information. At least a call number must be encoded in the <titleproper> element.

<profiledesc><creation><date>mm/dd/yyyy</date> encoder's name [optional] </creation> </profiledesc>

[The <date> subelement should contain the creation date of the digital version of the finding aid. The encoder is the person who did the SGML markup and is optional.]

<revisiondesc><change><date>mm/dd/yyyy</date><item><name> encoder's name [optional] </name></item> </change></revisiondesc> [optional]

[This element set holds date and (optionally) name information for revisions to the SGML-encoded finding aid. Its function is similar to that of a publishing history for a book, and it allows you to retain the information about when and by whom the original version was created, as well as verify the most recent version.]

</eadheader>

<frontmatter>

<titlepage>
<num> collection/accession number </num> [optional]
<titleproper> official finding aid title </titleproper>

[drawn from the MARC 100 and/or 245 field, if they exist, followed by a colon and words distinguishing this as descriptive material, not the material itself (e.g. register, contents list, guide, inventory, or finding aid). For example, Jane Doe Papers: A Guide.]

<author> repository name </author>
<publisher> Harvard University </publisher>
<date> date finding aid was created </date> [optional]
<p>© YYYY The President and Fellows of Harvard College</p> </titlepage>

</frontmatter>

Appendix 2 — *Harvard/Radcliffe EAD Application Guidelines—Continued*

<archdesc level=''collection''>
<did>

[NOTE: the following optional elements can be used in any order that makes sense for the finding aid in hand. Those marked ''optional, recommended'' are elements that will be required in the RLG union database, used to generate brief information about the collection.]

<repository> repository name </repository> [optional, recommended]
<unitid> call number, accession or collection number (can also be HOLLIS#) </unitid> [optional]
<physloc> shelving designation</physloc> [optional]
<unittitle> collection title [optionally can use a subelement for <date> dates of coverage </date>] </unittitle> [optional, recommended]
<unitdate> date(s) of collection materials </unitdate> [optional]
<origination> creator(s) of the collection, with or without dates. Names can be repeated if more than one creator was involved (use <persname>s; or <corpname>s, etc. </origination> [optional, similar to the MARC 100 field]

NOTE: the collection creator can be input as a <persname role=''originator''> name </persname> if this information is wanted for local indexing.

<physdesc><extent> information about the size of the collection (can optionally include a <num> element with a call number for a microfilm version, etc.) </extent> </physdesc> [optional, recommended]
<abstract> A very brief summary of the collection </abstract> [optional, recommended]

</did>

<admininfo> [optional]

<processinfo> [optional]

<head> ''Processed by:'' </head> [optional]
<p> collection processor (person who created the original finding aid) </p> [optional]
<p> date of creation </p> [optional, and additional <date> tags can be used in the <p> if desirable]

</processinfo>
<acqinfo> [optional]

<p><num> accession number, or details of acquisition </num></p> [optional]
<p><persname role=donor> donor </persname></p> [optional]
<p><date> accession date </date></p> [optional]

</acqinfo>

Appendix 2 — *Harvard/Radcliffe EAD Application Guidelines—Continued*

<accessrestrict> restrictions on access, if any </accessrestrict> [optional]
<userestrict><p> restrictions of use of materials, if any </p></userestrict> [optional]
</admininfo>

<bioghist> [optional]

<head> heading such as Biography or History of Organization </head> [optional]
<geogname, persname, etc.> Name [optional <date> dates </date>] </geogname, persname, etc.> [optional]
<chronlist> [optional]

<chronitem><date></date><event>...</event><</chronitem> [repeatable]

</chronlist>

NOTE: Use this approach, instead of the simpler <persname> approach, when the biographical note consists of a chronological list.

</bioghist>

<scopecontent> [optional, repeatable]

<head> heading such as Notes or Scope and Content Note </head> [optional]
<geogname, persname, etc.> Name [optional <date> dates </date>] </geogname, persname, etc.> [optional]
<organization> description of the structure of the finding aid, e.g. ''Organized into the following series: I. Correspondence; II. Biographical files.'' </organization> [optional]
<arrangement> description of the filing sequence, e.g. alphabetical, chronological (if in doubt, use the broader <organization>) </arrangement> [optional]

</scopecontent>

<dsc type=''insert appropriate value here''> [repeatable, type attribute value will usually be ''in-depth'']
<head> heading for collection-level info [recommended]

[Note: preferred to using <dsc><c><head>]

<c level=series, subseries, etc.>
<did>
<head> [optional]</did>
<scopecontent> </scopecontent> [optional]

Appendix 2 — *Harvard/Radcliffe EAD Application Guidelines—Continued*

<c level=file/item/etc.><did>

[optional and repeatable. The default assumption is that level=item, and that ''items'' are whatever is the lowest level of description that you have chosen to do (so, for example, if you only describe to the folder level, then you don't need to encode level=''file'' for each folder since the ''item'' display treatment should work equally well)]

<container> or <physloc> Box, etc. designation, or location; can go with the unitid information. This can go before or after the <unitid> element. </container> or </physloc> [optional]
<unitid> id number for box, folder or other physical unit. This can be the item number, if one is assigned, or an item range like 1-9, or any other information that points to the physical thing being described. </unitid> <unitdate> dates at the <c> level </unitdate> [optional]

[NOTE: <unitdate> can be placed inside the <unittitle> if appropriate, and will display inline with the title. For other kinds of dates, use the <date> element inside the <unittitle> or other <c>-level subelement.]

<unittitle> title information for box, folder, series name, title or description </unittitle>

NOTE: if your description has only a <unitdate>, put the <unitdate> within a <unittitle>. Use of the following tags is optional, but recommended, within <unittitle> for indexing purposes:

<persname></persname>
<corpname></corpname>
<famname></famname>
<genreform> Use terms from the DFAP list of recommended form and genre terms. </genreform>

<physdesc><extent> size of unit being described (eg. 1 folder, 12 folders, 2 boxes, etc.) </extent></physdesc> [optional]
<note> <p>... </note> </p> [optional]

</did></c> [for level=file, item, etc.]

</c> [for series components, if any]

<controlaccess> [optional]

[use for terms that should be indexed, but that do not appear explicitly in the finding aid (e.g. LCSH, NAF forms of names). All <controlaccess> terms are under authority control. <Controlaccess> can appear at many points in a finding aid.]

Appendix 2 — *Harvard/Radcliffe EAD Application Guidelines—Continued*

<name> ... </name> [optional, repeatable]
<famname> ... </famname> [optional, repeatable]
<persname> ... </persname> [optional, repeatable]
<corpname> ... </corpname> [optional, repeatable]
<geogname> ... </geogname> [optional, repeatable]
<occupation> ... </occupation> [optional, repeatable]
<subject> ... </subject> [optional, repeatable]
<genreform> ... </genreform> [optional, repeatable]

</controlaccess>

</dsc>

<add> [optional]

<index>

[<index> is a **list** of terms, usually at the end of a finding aid. Terms are not necessarily under authority control]

<indexentry><namegrp><name> ... </name><name> ... </name> </namegrp></indexentry> [optional, repeatable]
<indexentry><name> ... </name></indexentry> [optional, repeatable]
<indexentry><famname> ... </famname></indexentry> <ptr></ptr> [optional, repeatable]
<indexentry><persname> ... </persname></indexentry> <ptrgrp><ptr> </ptr><ptr></ptr> </ptrgrp> [optional, repeatable]
<indexentry><corpname> ... </corpname><ref target="source ID"> </ref></indexentry> [optional, repeatable]
<indexentry><geogname> ... </geogname></indexentry> <ptrgrp><ref> </ref> <ref></ref> </ptrgrp> [optional, repeatable]
<indexentry><occupation> ... </occupation></indexentry> <ptr></ptr> [optional, repeatable]
<indexentry><subject> ... </subject></indexentry> <ptr> [optional, repeatable]
<indexentry><genreform> ... </genreform></indexentry> <ptr></ptr> [optional, repeatable]

[Each variation of <ptr>, <ptrgrp>, and <ref> may be used in each element of an <indexentry>. Use these tags for internal links.]

</index>

</add>

</archdesc>
</ead>

Appendix 3
EAD Template for Houghton Library Finding Aids

The following template does not include all possible options, but only those elements for coding information usually found in Houghton finding aids. Text in [ ] is to be supplied by the cataloger; other text and punctuation marks outside the [ ] are required.

Macros are defined to repeat <c level="item"> ... </c> tags. Level="item" is the default value.

= =

<ead>
<eadheader>
<eadid>hou[nnnnn]</eadid>

<filedesc><titlestmt><titleproper>[Main entry, title, and inclusive dates of collection, as in MARC record; followed by the size designation (b,f,pf) & call number in parentheses].
Guide.</titleproper></titlestmt> </filedesc>

<profiledesc><creation><date>[mm/dd/yyyy] </date>[encoder's name]</creation>
</profiledesc> </eadheader>

<frontmatter>
<titlepage>
<num>[size designation and call number]</num>
<titleproper>[same as "titleproper" in "filedesc" above, without the size designation and call number in parentheses]. </titleproper>
<author>The Houghton Library</author>
<publisher>Harvard University, Cambridge, MA 02138</publisher>
<date>[year finding aid was created in form yyyy]</date>
<p>© [YYYY] The President and Fellows of Harvard College</p>
</titlepage>
</frontmatter>

<findaid>
<archdesc level="collection">
<did>
<unitloc>[size/shelving designation, e.g. b,f,pf]</unitloc>
<unitid>[call number]</unitid>
<unittitle>[use same title as in "titleproper" in "titlestmt"]. </unittitle>
<unitdate type="inclusive">[date(s) of collection materials]. </unitdate>
<physdesc><extent>[xxx] boxes ([xxx] linear ft.) </extent></physdesc>
</did>

Appendix 3 — *EAD Template for Houghton Library—Continued*

<admininfo>
<processinfo>
<head> Processed by: [your name here]. </head>
</processinfo>

<acqinfo>
<p><num>[accession number]</num></p>
<p><persname role=‘‘donor’’ or role=‘‘source’’>[donor name and/or source of collection (select corresponding attribute)]. </p>
<p><date>[accession date, in form YYYY]</date>[month day]</p>
</acqinfo>

<accessrestrict><p>[restrictions on access, if any]. </p></accessrestrict>
<userestrict><p>[restrictions of use of materials, if any]. </p> </userestrict>
</admininfo>

<dsc type=‘‘in-depth’’>
<c level=‘‘collection’’>
<c level=‘‘series’’>
<head>[I. Correspondence or Letters]</head>

<c>
<did><unitid>([item #])</unitid>
<unittitle><persname>[name of correspondent as in LCNAF: last name, first name], </persname></unittitle><unitdate type=‘‘inclusive’’>[YYYY-YYYY; or put in single date and change attribute to ‘‘single’’]. </unitdate><physdesc><extent> [#] folders. </extent></physdesc>
</did>
<note><p>[Note on contents, if needed]. </p></note>
</c>
</c>

<c level=‘‘series’’>
<head>[II. Compositions by xxx]</head>
<c>
<did><unitid>([item #])</unitid>
<unittitle><title>[title of work] : </title><genreform>[AMs, Ts, etc.], </genreform></unittitle><unitdate type=‘‘single’’>[YYYY]. </unitdate>
<physdesc><extent>[# of folders]. </extent></physdesc>
</did>
<note><p>[note on contents if needed. Markup names and genre/form as appropriate]. </p></note>
</c>
</c>

Appendix 3 — *EAD Template for Houghton Library—Continued*

</c>
</dsc>
</archdesc>

<add>
<index>
<indexentry><persname> ... </persname></indexentry>

</index>
</add>

</findaid>
</ead>

CHAPTER 9

Implementing EAD in the Yale University Library

NICOLE L. BOUCHÉ

Introduction

THE YALE FINDING AID PROJECT is a joint venture of Yale manuscript repositories and the Library Systems Office to create an integrated database of finding aids, accessible via the World Wide Web. The Yale website[1] contains finding aids from three Yale library units: The Beinecke Rare Book and Manuscript Library, Special Collections in the Divinity School Library, and the Manuscripts and Archives Department of Sterling Memorial Library. At the present time, the site contains over 350 SGML "instances" (i.e., finding aids) encoded using the beta version of Encoded Archival Description (EAD). HTML versions of the SGML files also are available. Additional finding aids are added to the site as they are completed, and in fall 1997 the Beinecke Library loaded almost three hundred preliminary finding aids in pre-formatted HTML, derived from plain ASCII text files. Files in other non-SGML "native" formats (e.g., WordPerfect, Microsoft Word) may be added at the discretion of the contributing repositories.

Although only three Yale repositories undertook initial development of the finding aid site, now that a core group of Yale "early implementers" has acquired sufficient expertise in implementing EAD, building the finding aids database and maintaining the server, we anticipate assisting colleagues at Yale in adding their finding aids to the site. Eventually, members of the Yale community, as well as researchers elsewhere, will have unprecedented access to an integrated source file of finding aids describing an extraordinary range of primary source materials scattered throughout Yale's various research and departmental libraries and museums.

A project of this scope has many facets; this case study will touch on only a few. First, I will describe the basic configuration of the finding aid site and review the project's history and accomplishments since its inception in 1995. I will then discuss the methods employed by the three participating units to mark up legacy files and to integrate EAD into their routines for creating new finding aids. Finally, I will close with a few recom-

---

N.B. "Implementing EAD in the Yale University Library," by Nicole L. Bouché, co-published simultaneously in the *American Archivist* (The Society of American Archivists) vol. 60, no. 4, pp. 408–19; and *Encoded Archival Description: Context, Theory, and Case Studies* (ed.: Jackie M. Dooley) The Society of American Archivists, 1998.

[1] <http:\\webtext.library.yale.edu>.

mendations, based on our experience over the past two years, for those who are considering an SGML/EAD encoding project of their own.

The Setup

Yale's EAD-encoded finding aids reside on an OpenText (OT) server running OT's search engine software LiveLinks. The finding aids are cross-indexed: one can search across the holdings of all three contributors or just the finding aids of a single unit. A finding aid can be accessed in three ways: via links on the repository's website, by directly searching the finding aid server, or by clicking on the linked 856 field in the corresponding MARC record in the Webpac version of Yale's on-line catalog, Orbis.[2]

The finding aids website supports both simple and more complex key word searches: standard Boolean operators (AND, OR, and NOT) and proximity qualifiers (WITHIN and FOLLOWED BY) are incorporated into the search forms. Searching the SGML-encoded files by specific EAD tag regions also is possible. At present, EAD tag regions defined and indexed for searching purposes across all SGML-encoded finding aids are Entire Document, Introductory Material, and Container List. A limited number of other tag-qualified search options is offered at the repository level, as indicated in pull-down menus on a unit's SGML-Encoded Finding Aids search form.

Although many other indexing and search configurations are possible, implementing them would greatly complicate file markup as well as the routines for loading and indexing the files on the server. For this reason, the EAD Implementation Group settled on this initial set of indexing and search options. We recognize that, in time, other configurations may be preferable, in which case the indexing structures, search forms, and results screens can be adjusted or redesigned accordingly.

Once a finding aid has been identified on the OpenText server, it must be brought up on the individual's PC by means of an appropriate Web browser (e.g., SoftQuad's Panorama viewer for the SGML-encoded files, or Netscape for the simple ASCII and HTML files). Files in other "native" formats such as Microsoft Word or WordPerfect similarly require the operator to select an appropriate application to display the file. As with other Web queries, a search for a specific term or phrase used initially to identify finding aids on the OpenText server must be reinitiated within the finding aid itself to locate specific occurrences of the search term(s).

Project History to Date

In the early days of the Berkeley Finding Aid Project (BFAP), from which EAD evolved, the Manuscripts and Archives Department in Sterling Library was one of several repositories in the United States that supplied copies of finding aids to the Berkeley group so they could study the feasibility of developing a national standard for finding aid encoding and Internet delivery. The Yale library as a whole, however, did not become involved in the project until after the Berkeley Finding Aid Conference, held in April 1995. Richard Szary, Head of Manuscripts and Archives, and I, representing the Beinecke Library, attended the conference, and we were much intrigued by the progress that the Berkeley team had made. After reporting back on their findings to our colleagues at Yale, we received enthusiastic support for the Yale library to become one of the early imple-

[2]<http:\\webpac.library.yale.edu>.

menters of the new encoding standard. It was fortunate that the BFAP conference and the subsequent release of the FindAid Document Type Definition (DTD) for wider testing and evaluation by the archival community coincided with a growing interest in the Yale library in installing an SGML-capable server to enable the library to expand the repertoire of on-line reference tools and services that it offers.

Consequently, within a few weeks of the Berkeley conference, the Beinecke Library had committed funds to purchase an SGML server and the necessary start-up software, and a hardware/software selection task force had been appointed. Three Yale library units volunteered to be the Yale "early implementers," and essential technical expertise was assigned to the project from the library systems office. By fall, the technical task force had selected a start-up set of hardware and software that included an OpenText server, SoftQuad's suite of SGML authoring, publishing, and Web-browsing software, and an SGML-enabled version of WordPerfect. With all the basic tools in hand, a formal EAD Implementation Group was appointed in February 1996. The team included representatives from the three participating repositories, the library systems office, and two additional staff members representing the public services department in Sterling Library and the Social Science Library. (The latter was interested in other forms of SGML implementation.) Within a matter of weeks, however, as the mechanics of simply getting an EAD site up and running became clearer, the task force had narrowed itself down to a core group of EAD implementers.

Although the archivist/librarians on the implementation team were well versed both in finding aids and in the research and reference patterns for their departments, our knowledge of SGML was virtually nonexistent, and our experience with Web publishing was limited at best. Although all of the participants were producing finding aids in machine-readable form, only Beinecke's guides were available to researchers on-line, both locally in a stand-alone database and on the Internet via the Yale Gopher. As a general rule, project staff had little experience searching finding aids in an on-line environment or maintaining them on a server. With one key exception (Beinecke), no one had any real experience in programming or writing macros for data processing: it became clear fairly early that the Divinity Library and Manuscripts and Archives Department would need to recruit additional technical assistance from outside their units, while Beinecke would have to draw on additional in-house expertise.

As one might expect, the systems personnel assigned to the project knew little about archival practice, patterns of research in archives, or the creation and use of finding aids; their contributions came in the form of an invaluable range of experience in library automation. Beyond the obvious assets of programming and technical expertise, the systems staff had experience in the routine maintenance and ongoing development of the library's OPAC and in the installation and maintenance of other library servers. They also had recently installed the first Web version of Yale's on-line catalog.

From February through summer 1996, the EAD Implementation Group met weekly to work out the mechanics of everything from basic SGML encoding to HTML search form design for the website. The process of mastering and implementing EAD was very similar to the early days of learning MARC AMC, before there were workshops or full-blown documentation with examples. When we started, the tag library wasn't even available. (It came later, with the alpha release of the EAD DTD.) All we had to work with were the FindAid DTD (which, at first glance, was utterly unintelligible), later the alpha EAD, and a handful of sample finding aids, including a few of our own, which the Berkeley team had marked up the previous April.

At the repository level, task force members reviewed current finding aid practices and experimented with markup by hand. (Virtually from the outset, we had determined that markup would have to be automated, so this initial manual work was simply to become accustomed to SGML and to EAD, as well as to devise our tagging protocols.) At weekly task force meetings, the three teams compared results and revised and clarified tagging practice to achieve consistent tag interpretation, if not uniform finding aid style. We eventually settled on a core group of 44 tags to be used for Yale finding aids out of a beta EAD tag library of approximately 135 tags. The more technically proficient members of the task force also began to experiment with the various authoring and publishing software packages that had been acquired as part of our start-up package. Eventually they mastered the SGML publishing routines of Panorama and developed preliminary style sheets and navigators for each repository.

Meanwhile, systems personnel worked to install and configure the server and search engine. An initial group of test files using the EAD alpha version was loaded in early summer 1996. Finally, a year into the project, we began to get a sense of how all the pieces might actually fit together as an integrated, Web-based source file of Yale finding aids. Having acquired a working knowledge of both EAD and of Panorama, and with our basic tag library and tagging sequences mapped out, the teams in each unit turned their attention to more systematic encoding methods. We spent the summer of 1996 developing more efficient automated tools to mark up legacy files and to introduce SGML-encoding into our respective routines for producing new finding aids. As with our early experience with tagging, there was considerable discussion and exchange of ideas about strategies for writing macros to expedite markup as each unit worked out methods and tools appropriate to its particular circumstances.

At this point in the project, however, the experience of the three repositories began to diverge because of fundamental differences in both established routines for creating new finding aids and the scope and character of our legacy files. At Beinecke, conversion of legacy files surged ahead, and mechanisms were readily put in place to integrate SGML encoding into routines for producing new finding aids. Work in the Divinity Library and Manuscripts and Archives Department proceeded more slowly, especially in Manuscripts and Archives, which faced the largest and most complex backlog of legacy files (estimated at eighteen hundred finding aids.)

In August 1996 the Yale Finding Aid Project website, containing fifty EAD instances, was announced in "test" mode to the EAD listserv.[3] Between that time and May 1997, when the site was announced to the archival community at large, file conversion continued in each unit to the extent possible, given staff availability and the inherent difficulties of file conversion. Overall, the project weathered a string of technical modifications and upgrades that affected both the OpenText server and the various components of SoftQuad's suite of SGML publishing and browsing software. Relatively late in the game we decided to provide HTML versions of EAD instances for the benefit of those unable to access the SGML-encoded files, and so a parallel set of files was created and added to the server.

[3]The EAD forum is an electronic mail posting service created to facilitate the exchange of information about the SGML DTD being developed for archival finding aids. Developers and implementers of the EAD DTD are welcome to join the forum and share their ideas and experiences with using SGML for finding aids. To subscribe to the EAD forum: From the e-mail account you intend to use, send a message to listserv@loc.gov containing the message: subscribe ead [Firstname Lastname].

When the Yale Finding Aid Project site finally went public in May 1997, it contained 323 EAD instances: 260 for Beinecke, 46 for Divinity, and 17 for Manuscripts and Archives. Development work on the overall site is ongoing, and we continue to build the database with new and updated files.

Some Key Early Decisions

Besides generally accepting the logic of the EAD DTD and the content of the beta EAD tag library, the Yale EAD Implementation Group also made some strategic decisions in the early days of the project that influenced our selection of hardware and software, the character of our EAD instances, the configuration of files and indices on the OpenText server, and the formatting of search and results screens. These decisions, once made, enabled us to proceed fairly expeditiously to our greatest challenge—file conversion—without any of the contributors having to significantly modify either the format of their finding aids or their workflow to accommodate our EAD implementation.

Our selection of the initial suite of hardware and software (within what was admittedly a rather small universe of commercially available options) was guided to a great extent by two key considerations. First, the Yale library wanted to install a powerful server that could deliver large and complex files in a variety of formats, including but not limited to SGML-encoded documents. (The Beinecke Library already had anticipated including preliminary and other nonstandard finding aids in ASCII text format along with its EAD instances.) For its part, the Yale EAD team wanted to provide the widest possible access to the SGML instances. This meant we would have to find an alternative to the proprietary software/server model embodied in the Dynatext/DynaWeb package that was being tested by other early implementers, including the Berkeley team.

Given our requirements, a package that included an OpenText server and SoftQuad's SGML authoring, publishing, and Web-browsing tools, including the freeware browser PanoramaFree, was the most logical choice. The OT server had the capacity to manage and deliver files in various formats, and we were told it was fully compatible with SoftQuad's products. A version of WordPerfect with SGML editing capabilities also was included in our start-up group of software: it would be tested by Divinity and by Manuscripts and Archives, who were already using WordPerfect to produce their finding aids, while Beinecke would experiment with SoftQuad's Author/Editor.

We have since discovered that vendor claims, however confident, do not always pan out quite as expected. "Compatibility" is a relative term, and local circumstances can influence just how well all the pieces fit together, in ways that cannot always be anticipated. And, yes, on occasion some features simply do not work as advertised, and you may be the first to point out a problem to the product developer! Similarly, the proliferation of SGML-enabled Web browsers, which many at the Berkeley conference predicted was just around the corner, has been slow to materialize. Even SoftQuad has wavered on its previous assurances that it would maintain a freeware version of its SGML Web browser.

But, as we also learned, all of this is part of the price one pays for being an early implementer. On the other hand, the members of the Yale task force acquired a much better understanding of the range of technical issues associated with a project of this type than would have been the case if things had gone as smoothly as we had originally envisioned. In the long run, although the learning curve was steep (and at times extremely frustrating) and numerous unanticipated hurdles had to be overcome, it was worth the effort and will stand us, and Yale, in good stead. In the meantime, we will continue to work with the hardware and software vendors, as well as with other interested parties in the archival and computer science fields, confident that in time the glitches will be resolved and products that fully meet our requirements will emerge. Fortunately, in this we are not alone.

Another of our key early decisions was that we would build the database as quickly as possible. We were determined that the Yale site would become an effective research tool and not languish as an innovative but not very useful oddity in the universe of on-line resources that we offer to researchers, students, and staff. As much as was possible, both legacy file conversion and the encoding of newly created files had to become priorities. We followed the advice of experienced SGML consultants, who encourage those facing massive legacy file conversions to keep the markup simple and to focus on tagging structure, not content.[4] This was not a difficult choice to make: we had considered both the tagging and authority control issues associated with in-depth content tagging and were already inclined to take a ''wait and see'' approach to the question of content markup. We were, and remain, skeptical that the benefits to be gained by further enhancing access to specific data elements within the text of existing finding aids, beyond that already provided for in our local practice (e.g., using *AACR2* forms of headings for key names in lists of correspondents), will outweigh the effort involved and justify the allocation of scarce resources to such an indexing and authority control effort, particularly given the sizable backlogs of unprocessed and inadequately listed collections most of us face.

With these priorities in mind, we developed our markup tools and strategies to maximize automated functions and minimize the need for time-consuming manual intervention. We eventually rejected both SoftQuad's Author/Editor and WordPerfect's SGML editor, which we found cumbersome and particularly ill-suited to legacy file conversion; finding aid creation is an ongoing process of composition and editing, and we did not want to burden staff with the details of encoding at the same time they are writing a finding aid. All in all, we found it easier to stick with our current practices for creating finding aids and augment them by use of encoding macros or templates.

A third important early decision was to retain a measure of autonomy for each of the departments by providing for searches that take into account similarities and differences in finding aid practice, as well as in patterns of collecting and in research use of our collections. To this end, we developed both an all-Yale search form and unit-specific search forms, and we indexed the database in a parallel manner. Also, in the few cases where content markup varies by unit, the query boxes in the pull-down menus of the unit-specific search forms prompt those options. We also agreed that strict conformity to a single finding aid ''look'' or practice was neither desirable nor necessary, and as a result, each unit was allowed to design its own style sheets and navigators.

[4]Briefly, structural markup is markup that codes the physical (and intellectual) structure of the document, such as series headings and cross references, the front matter (e.g., table of contents, biographical note, narrative description of the collection) and the container list (the box and folder inventory of contents). Generally, if a document conforms to a well-defined format or template, structural markup can be readily automated. Content markup, in contrast, focuses on the text of the document itself as the basis for locating specific occurrences of a given proper name or corporate name, or to distinguish a date from other forms of numeric or alphanumeric combinations. Content markup is less readily accomplished using automated techniques such as macros; accuracy of markup, which is essential for meaningful indexing of content tags, usually requires human intervention to verify the meaning of the text and establish correct tag assignments. When content and structure converge (as in the Beinecke case, where folder dates always occur at tab 63 in a printed finding aid), tagging for content can be accomplished with macros with considerable accuracy and little or no need for manual review.

Local Finding Aid Practice and File Conversion Strategies

As previously stated, all three units were creating finding aids in machine-readable form when we embarked on the EAD project. Beinecke had approximately 250 finished finding aids, all in machine-readable form, that had been produced using a powerful DOS-based text editor, Edix/Wordix.[5] The Divinity Library and Manuscripts and Archives Department had been using WordPerfect for some time, but 50 percent of the Divinity Library's seventy legacy files and 90 percent of Manuscripts and Archives' estimated eighteen hundred legacy files still existed in paper form only. While the Divinity Library was able to convert its remaining thirty-odd paper files to WordPerfect in relatively short order using optical character recognition (OCR), the bulk of Manuscripts and Archives' files, including all of the paper-based legacy data, has yet to be converted.

As we shall see, differences in the character and scope of the legacy files, combined with current practices for creating and maintaining finding aids in machine-readable form, had a decisive impact on the methods adopted for encoding both new and existing files, as well as on the rate at which legacy files could be converted. As much as anything, it is these differences that account for the fact that, from the outset, the majority of EAD instances on the Yale site have been Beinecke files.

Divinity Library and Manuscripts and Archives Department: From WordPerfect to Macros and Templates

During the summer of 1996 staff in the Divinity Library and Manuscripts and Archives Department successfully encoded a group of files using macros they had written for WordPerfect. They have since opted for a template-based method for both legacy file conversion and the encoding of newly created finding aids.[6] Each archives found that subtle (and not so subtle) differences in the structure of finding aids generated in their units made it impractical to take a direct macro-based approach to the encoding of files; a template proved to be a more efficient and reliable method for legacy file conversion and for encoding new files. Moreover, this work can be done by staff who have only a general awareness of SGML or the specifics of EAD, because the tagging is inserted "behind the scenes," as output from the template. Although the switch to a template has made conversion easier, the process remains fairly labor intensive and does not lend itself very well to the sort of batch treatment of legacy files that proved to be such an advantage for file conversion at Beinecke.

The Beinecke Library: Macro-based Conversion and Batch Processing of ASCII Files

The Beinecke has used sophisticated automated routines to create its finding aids since 1986. This has been possible because the structure of the finding aids conforms to a rigid format predicated on the placement of specified data elements at fixed tab locations. For example, box numbers flush left, folder numbers at 6, series names at 16, subseries

[5]This software package, which came out in the early 1980s, is no longer commercially available. It proved so effective for finding aid production, however, that Beinecke has continued to use it. We are investigating options for migrating to a more current software package; one that will allow us to preserve the inherent logic and functionality of our Edix/Wordix based system, while also employing a standard, nonproprietary programming language.

[6]For further information about the Divinity Library and Manuscripts and Archives Department EAD conversion templates, contact Martha Smalley, Research Librarian, Yale Divinity Library (martha.smalley@yale.edu) or consult the Yale Divinity Library's in-house training guidelines on the Web, <http://www.library.yale.edu/div/sgmanual/htm>.

at 18 and 20 (sometimes 22), folder descriptions at 22 (sometimes 24), notes at 24 (sometimes 26), and folder dates at 63 (see Figure 1).[7] Guidelines for formatting text within the data elements (such as how to handle wrap-around text in notes or to format date information at the file level) further assure a very uniform structure, both within and across a wide range of finding aids. The layout of the front matter, though less structured, is equally precise.

In addition to prescribing the precise location and formatting of specified data elements, each of Beinecke's finding aids is made up of two ASCII text files: a front matter file ([filename].frn) and a box and folder list file ([filename].box); an optional appendix file ([filename].app) is provided for but rarely used. Staff process the two files through a series of locally defined Edix and Wordix programs and macros to manipulate the front matter file and box and folder list into a variety of useful forms: an output to screen of the document, stripped of diacritics, that is used in an in-house full-text database; a printer-ready file, including diacritics; and sets of folder and box labels. A set of diagnostic macros tests for errors in data placement and in box and folder numbering; another macro automatically assigns folder numbers in sequence. Printed and on-screen reports of the diagnostics are output for staff review.

All of this data processing and various paper-based and machine-readable outputs are possible because the structure of the finding aid conforms to well-established and rigorously enforced specifications. When it came to doing SGML markup, it was therefore a relatively straightforward matter of building on the existing logic of our finding aid routines. We wrote new Edix/Wordix programs and macros to parse the .frn and .box files and to insert EAD tags at appropriate locations in each file structure. Some manual follow-up was necessary to review the markup, insert unique data (such as addresses for hypertext links within the document), or resolve problems, but this was a relatively minor task compared to the encoding of the files overall, many of which exceeded one hundred pages in length.

The basic division of front matter and container list into separate ASCII files had the added advantage of allowing us to batch the SGML markup and process large numbers of files in sequence with minimal manual intervention. Similarly, when we were preparing files for encoding, we were able to write macros to pinpoint formatting errors or other trouble spots (which early testing had identified as being problematic for automated markup) and to make the necessary corrections globally across dozens of files.

[7]Summary of .box file tab specifications for Beinecke finding aids:

Flush left (tab 0)............for BOX NO.

Tab 6..............................for FOLDER NO.

Tab(s) 16, 18, 20, (22)..for HEADINGS (series, subseries, sub subseries, and sub sub subseries).

Headings at 16, 18, and 20 should not extend beyond tab 70 and must not exceed one line in length. Headings at 22 should not extend beyond tab 60 but may extend beyond a single line.

Tab(s) 22, (24)...............for FOLDER TITLES

Folder descriptions should not be placed at a tab value higher than 22; if tab 22 is functioning as a sub sub subseries heading, folder titles go at 24. Folder description text should not extend beyond tab 60.

Tab(s) 24, (26) ....for NOTES, CROSS REFERENCES

Notes and cross references should not be placed at a tab value higher than 24; if tab 24 is functioning as a folder title, notes and cross references go at 26. Do not set additional tabs beyond 26. Text of notes and cross references should not extend beyond tab 60.

Tab 63...........................for DATE

Date information should not extend beyond tab 76.

Tab 78.............................RIGHT MARGIN

```
REGISTER TEMPLATE
                    1 1 2 2 2 2                          6 6   7   7
1      6            6 8 0 2 4 6                          0 3   0   8
|      |            | | | | | |                          | |   |   |
                    Series heading______________________________
                        Note____________________________________
                        Note____________________________________
                        ________________________________________
                     SUBSERIES heading__________________________
                        Note____________________________________
                      Sub subseries heading_____________________
                        Note____________________________________
Box#   Folder#          Folder title_______________________  Dates_____
       Folder#          Folder title_______________________
                              _____________________________  Dates_____
                         Note______________________________
                            _______________________________
       Folder#          Folder title_______________________  Dates_____
                              _____________________________
                         See also: cross-reference_________
                        Folder title_______________________  Dates_____
                         See: cross-reference______________
                      Sub subseries heading_____________________
                        Sub sub subseries heading__________
       Folder#            Folder title_____________________  Dates_____
       Folder#            Folder title_____________________  Dates_____
                              _____________________________
                            Note___________________________
                            See also:______________________
```

Figure 1. Excerpt from the Beinecke Library Manuscripts Unit's *Microcomputer Manual for Registers.*

Because of the consistency of our file format and the capacity for batch processing, basic structural markup of Beinecke's 260 files, encompassing thousands of pages of text, was accomplished in a few days.[8] The container list markup (by far the largest and most complex portion of any finding aid) took only a few hours. The rest of the time was spent

[8]A recent test run to encode a finding aid composed of a box and folder list with 245 file entries, plus standard front matter, took fifteen minutes. Basic encoding of the container list took ninety seconds; the remainder of the time was spent inserting internal hypertext links (e.g., cross references) using a combination of a special macro and manual markup, other follow-up work, verification, troubleshooting, validation, file naming, and exporting the file to the load queue on the server.

marking up the front matter; providing the necessary internal cross-reference links; reviewing, troubleshooting, and validating the files; and sending them to the server to be loaded and indexed.

Some Words of Advice for Others

With more than two years of work now behind us, what have we learned that might be of use to others who are considering embarking on an EAD project of their own? A great many things could be mentioned, but a few stand out as being particularly important.

If you have written guidelines and/or formatting templates for finding aids, review them, improve them if needed, and enforce them. If you don't have written guidelines, create them and enforce them. Similarly, once you determine your EAD-encoding practice and tag set, document it and keep it up to date![9]

Beyond formalizing and enforcing formatting guidelines for newly created machine-readable files, unquestionably the single most important piece of advice we can offer is to define your priorities. How much time, really, are you willing and able to devote to the project? Be realistic and set your goals accordingly; to get even a few files up and running may entail a significant investment in time, especially when you are just starting out and are still learning the ropes. Is legacy file conversion a priority? Or are you primarily interested in working EAD into your routines for creating new files? These are critical questions; your answers will determine how you proceed, the kind of resources you will have to commit, and the type of technical support you will require.

Remember, too, that the priority you are able to give to legacy file conversion may determine the utility of your on-line files for general research and reference use. If you have a significant body of legacy data to convert, you should therefore consider carefully the level of markup that you should attempt. The number of EAD tags that are *required* is about twenty (all of them structural, plus a few that are required to create a valid EAD instance). Twenty out of a tag library of 135 may not sound like much, and hardly worth the effort, but you might be surprised to learn that a very useful result can be obtained even with a minimal amount of tagging. If your finding aids have not previously been available on-line, even the simplest markup will be a great step forward. If you get through converting all of your data and feel the need to do more, there's nothing to stop you. You may well find, however, that a minimalist approach to EAD tagging is quite sufficient.

When planning legacy file conversion, carefully assess the degree of standardization present in those files. Wherever possible, find ways to group files of like type so as to take advantage of any potential that may exist for batch processing. Set your goals for legacy conversion, as compared to encoding of newly created files, by taking into account your levels of standardization; this will determine your capacity to convert files quickly. Don't set yourself up for defeat by aspiring to a rate of conversion that you cannot sustain given your resource base and/or the relative lack of standardization in your legacy data. As the Beinecke experience amply demonstrates, standards for data input are a key factor in being able to employ macros for markup; the more idiosyncratic the format of the finding aid, the more sophisticated your macros and programs must be, and the fewer your options for using macros at all.

---

[9]To view the Beinecke Library's draft SGML/EAD Instructional Guidelines for staff, see: <http://www.library.yale.edu/beinecke/manuscript/sgmlmain.htm>.

If you anticipate having to develop your own markup macros or other tools rather than using existing SGML authoring tools, do you have the requisite technical knowledge for writing the macros and programs you will need? It seems highly unlikely that you will be able just to adopt a template (or macros) written for another institution's finding aids and, wholesale, apply them to your own; some tweaking, if not major rewriting, will almost certainly be required. If you do not have this expertise yourself, or elsewhere in house, you will have to obtain the assistance of someone with a fairly sophisticated understanding of the tools you propose to use for writing the macros. That person also must have, or acquire, a fairly sound understanding of your finding aid practice.

Finally, hardware is a consideration not to be underestimated, especially if your files are large and complex. The power of the CPU and the size of the display screen can make a world of difference in retrieving, navigating, and viewing files.[10] If, as we did, you plan to install a server, or if you will be working with new or unfamiliar hardware and software components, expect to spend more time than you anticipate dealing with the consequences of products that do not function as advertised (at least not in *your* systems environment) or that may not become available as projected. After all, EAD implementation, especially on the Web, in many ways is still a work in progress for us all.

Conclusion

It is often said that ''Fools rush in where angels fear to tread.'' Certainly the Yale EAD early implementers have had reason to recall this saying on several occasions and to wonder in which camp we stood. As I have suggested, our EAD/Web server initiative proved to be a vastly more complex and time-consuming project than we had envisioned; the learning curve was steep and at times frustratingly slow. And as if our own inherent ''weaknesses'' of limited experience with SGML, Web publishing and the like were not enough to contend with, it seemed on more than one occasion that an unending stream of technical ''glitches'' and exceptions to the claims of functionality made by product vendors might defeat us. But in spite of all that, we prevailed, and there is general agreement that the experience has been worth the effort, and not just for the specific results embodied in the current Yale Finding Aid Project database and website. EAD, and Web distribution of SGML-encoded documents in general, are still undergoing development, and it is not yet clear just where we will arrive when all is said and done. What is fairly sure, we think, is that with this initiative the Yale library has entered into a new and powerful world of electronic and hypertext document delivery to expand awareness of and access to Yale's remarkable array of special collections, and that there is no turning back. We have achieved a hard won but critical first step in the right direction on behalf of ourselves, as library and archival professionals, for the collections entrusted to our care, and for the students, faculty, and research public who use these collections and who unquestionably will benefit from Web-based access to information about Yale's archival and manuscript holdings.

As to where we go from here, stay tuned....

[10]For our current recommended technical specifications, see ''System Requirements for Panorama browsers'' on the Yale Finding Aid Project website <http://webtext.library.yale.edu/#view>.

CHAPTER 10

EAD Testing and Implementation at the Library of Congress

MARY A. LACY and ANNE MITCHELL

Introduction

THE LIBRARY OF CONGRESS (LC) is one of several institutions that tested the alpha and beta versions of the Encoded Archival Description (EAD) Document Type Definition (DTD) in 1996 and 1997. The library's goals were to explore the use of Standard Generalized Markup Language (SGML) as a tool for encoding finding aids, to evaluate the EAD DTD's structure, noting any problems or inconsistencies, and to see how well EAD could accommodate a variety of finding aid formats. Staff also sought to determine the ease or difficulty of converting a finding aid to EAD.

LC has an immediate interest in using EAD. As it begins to digitize its extensive special collections, the digital object-linking features of EAD offer a promising approach for its National Digital Library Program (NDLP) projects, given that many of LC's special collections are far too large for each component to receive individual cataloging.

In addition, LC is interested in making its finding aids broadly available whether or not a particular collection's contents are digitized. LC has formally published selected registers over the last forty years, and since 1995, its special collections divisions have made additional finding aids available on the Internet through LC's Gopher and World Wide Web sites.[1] LC is using SGML encoding, however, as a better and more lasting investment than it would be to encode finding aids using HyperText Markup Language (HTML). As an SGML DTD, EAD is platform- and program-independent and provides a stable storage environment for data. By supporting more sophisticated display and navigation than is possible using either HTML or plain ASCII text, EAD helps the hierarchical structure of a finding aid convey the depth and complexity of an archival collection in an intelligible way. In addition, EAD-encoded finding aids offer researchers an opportunity to simultaneously search multiple finding aids within and among institutions.

N.B. "EAD Testing and Implementation at the Library of Congress," by Mary A. Lacy and Anne Mitchell, co-published simultaneously in the *American Archivist* (The Society of American Archivists) vol. 60, no. 4, pp. 420–35; and *Encoded Archival Description: Context, Theory, and Case Studies* (ed.: Jackie M. Dooley) The Society of American Archivists, 1998.

[1]As of September 1997, the Manuscript Division has made ASCII versions of over one hundred finding aids available through Gopher and Web gateways. The American Folklife Center, the Prints and Photographs Division, the Music Division, and the Motion Picture, Broadcasting, and Recorded Sound Division also have made numerous finding aids available via LC's Gopher and websites.

LC has found EAD to be a worthwhile method of automating finding aids in several divisions and has benefited from participation in the alpha and beta testing of the DTD. Staff learned to use the EAD DTD by experimenting with various approaches to tagging and learned that encoding can progress rapidly once finding aid creators are familiar with the tags and structure of EAD. The learning curve has been steep, however, and substantial technical support has been needed to understand how to configure the SGML files to interact properly. LC has tested varying approaches and strategies for converting existing finding aids and now has thirteen encoded finding aids. LC's EAD Task Force is disseminating information internally about EAD and finding aids; fostering discussion of common standards for content, coding, and display; and investigating how best to distribute EAD finding aids via the World Wide Web.

This case study focuses on LC's participation as one of several institutions that tested EAD by encoding finding aids.[2] The first section addresses LC's test of the alpha version of the DTD, describing common activities and decisions; the differing approaches to tagging taken by the Manuscript and the Prints and Photographs divisions in encoding sample finding aids is also analyzed. The second section describes the encoding activities of the Manuscript, Prints and Photographs, and Music divisions following the alpha test. The final section discusses organizational and technical issues in the cooperative exploration of EAD at LC and summarizes the authors' conclusions, based on their two-year involvement with EAD at LC.

Alpha Testing at the Library of Congress

Group Activities and Decisions

Three divisions at LC participated as early implementers of EAD beginning in January 1996. By May 1996 (no one worked full time on the project), LC had two prototype finding aids on-line. Finding aids selected for conversion included the moderately sized traditional register for the Shirley Jackson Papers (Manuscript Division) and the larger finding aid for visual materials from the NAACP Records (Prints and Photographs Division). The very large finding aid for the Federal Theatre Project (Music Division), begun during alpha testing, was completed during beta testing and will be discussed in a later section.

The participants took a group approach, blending the skills of staff in NDLP and Information Technology Services, who were familiar with SGML from tagging book texts, with the skills of staff in the Manuscript and the Prints and Photographs divisions, who were familiar with finding aids. The number of EAD tags was a shock! It gradually became apparent that finding aids often merit more markup than the historical narrative texts that were tagged in the NDLP projects because finding aids, which are documents about other documents, have more structure and more varied content. It also became clear that staff members who were unfamiliar with finding aids would have a hard time doing markup. The parts of finding aids cannot be as easily identified as a chapter, heading, or paragraph in a book, for example, and the headings for each finding aid section do not always match the generalized EAD tag names (e.g., "Description of Series" vs. "Description of Subordinate Components").

[2]This case study does not describe LC's participation in the Berkeley Finding Aid Project or on the team of researchers who worked at the Bentley Historical Library on the transition from the FindAid DTD to EAD, or in pre-alpha testing of EAD. Neither does it address the role of LC's Network Development and MARC Standards Office as the maintenance agency for EAD in conjunction with the Society of American Archivists.

The participants gained some familiarity with SGML and EAD by looking at standard SGML reference sources,[3] the pre-alpha EAD DTD, and eventually the alpha DTD and tag library. Marking up finding aids on paper at this stage helped the testers learn the DTD structure and tag library before going on-line. A four-day SGML overview course offered by NDLP later in 1996 helped some staff. LC found, however, that once software is configured and sample EAD finding aids exist, the training focus for most staff can be on EAD itself.

At first, all tagging was done at one digital library development workstation on which two software tools, SoftQuad's Author/Editor and Panorama PRO (SGML editor and viewer software) had been installed. The alpha version of the EAD DTD was loaded, and rules files were generated to enforce the syntax of the DTD during tagging. As additional copies of software were installed, alpha testers were able to work with the SGML editing software in their own divisions, while continuing to work with the SGML viewer on the digital library workstation.

The earliest encoding was done in weekly "play sessions" attended by staff from the three divisions that were encoding finding aids; staff with technical expertise also participated.[4] Working without adequate documentation was difficult (the alpha tag library became available in late February 1996), but testers were aided by the expertise of two LC participants in the Bentley Fellowship Program who were available to help interpret the DTD.[5] Additional insights were gleaned from postings on the EAD listserv.[6]

Staff in each of the divisions invariably focused on different encoding problems, and these informal, experimental sessions were excellent opportunities to see things from another angle, to pick up practical tips, and to resolve many issues. Topics included tagging dilemmas, use of WordPerfect macros to insert tagging, SGML conventions, how to configure the different components (i.e., the DTD, entity files, finding aid files, and files required by the viewing software) to interact on-line, and how to create and edit style sheets and navigators.

An important part of the test was making provisional decisions about how to encode; specifically, how to interpret the tags and how intensively to code the finding aids. Data retrieval and navigation needs were considered as much as were data display features. Staff purposefully explored different encoding options, with the hope of demonstrating by experimentation that EAD could be applied at various levels of detail. The register for the Shirley Jackson Papers was marked up by the Manuscript Division at a high level of

[3]Charles F. Goldfarb, *The SGML Handbook* (New York: Oxford University Press, 1990); Eric Van Herwijnen, *Practical SGML* (Boston: Kluwer Academic Publishers, 1994).

[4]Many specialists from throughout LC advised staff during these sessions: National Digital Library Program staff lent their expertise in SGML and SGML software, gained from implementing the American Memory DTD; Automation Planning and Liaison Office staff installed and configured the required hardware and software; and Information Technology Services staff assisted with configuring software to read the EAD DTD, creating the navigator, and testing ways to point from the finding aid to the Prints and Photographs Division home page.

[5]Janice Ruth (Manuscript Division) and Helena Zinkham (Prints and Photographs Division) were members of a team of experts in archival descriptive standards sponsored by the Bentley Historical Library Research Fellowship Program, which first met July 1995 in Ann Arbor, Michigan. The team collaborated in the production of finding aid encoding standard design principles, a revised finding aid data model, a revised finding aid Document Type Definition (which became EAD), and finding aid encoding guidelines and examples. This group continued to shape the development of EAD; most members now belong to the Society of American Archivists' Committee on Archival Information Exchange EAD Working Group, which maintains intellectual ownership of EAD.

[6]Information on the EAD listserv and instructions for subscribing are available at <http://www.loc.gov/ead/eadlist.html>.

specificity up until the container list. The Prints and Photographs Division explored a briefer tagging style, ''EAD Lite,'' for its longer NAACP finding aid, which included an index, an image sampler, and additional material. The Music Division's Federal Theatre Project finding aid, discussed below, minimized its container list, tagging even less than the others to reduce the bulk of this very long finding aid.

The alpha group agreed to certain common practices. All appropriate data would be supplied in the EAD Header <eadheader>, the tag which holds information identifying the finding aid. The Manuscript and the Prints and Photographs divisions agreed on a title page display generated from the header that would provide a uniform look and feel to on-line LC finding aids.

All LC EAD finding aids begin with summary elements in the Archival Description-level Descriptive Identification <archdesc><did> element to give researchers a quick, general sense of what each collection includes. These elements, not previously found in LC's paper finding aids, ensure that basic data can be readily located on-line; EAD encourages inclusion of this data in all finding aids. The extent statement was moved from the administrative information page of the paper finding aid to the descriptive identification element. In other words, the use of EAD is changing and improving former paper finding aid practices.

Both divisions chose to enrich their finding aids with a list of Controlled Access Headings <controlaccess>, which are authorized forms of names, topical subjects, and other terms taken from the USMARC catalog record for a collection. Finding aid searches limited to these specific fields will retrieve collections which are particularly strong sources of material for these subjects. The working group decided that detailed tagging of names, dates, and places in the container list would be unlikely to yield enough retrieval benefits to justify the time required by available tagging methods.

Finally, the two divisions chose to enhance navigability among the sections of the finding aid by using reference tags to provide hypertext links between the scope and content note and description of series, and between the description of series and container list. Cross-references in the container list also were linked.

Manuscript Division: Shirley Jackson Papers

For purposes of the alpha test in early 1996, the Manuscript Division focused on finding aids previously converted from WordPerfect to plain ASCII for mounting on the LC Gopher site. The register for the Shirley Jackson Papers is typical of a finding aid for a literary author; at nineteen pages, it is of moderate length and complexity.

Tagging began by importing an ASCII version of the register into Author/Editor. The SGML editor enforced correct tagging and prompted participants with the tags available at any point; this interactive method allowed the group to learn the DTD thoroughly while making tagging choices. Once the tagged finding aid was validated, it served as a model from which to devise more efficient tagging procedures.

In order to use as many different elements as possible to evaluate their usage and to suggest changes for the beta version, the Manuscript Division coded personal <persname>, corporate <corpname>, family <famname>, and other names, geographic places <geogname>, and dates <date> in the Administrative Information <admininfo>, Biographical Note/Agency History <bioghist>, and Scope and Content Note <scopecontent> elements. Bibliographic references <bibref> were coded throughout the finding aid, as were titles of works <title>; for the latter, attributes were used to distinguish between titles which should be rendered in italics (e.g., book titles) or with quotation marks (e.g., article titles). Detailed tagging of names, dates, and places in the container list was deferred.

Paragraphs in the Administrative Information <admininfo> section were coded as Acquisition Information <acqinfo>, Processing Information <processinfo>, and Restrictions on Use <userestrict>, as appropriate, although coding them as Paragraphs <p> also would have been acceptable.

Both the Description of Subordinate Components <dsc type="analyticover"> and the Container List <dsc type="in-depth"> were coded with numbered rather than unnumbered components (e.g., <c02> rather than <c>) for ease of tag tracking and proofreading. The register for the Shirley Jackson Papers contains five nested levels of components, and many other finding aids feature even deeper hierarchical nesting. Unit dates <unitdate> were tagged only at the series and subseries level.

The Manuscript Division staff chose to code the container list using Display Rows <drow> and Display Entries <dentry> in hope of enabling a tabular display of data, with container numbers in a left column and contents in the right column. This model was an attempt to impose tabular display while tagging the components of the container list according to their hierarchical value.

Prints and Photographs Division: NAACP Finding Aid

The sixty-seven-page print version of the finding aid for the visual materials in the National Association for the Advancement of Colored People (NAACP) Records, completed in 1994, was created in a traditional finding aid format. The Prints and Photographs Division selected this finding aid because the NAACP collection is of high interest to the division's users, and staff hoped that the navigation and searching capabilities of SGML browsers would allow researchers easier access to specific information in this long document. The finding aid's traditional format facilitated mapping to EAD.

Division staff explored four main issues while encoding the NAACP finding aid: testing "EAD Lite,"[7] developing techniques for converting a traditional-style paper finding aid into an on-line version, showing how EAD accommodates some special qualities of pictorial collection finding aids, and examining the linking of digital images to finding aids on the Web.

"EAD Lite" is an attempt to save time (and thereby reduce costs) by avoiding tagging that would result in relatively few display and retrieval benefits; staff can create more EAD finding aids by tagging each at a basic level. They can focus on understanding EAD core structures, and nonarchivists can successfully be employed to provide basic tagging. The full EAD DTD allows for very detailed content tagging when more intricate retrieval is needed (for example, every instance of "NAACP" as a corporate name, and all personal names could be tagged as <persname>). "EAD Lite," in contrast, permits paragraph-level information to be tagged as minimally as possible; attributes are seldom used. The focus is on links, collection summary elements, and large structures rather than on tagging every personal name and date.

---

[7]Available as an appendix in Anne J. Gilliland-Swetland, *Encoded Archival Description Document Type Definition (DTD) Application Guidelines* (Washington, D.C.: Library of Congress and the Society of American Archivists, 1996). Unpublished draft available from <http://scriptorium.lib.duke.edu/findaids/ead/guidelines/index.html>.

''EAD Lite'' stresses the importance of ''heads'' and ''links'' to ensure easy navigation within the parts of the finding aid. Prints and Photographs Division staff created hotlinks on call numbers in the series description to lead users directly to more detailed information in the contents list, as well as on call numbers in the Photographer Index to lead users to the series-level description. These links were created by tagging the call numbers as references.

The ''Contents List'' in the NAACP finding aid was encoded as a minimalist container list to test the use of nested, unnumbered components. Staff found it difficult to keep these unnumbered components properly nested. They also discovered the hazard of components that appear to be at two different levels because they are displayed on two lines in the paper finding aid, but which are, in fact, only a folder title and subtitle of the same component. The Prints and Photographs Division's finding aids will use numbered components in the future.

Tagging was done using Author/Editor and WordPerfect software. It helped to manually key tags for ''large'' elements (e.g., <ead>, <archdesc>, <findaid>) before importing the text to Author/Editor in order to side step the time-consuming ''wrapping'' of text. WordPerfect's search-and-replace function was useful for inserting tags in long lists when the tags could be applied consistently.

The division developed an ''Image Sampler'' (or digital archival object group <daogrp>) of eight images to give researchers an idea of the typical images in this collection (Figure 1). (Paper finding aids similarly often include photocopies of images because visual data for visual images is so important.) The division will continue to link digitized images of items in collections to its EAD finding aids, highlighting the images of most interest to researchers.

Within the <daogrp>, the digital archival object <dao> points from the document to an individual ''gif'' file for each image. The sampler featured images of approximately 50 KB each rather than thumbnails. Entity references were declared for each image at the beginning of the SGML document. (An SGML declaration document file would be used to handle the entity references for names of digital image files if more than ten images are included.) Naming conventions for digital image files are still evolving.

Unfortunately, these images cannot be included in the version of the finding aid that is currently mounted on LC's public website because they were produced within the last fifty years, in some cases by unknown photographers, and the rights to most of the images are not clear. Therefore, the version with the images is available only on LC's internal ''intranet'' website.

Results of alpha testing

The most concrete result of alpha testing at the Library of Congress was a preliminary version of the register for the Shirley Jackson Papers, which was loaded on the American Memory website on April 26, 1996; the NAACP register followed on May 22. These registers have been revised to conform to the beta EAD DTD released in fall 1996. The third finding aid, for the Federal Theatre Project Records, was made available in February 1997. The Shirley Jackson Papers register was submitted as an example for use in the EAD application guidelines.[8]

[8]Gilliland-Swetland, *Encoded Archival Description Document Type Definition (DTD) Application Guidelines.*

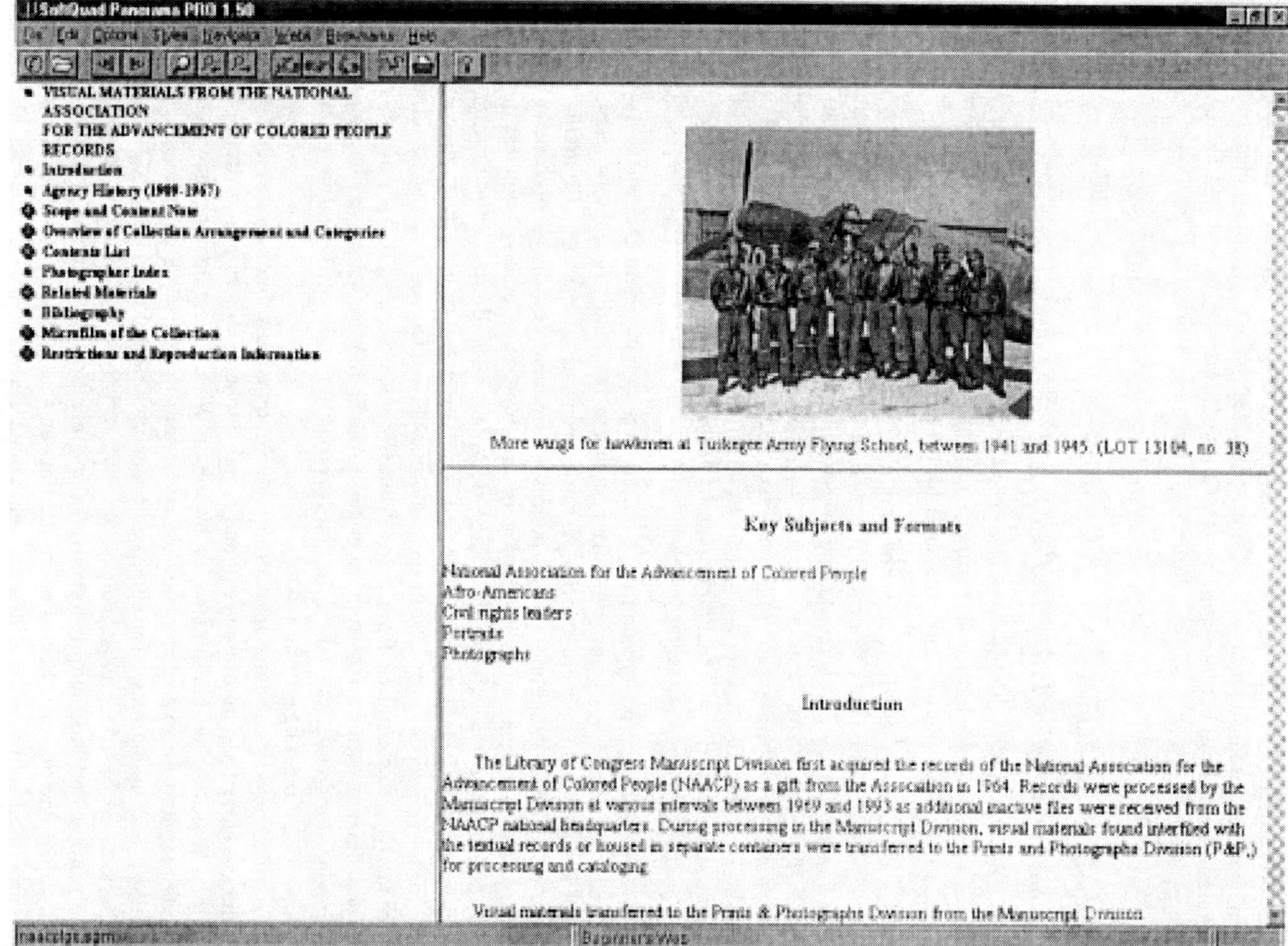

Figure 1. Image Sampler, NAACP Finding Aid, displayed in Panorama.

The basic EAD structure seems to fit LC finding aids well. LC reported only a few problems and proposed a number of minor changes to the EAD DTD, most of which were implemented in the beta version. Most of these DTD changes resulted in new names for elements and attributes, and the alpha EAD finding aids were updated with simple search and replace procedures.

Divisional Case Studies

Manuscript Division: EAD Pilot Project

In September 1996 the Manuscript Division approved an EAD pilot project. In support of EAD's long-term goal to improve onsite and remote access to information contained in archival finding aids, the short-term objectives of the project were:

1. To increase the division's production of encoded finding aids, giving LC a larger pool of documents from which to test searching methods, linking mechanisms, and other display and access questions pertinent to LC's implementation of EAD;
2. To identify strategies, staffing levels, and workflow patterns that the division may wish to implement for full-scale production of EAD finding aids; and
3. To gather additional comments, criticisms, and recommendations about the beta version of EAD. (In fact, few comments resulted from the beta testing, due to the success of alpha testing.)

The Manuscript Division pilot project was conducted in the fall of 1996 and was largely completed by spring 1997. Ten finding aids already available in plain ASCII and WordPerfect versions were identified by reference and subject specialist archivists as being of high research value and general interest. An advisory group of division reference and processing managers, curators, catalogers, and processing archivists met at the beginning of the project to reevaluate the coding decisions made during alpha testing. The group continued to advise on levels of specificity and extent of tagging in an attempt to balance the improved access provided through more sophisticated searching against the decreased productivity that resulted from more detailed content tagging. Group members also provided input in editing the style sheet for EAD finding aid display. Manuscript Division catalogers reviewed the ten collection-level cataloging records and completed authority work for all headings in the records.

The project coordinator worked with the division's automated operations archivist, who developed a suite of powerful and creative macros to perform the bulk of the tagging within WordPerfect. These macros were run on WordPerfect documents which had already been prepared for export as plain ASCII versions by removing page headings and substituting "fake underlines" for emphasis codes such as bold and italic. Conversion macros inserted tags based on tabs, indents, and other "hooks;" the macros relied upon regular tab settings and hard returns to convert the context of the container list from white space to tagged components. Each finding aid, tagged thusly within WordPerfect, was ready to be imported into Author/Editor for validation. Conversion of documents to SGML was facilitated by the prior existence of detailed divisional guidelines for consistent preparation of registers and by extensive use of word processing macros and templates in the production of the original WordPerfect finding aids.

The project coordinator trained and directed a manuscript technician, who worked half-time on the project for its duration and ably encoded the ten selected finding aids. The technician kept a careful record of the time required for each step in the project, which helped the project team streamline the workflow and improve the evolving macros and documentation.

After the tagged WordPerfect finding aid was printed out and proofread against the original document using an editing checklist, it was exported as generic ASCII text and imported into Author/Editor; this process identified additional errors. Staff then added appropriate content tags to names, places, bibliographic citations, and types of information in the <admininfo> section using Author/Editor (this step requires intellectual input and is not easily done by conversion software). Where links were needed for navigation or container list cross-references, the technician wrote on the paper finding aid a short name for the attribute called "id" for each element to which a reference pointed; those values were added to the EAD finding aid in Author/Editor. After work in Author/Editor was complete, the coordinator reviewed the Panorama display of the finding aid against the original paper finding aid and selectively checked tagging in Author/Editor. The Panorama style sheet, a file that controls how the data is displayed, was edited as needed.

Substantial experimentation was done with the Panorama style sheet and the navigator file, a file which determines which EAD elements are pulled into the on-line table of contents. The division wished to convey the finding aid information as clearly as possible, and staff attempted to replicate, on-line, the tabular appearance of the printed container list. This tabular formatting could be approximated on-line using either <drow> or <did> (Figure 2), but true tabular formatting required the assignment of empty <dentry> tags contrary to the DTD. The division thus decided to abandon this <drow><dentry> approach and changed all eleven Manuscript Division finding aids to a <did> presentation.[9] This simpler approach makes coding and proofreading easier, as well as decreasing total file size. Once staff identified the necessary file directory structures and had server space assigned, the EAD finding aids were loaded and made available via the Manuscript Division finding aid page on the LC website.

The pilot program's preliminary strategy, therefore, tested the use of existing software, equipment, and staff for the retrospective conversion of current finding aids already available via LC's Gopher and websites in ASCII text. The division identified minor changes to paper finding aids which ease the conversion process and more accurately reflect the content of sections of the finding aid. Converting a finding aid to EAD should be viewed as the final step in processing collections and creating, inputting, and editing the registers. The time required to complete this step will continue to decrease.

In the summer of 1997 the Manuscript Division identified additional high-priority finding aids for SGML conversion; staff also scanned or rekeyed registers not yet in machine-readable form in preparation for EAD encoding. The division will encode these finding aids by the methods already developed. Staff expect to refine the process and streamline workflow; identify hardware and software needs; design styles, macros, and templates; and investigate autotagging software to speed document conversion. Word processing operations are being transformed to make EAD conversion faster and more reliable. Concurrently, LC is upgrading its WordPerfect software to versions which include SGML modules.

[9]For instance, a line of the finding aid that had been encoded:
<c04><drow><dentry spanname="c8-20"><unittitle>Letters sent</unittitle></dentry></drow> </c04>
was encoded more simply: <c04><did><unittitle>Letters sent</unittitle></did></c04>.

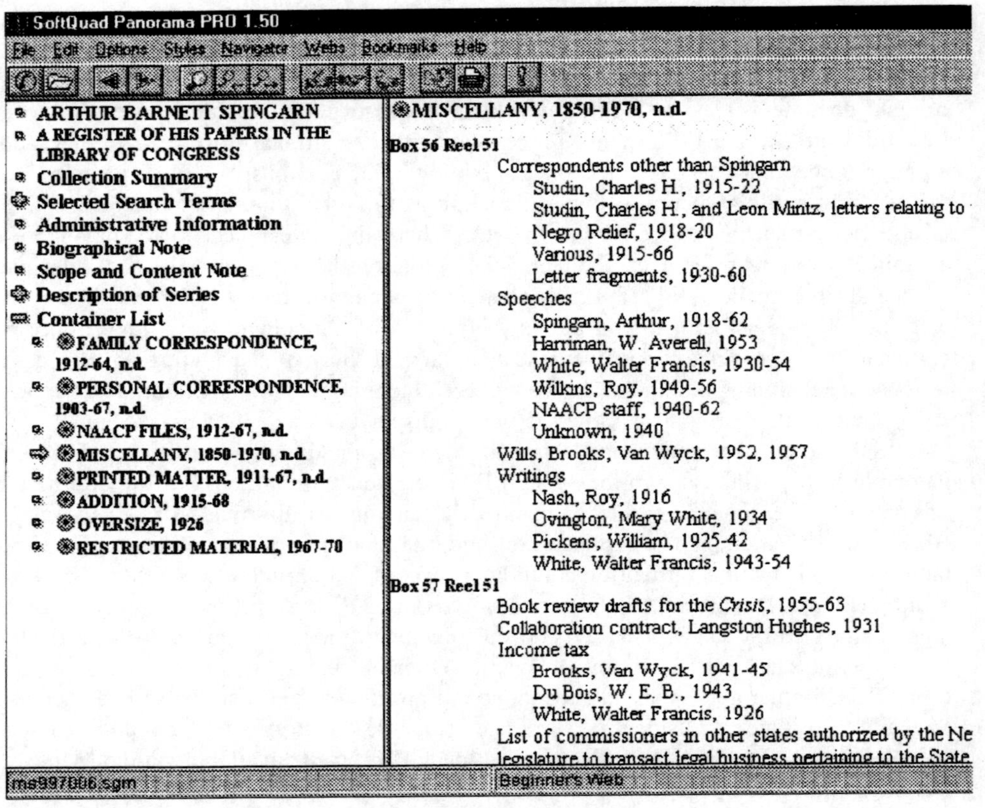

Figure 2. Style sheet and navigator displays of finding aid in Panorama. The navigator panel (left side) is controlled by the navigator file. The Container List entry has been expanded to show the series title; the arrow points to the user's place in the document. The display of the right panel is controlled by the style sheet. Labels have been supplied for box and reel numbers, which do not appear on the same line as the corresponding titles.

Still to be determined is the best method of creating new finding aids from which both the paper and electronic EAD products can be efficiently derived. LC also will explore methods for storing, indexing, and retrieving EAD finding aids as part of its NDLP repository efforts. How EAD best meets reference needs also will be evaluated.

Prints and Photographs Division: Experiments with Alternate Finding Aid Formats

Encoding activities in the Prints and Photographs Division following the completion of alpha EAD testing have centered on experimentation with a variety of divisional finding aids for photographic and other pictorial collections.

Test encoding of the finding aid for the Chadbourne Collection of Japanese Prints explored how well EAD could accommodate detailed item-level descriptions for each of the 188 prints in this collection (this level of description also could be handled by item-level USMARC records, but the descriptions in this finding aid are preliminary and more informal than those in the division's USMARC catalog records). Staff included USMARC encoding analog attributes in element tags, but individual names and titles are not constructed in the same way as the terms found in library catalogs. The division believes that EAD finding aids provide the flexibility to accommodate those cases in which it is necessary, perhaps only selectively, to provide fairly detailed item-level descriptions; examples could include caption lists or other types of pictorial inventories. The Chadbourne finding aid contains consistent categories of information, and so most tags could be inserted fairly quickly using WordPerfect macros and the search/replace function. Staff also tested use of EAD's label attribute to improve users' comprehension of the meaning of specific information categories (for example, to explain that a particular name is an "artist").

A finding aid currently is being compiled for the division's baseball card collection containing 2,100 early baseball cards. This collection also is being digitized; images of both the front and back of each card will be available on the American Memory website. The finding aid contains an item-level caption list for each card that includes the player's name, position, date, city, team name, and the card's call number. Because this information has been organized in a Paradox database, nearly all of the tagging can be generated from a database report. Staff constructed a hierarchical report form that reflects the four levels of nesting in the finding aid. Tags were added to the form after determining valid tag structure for the finding aid. The finished report is imported into SGML authoring software as an ASCII file for final tagging.

Other finding aids are slated for EAD conversion in the next few years. The division's finding aids come in a wide range of formats: some are straightforward lists containing detailed item-level descriptions (such as that for the Chadbourne Collection of Japanese Prints); others contain long lists of folder-level headings (such as the finding aid for the photo morgue of the *New York World Telegram and Sun* newspaper). The division also creates finding aids in a more traditional finding aid format. Most describe collections at the folder- or item-level, since visual materials often lack captions, and the finding aid serves as a caption list. Reference staff have found that providing more detailed description reduces the need to browse original images.

These projects will present new challenges. Encoding the finding aid for the *New York World Telegram and Sun* photo morgue will require the creation of multiple SGML files, given that it consists of a ten-thousand-page folder list for the one-million-item collection. Creating multiple files will help address concerns about how well Web browsers can handle such an enormous finding aid.

Test encoding of the NAACP finding aid has demonstrated that EAD is flexible enough to accommodate finding aids for photographic and other pictorial collections, even though these finding aids do not always fit the traditional finding aid structure. The EAD structure is standardizing the use of core finding aid elements across LC. The Prints and Photographs Division has begun to include some important pieces of information not currently found in some of the division's older finding aids, such as the collection summary information mentioned earlier in the Manuscript Division context. Researchers using EAD finding aids on the LC website will not have access to reference staff who assist researchers onsite, so remote access adds the new requirement to provide a fuller context for understanding and using these collections.

Music Division: Federal Theatre Project and Digital Images

The Music Division, assisted by the National Digital Library Program, has encoded LC's largest EAD finding aid to date, the three-hundred-page published register for the Federal Theatre Project (FTP) Records. This finding aid was selected because significant parts of the collection are being digitized—by 1998 more than thirty thousand digital objects should be on-line. The finding aid does not currently link to these digital objects, but links will be added in the next few years.

The first part of the markup project, begun during EAD alpha testing in 1996, involved the overall view of the document structure—how it was organized and how much "nesting" of information was involved. The FTP finding aid has an introduction and an extensive container list with many layers of description. This structure suggested using <did> rather than <drow><dentry> to decrease the number of tags required, as well as numbered rather than unnumbered components to keep better track of hierarchical levels in the extensive container list. Thus the basic pattern was set for the markup: determine the outermost boundaries first, then fill in the details.

The question, "What are the research needs?" guided the tagging philosophy for this finding aid, which evolved over several months. After initial uncertainty regarding how to use the Physical Description <physdesc> tag for folder counts, staff decided to use it only for titles that overflowed into multiple containers to avoid using an excessively large number (and possible overload) of tags. Names and dates were tagged only in <admininfo> and <chronlist>.

The markup of this document required several phases. It was crucial to do a preliminary markup on paper, highlighting the higher-level elements (the <c01>s and <c02>s) before tagging in Author/Editor, as it was much easier to see the breakdown of the sections on paper than on-line. The finding aid was divided into five files during encoding: one file for the introductory material and four separate files for the container list. Smaller files were easier to manage in both word processing software and Author/Editor; and also allowed more than one person to do markup simultaneously. A "fake" SGML heading, including the SGML declaration and header for each of the smaller files, was added to permit the sections to be validated independently. Once the tagging was finished, these files were reconnected by eliminating the temporary headers to make a single document, which was nearly one megabyte in size.

Because of the large amount of data, it was easier to manipulate the finding aid first in a word processing program. Preliminary tagging was accomplished through the use of WordPerfect macros. The combinations of indents and returns already present in the electronic document were searched and replaced with strings of SGML tags, thus enabling much of the tagging to be automated. The text editing software Codewright, which includes features to facilitate autotagging, was used concurrently with word processing software. Codewright was faster to use than word processing software, as it is capable of more elaborate search and replace functions, but it required that staff learn to use yet another program.

The SGML editor was used mainly for validation of the files. The WordPerfect files invariably contained formatting errors which translated into errors in the initial tagging. Cleanup of these errors, as well as refining the tagging, required a time-consuming line-by-line check of the entire document.

The finding aid for the Federal Theatre Project Records was made available on the American Memory EAD website in February 1997. On June 28, 1997, the NDLP unveiled the initial version of "The New Deal Stage: Selections from the Federal Theatre Project, 1935–1939." Access to ten thousand digital objects is currently being provided through indirect HTML links, pending resolution of LC digital repository issues to facilitate direct links between the finding aid and the images.

LC EAD Task Force

In June 1996 the acting director of Public Service Collections (PSC), the directorate to which LC's special collections belong, charged a joint task force of National Digital Library Program and PSC representatives to further expand LC's EAD implementation. The group's charge included the following: identify types and quantities of finding aids that should be encoded; help each division that compiles finding aids to establish appropriate work flows to convert or author EAD finding aids; establish software and hardware needs; determine training needs; work with the NDLP, LC's Automation Planning and Liaison Office, and Information Technology Services to implement finding aid server capability that can be accessed by each LC reading room and by offsite users; and assist each division in establishing a work plan, as well as contributing at least one finding aid to the LC EAD website.

The task force learned that each of LC's seven special collections divisions has created archival finding aids to control some portion of its collections. The Manuscript Division has by far the most finding aids, and creates the most new finding aids each year. LC's earliest candidates for conversion to EAD include the almost two hundred on-line finding aids already available in plain ASCII format. The universe of paper finding aids is much larger: there are more than 2,000 finding aids in the Manuscript Division alone, another 100 in Prints and Photographs, and about 125 total among the American Folklife Center; Geography and Map; Motion Picture, Broadcasting, and Recorded Sound; Music; and Rare Book and Special Collections divisions. The size of these finding aids ranges from one page to ten thousand pages and more.

One of the EAD Task Force's charges is education, and monthly meetings have served to educate members from the participating divisions. One such educational activity was the "live" tagging of a finding aid from the American Folklife Center using Author/Editor. A subgroup identified training opportunities using LC and external resources such as the Research Library Group's FAST (Finding Aids Archival SGML Training) course. A half-day EAD overview workshop developed by LC staff was taught first at the Mid-Atlantic Regional Archives Conference (MARAC) in Charlottesville, Virginia in May 1997, and is now being offered to staff throughout LC, as well as at subsequent MARAC meetings.

The conversion of finding aids to EAD has slowed while a number of underlying technical issues are resolved. LC's EAD Task Force appointed a technical issues subgroup in March 1997 to address questions relating to the library's digital repository, including digital object naming; indexing schemes; structural and administrative metadata; levels and types of description; and relationships among USMARC records, EAD finding aids, related description files, and the digital objects to which finding aids can be linked. Links between LC's catalog records and finding aids are central to the successful integration of these bibliographic and descriptive tools. LC is implementing a digital repository which assigns permanent names called "handles"[10] to EAD finding aids and digital objects; this is in lieu of Uniform Resource Locators (URLs), because the latter change too often to be practical addresses in a digital repository.

Accomplishments of the technical subgroup thus far include formulation of a method of creating unique identifying names for the mandatory <eadid> element to make it

[10]"Handles" are Uniform Resource Names (URNs) developed by the Corporation for National Research Initiatives (CNRI), Reston, Va. CNRI is working with the LC to build a prototype digital repository system.

compatible with LC's naming scheme for objects in its digital repository, and the development of an SGML file system for central storage of the DTD, entity files, style sheets, navigators, and image files which are shared by finding aids stored within each division's file structure. The Manuscript Division created a model file structure for its finding aids and edited "catalog" and "entityrc" files to point to the SGML file system. Files are made available for internal use by divisions wishing to adapt these for their own needs, as well as for use from outside LC via anonymous file transfer protocol. A new LC EAD webpage,[11] released in August 1997, provides access to all EAD finding aids at LC and also leads researchers to other LC on-line finding aids and special collections information. This webpage supplements the EAD home page maintained by the Network Development and MARC Standards Office, which makes available the EAD DTD, guidelines, and other background information.[12]

There are still many issues to be resolved at the Library of Congress. LC's reading rooms only recently introduced public access Internet stations, and efforts to obtain user feedback about on-line finding aids has been limited thus far. Also, a freely accessible method of delivering finding aids on the Web is not yet in place; in general, industry development of SGML viewers has lagged behind expectations. For now, users must download a free version of Panorama, an SGML viewer that currently runs only under Windows, and not all potential users are willing or able to download this software. One way around this problem is to convert SGML documents to HTML versions for display, but to facilitate retrieval by allowing users to search the original SGML versions and to formulate search queries which take advantage of the rich structural SGML tagging. It seems that EAD finding aids may be convertible to Extensible Markup Language (XML), an emerging standard that promises to serve SGML on the Web as readily as HTML, while taking advantage of SGML tagging. Finding aids would be delivered by XML viewers currently under development by commercial vendors.

Searching SGML documents at LC presents additional problems at present. LC uses INQUERY from Sovereign Hill Software to index and search NDLP collections. INQUERY cannot read a DTD and lacks the capability to exploit some basic SGML features, such as nested searches or querying on attributes. Not until indexing issues are resolved will it be possible to create search forms that allow researchers to exploit the rich SGML tagging without expert knowledge of the tags.

Other SGML users at LC confront similar issues of indexing, conversion, and document management. SGML activities at LC include developing the American Memory DTD that the NDLP uses to encode historical documents, development of the USMARC DTD by the Network Development and MARC Standards Office, and several Congressional Research Service projects such as encoding the *Bill Digest.* LC's SGML Working Group facilitates the exchange of information among those divisions working with SGML and helps users address SGML needs and issues.

Conclusion

The Library of Congress's "early implementers" of EAD were provided with an opportunity to collaborate with other divisions at LC—the National Digital Library Program, the custodial divisions of LC, and automation and cataloging offices—and to com-

[11]<http://lcweb.loc.gov/rr/ead/eadhome.html>.

[12]<http://lcweb.loc.gov/ead/>.

municate with others from across the profession involved in creating finding aids and testing EAD. Finding aid creators are beginning to discuss common standards for content, coding, and display, and to develop models for encoding finding aids across LC. Knowledge of and interest in archival collections and finding aids has been raised to new prominence in LC. The project also has raised awareness of the benefits of SGML.

What value do these experiences have for newcomers to EAD? What elements of this journey of discovery can the authors recommend for others? First, one should analyze current finding aids in the context of EAD. Do they meet the needs of researchers? Does the EAD model point to ways they can be improved? Consider to what level finding aids should be encoded. Examine printed copies and attempt to mark at least one representative sample manually as a template for future encoding. Use the authoring software as a learning and validation tool.

There are now many resources available to help institutions embark on encoding finding aids with EAD. Most of the work of the early implementers was done with little available documentation and few examples, although the alpha version of the EAD tag library was invaluable. Institutions now have the benefit of the Research Library Group's training manuals that were created for its FAST workshops, draft EAD application guidelines, and a revised tag library. The authors also recommend that implementers study the retrospective conversion guidelines and toolkits prepared by the American Heritage Virtual Archive Project[13] and the University of California EAD projects,[14] and adapt or use them accordingly. Examination of EAD websites and study of the markup of selected finding aids available on-line are useful ways of keeping current with EAD practice. Participation on the EAD listserv continues to be a valuable source of information for EAD implementers as well. As more institutions become involved in using EAD, this pool of resources will continue to expand.

---

[13]<http://sunsite.berkeley.edu/amher/>.

[14]<http://sunsite.berkeley.edu/FindingAids/uc-ead/>.

CHAPTER 11

Multi-institutional EAD: The University of Virginia's Role in the American Heritage Project

DAVID SEAMAN

THE AMERICAN HERITAGE PROJECT is a consortium funded by the National Endowment for the Humanities and consists of project teams at the University of California at Berkeley, Duke University, Stanford University, and the University of Virginia. The goals of the consortium are:

- To produce a large number of EAD-encoded finding aids documenting American history and culture;
- To work collaboratively to ensure that these finding aids coexist effectively as part of a multi-institutional "union database;" and
- To examine and report on the intellectual, political, technical, and economic issues that surround the creation of EAD guides.

More information about the project and its participants can be found at the project's website.[1] This chapter will focus on the University of Virginia's portion of the American Heritage Project.[2]

The NEH grant provided the University of Virginia's Special Collections Department with a full-time staff member and several graduate student assistants for one year to work exclusively on the conversion to EAD of guides that already existed in electronic form (mostly in WordPerfect format). The Special Collections Department handles the selection and conversion of the guides, and the Electronic Text Center provides SGML training and the on-line search-and-delivery tools, thereby effectively combining our various skills and drawing on lessons learned in the past five years of full-text SGML and archival image production at the University of Virginia.

Since 1992, the Electronic Text Center has been serving SGML data on-line, using the OpenText search engine in conjunction with our locally written interface forms and

N.B. "Multi-institutional EAD: The University of Virginia's Role in the American Heritage Project," by David Seaman, co-published simultaneously in the *American Archivist* (The Society of American Archivists) vol. 60, no. 4, pp. 436–44; and *Encoded Archival Description: Context, Theory, and Case Studies* (ed.: Jackie M. Dooley) The Society of American Archivists, 1998.

[1] <http://sunsite.berkeley.edu/amher>.

[2] The University of Virginia's EAD guides can be found at <http://www.lib.virginia.edu/speccol/ead/>.

HTML filtering programs. This ongoing activity, mostly focused to date on the use of the Text Encoding Initiative (TEI) Guidelines, has provided a firm basis for the work we are now doing to manage and deliver EAD-encoded data.[3] There are points of similarity between EAD and TEI, especially in the formation of the <eadheader> and in the cross-referencing mechanisms. These similarities helped us deploy EAD rapidly and to convert the TEI authoring and delivery tools to EAD tools.[4]

Methodology

In October 1996 representatives from the four American Heritage institutions met in Berkeley for an intensive series of workshops out of which emerged an ''acceptable range of uniform practice'' for us to follow in our EAD encoding. This meeting was vital to focus and coordinate the work that we all have gone on to produce. Even for a single-institution EAD project, there is much to be gained by spending significant time examining and discussing with colleagues the level of detail one wishes to achieve in tagging and in the details of production.

Our series of workshops led to the preparation of an ''acceptable range of uniform practice'' document, produced by Daniel Pitti for the American Heritage consortium[5] and, for us, to the preparation of a local workflow document for the Virginia data converters to follow.[6] Writing this local document required us to codify—and in doing so, to examine and justify—day-to-day workflow practices in a variety of areas, including:

- file naming,
- file management,
- Unix utilities,
- level and nature of our tagging, and
- indexing and browsing.

Despite being project-specific, we hope these ''acceptable range of uniform practice'' and workflow documents may serve as useful starting points for other EAD projects.

The formulation of a written manual is highly recommended on such a project for a number of practical reasons, not least of which is project continuity when a key member leaves for another job. This happened to us five months into the project, and the ''corporate memory'' of the project that the workflow document encapsulates greatly eased the transition period for a new full-time EAD staffer. Our experience repeatedly has been that the time spent building such a ''project manual'' is one of the best investments one can make in a new project.

The current finding aids at the University of Virginia library exist variously in paper format, plain ASCII text, and WordPerfect. Fortunately, we have enough guides in electronic format to cover most of our production needs for the American Heritage Project, and so we are converting few guides from paper as part of this project. In the year since the project began, we have set up the operation, trained the staff, coordinated with the

[3]For examples of full-text databases at the University of Virginia's Electronic Text Center, see <http://etext.lib.virginia.edu/uvaonline.html>.

[4]The conversion of the TEI Web forms to EAD was performed by Susan Munson, the Electronic Text Center's senior programmer/analyst.

[5]See <http://sunsite.berkeley.edu/amher/upguide.html> for the EAD ''Retrospective Conversion Guidelines'' intended to represent an ''acceptable range of uniform practice.''

[6]The Virginia guide to EAD conversion can be found at <http://etext.lib.virginia.edu/ead/eadguide.html>.

other institutions, and converted over one thousand guides, including parsing and proofing the results after they appear on the Web.

Conversion

We employ two methods to create and convert our EAD guides: 1) For the EAD header and front matter, we use fill-in-the-blank Web forms, and 2) for the body of the text (main scope and content summaries, and the item-by-item summaries), we use WordPerfect conversion techniques.

1. Web forms for the EAD header and front matter. The use of Web forms for standard sections of an SGML document such as the "metadata" header (the <eadheader> element in EAD) has been a practice for several years at the University of Virginia (UVa), in particular for the TEI header we complete for each electronic text that we build. The system we use is a locally produced program, written and distributed by the Institute for Advanced Technology in the Humanities, and adopted gratefully by the Electronic Text Center. In return, we plan to spend some of the center's programming time in late 1997 to augment and develop this program to perform the following additional functions:

- Radio buttons and/or pull-down menus on the Web form for boilerplate text; and
- The ability to enter both text and tags into the Web form fields (at present one can enter only text). For simple documents, it may well be possible to use the form to enter not only the header and front matter, but also the Description of Subordinate Components <dsc> information.

Even as it stands, the Web form is a very useful tool. The program reads an SGML template file and configures itself accordingly, providing fill-in boxes for some or all of the tagged fields in the template. If the template file contains boilerplate language for certain fields, that material also appears on the form. Therefore, it is not a "hard-coded" form that knows only one set of fields, which means that we can use it for other projects simply by providing it with another set-up template. Moreover, one does not need to complete a form at one sitting; an encoder can come back the next day and pull the half-completed data back into the Web form, or call up a completed draft to make revisions. The completed form is saved directly to the Web server. (For the Text Encoding Initiative headers we create for our electronic texts, the Web form also automatically creates a MARC record from the SGML file, and this may be possible for the EAD guides as well.)

The use of such Web forms for data creation has three major advantages:

- An encoder cannot inadvertently create invalid tags, because the tags are hidden from the user and supplied by the form;
- The documents created through the forms have an absolutely consistent similarity of structure, which makes them easier to change programmatically at a later date; and
- The data is saved directly to a directory on the Unix Web server, which has higher-level data security backup mechanisms in place than we typically have on our desktop computers, and which also makes file sharing easier.

2. WordPerfect macros. Predictably, the WordPerfect "legacy data" finding aid files vary somewhat in their coding and layout, but they are similar enough in design to be converted to EAD-tagged data by a combination of WordPerfect macros, search-and-replace operations, and manual tidying up. This process is eased by the fact that our paper guides are rarely tabular in their layout, but rather, are organized in a list format. While EAD provides detailed support for tabular layout, the tagging is complex and is currently difficult to deliver on-line, because both Web browsers and the current popular SGML viewer, Panorama, have difficulty dealing with large tabular documents. I suspect that even if our guides were in tabular layout on paper, we would think seriously about the desirability of continuing that layout into the electronic versions.

We are not using an SGML editor for retrospective conversion. While either WordPerfect 7 and 8 or Author/Editor would be good candidates for authoring new documents (and it is likely that we will use one or both of them for that purpose in the future), these editors are not document-conversion tools; they are at their best when one is writing a new finding aid and encoding it in EAD from the outset.

On-Line Delivery

As with the Web data-entry forms, the search interface, HTML "on the fly" filter, and the Table of Contents generator described here all are items that we have developed over the past five years for handling our full-text and image databases. We have been very pleased to discover that the heavy investment that the Electronic Text Center has made in these software tools continues to transfer to new projects and new SGML Document Type Definitions (DTDs).

1. Searching. In order to search the growing archives of EAD guides, one simply fills in a Web search form that allows the user to search for words, phrases, and items in some proximity to one another, and then to limit further by EAD tags or collection names.[7] For example, one may look for "Chicago" everywhere in the collection of finding aids or limit the search term only to the UVa Mark Twain collection (see Figure 1). The Web form passes the query back to the OpenText search engine, which executes the search; the results come back from the search engine and are piped through an HTML filter and sent out to the user.

What one sees first is a Keyword-in-Context (KWIC) display—the search results with a small amount of surrounding context and the name of the collection from which the results came. The user can then choose to go on to larger and larger contexts around the search term: the section in which the term appears, the entire description of items, or the entire guide. In this fashion we make use of the hierarchical nature of SGML to display the search term in different contexts.

2. Browsing. An alternative way of accessing the collection of finding aids is to go to a browseable list of titles and simply select one.[8] A program written at the University of Virginia builds these pages of links dynamically, drawing on SGML fields in the EAD-encoded data. When we add a new guide, we rerun this script, and the pages are updated. The script pulls out titles, which it arranges alphabetically by surname, with each title followed by accession numbers and file size.

Here again the conversion of the EAD tags to HTML is achieved "on the fly" as it is displayed to a user. This means that we do not need to maintain a static HTML copy of a guide on the server in addition to the SGML version, thus avoiding all the attendant problems of tracking and updating two copies of a file.

---

[7]To try this, see the "Search UVa Guides" choice at <http://www.lib.virginia.edu/speccol/ead/>.

[8]To try this, see the "Browse UVa Guides by Name/Title" choice at <http://www.lib.virginia.edu/speccoll/ead/>.

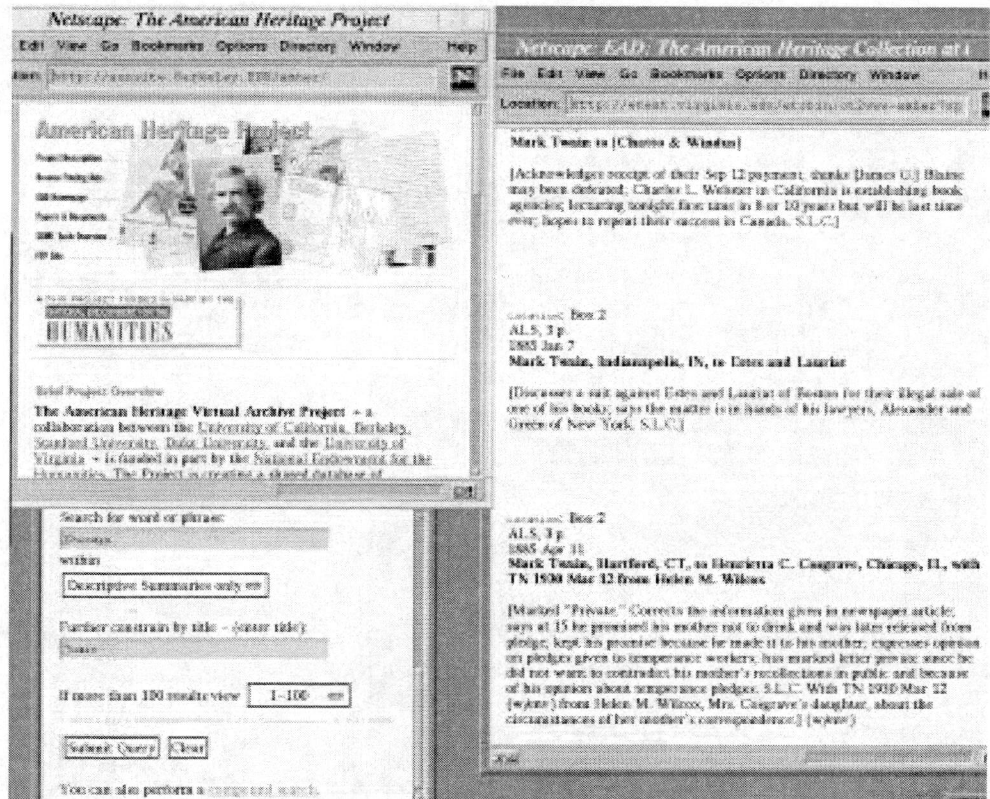

Figure 1. A search for the words "Chicago" and "Twain," each within specific finding aid segments.

3. Automatic Table of Contents Generation. As an alternative to retrieving the entire file, one can use a Table of Contents generator—the "TOC" choice displayed at the end of each entry in the lower left corner of Figure 2. This program takes advantage of SGML's predilection for hierarchical nested structures and predictable title and caption fields: it breaks out "on the fly" the hierarchical structure that exists in the EAD guide and builds a table of contents page that allows one to choose to view only a portion of the file—for example, the front matter or a <c01> or <c02> section of the container list. As a navigational aid, the TOC program prints out for each choice the <head> or <unittitle> that belongs to it (an example can be seen in Figure 3). The ability to browse only a part of the file really comes into its own with a large file such as the Mark Twain Collection.

4. HTML conversion "on the fly." Whether one chooses to search across our collections or to browse a single collection (or some piece of it from the Table of Contents generator), the results are delivered through the same EAD-to-HTML filter, giving the results a uniformity of appearance. The results of a browse or a search are piped through a perl script that substitutes the EAD tags for HTML tags. A simple example follows:

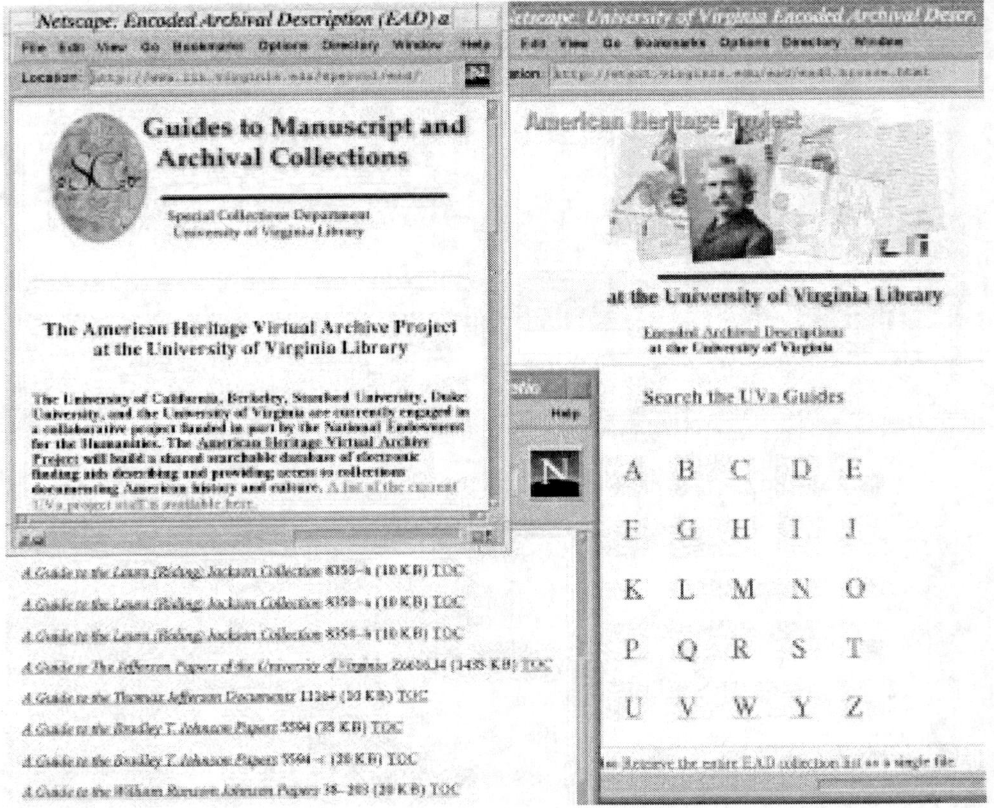

Figure 2. Use of the table of contents generator.

The perl script

```
s/ <unittitle> / <center><h2> /g;
s/ <\/unittitle> / <\/h2><\/center> /g;
```

would convert the EAD tags

<unittitle> Manuscripts </unittitle>

to the HTML tags

<center><h2> Manuscripts </h2></center>.

An obvious advantage of this is that we can make global changes to the appearance of our documents simply by changing a line or two of instructions in the filter.

We do not rely on SGML helper applications such as Panorama because they do not solve any particular issues for us, and, in fact, they create some problems:

- Users resent having to set up another piece of software on their client machines simply to look at a single finding aid;
- Unix, Mac, and VT100 users are excluded, as no version of Panorama exists for these platforms; and

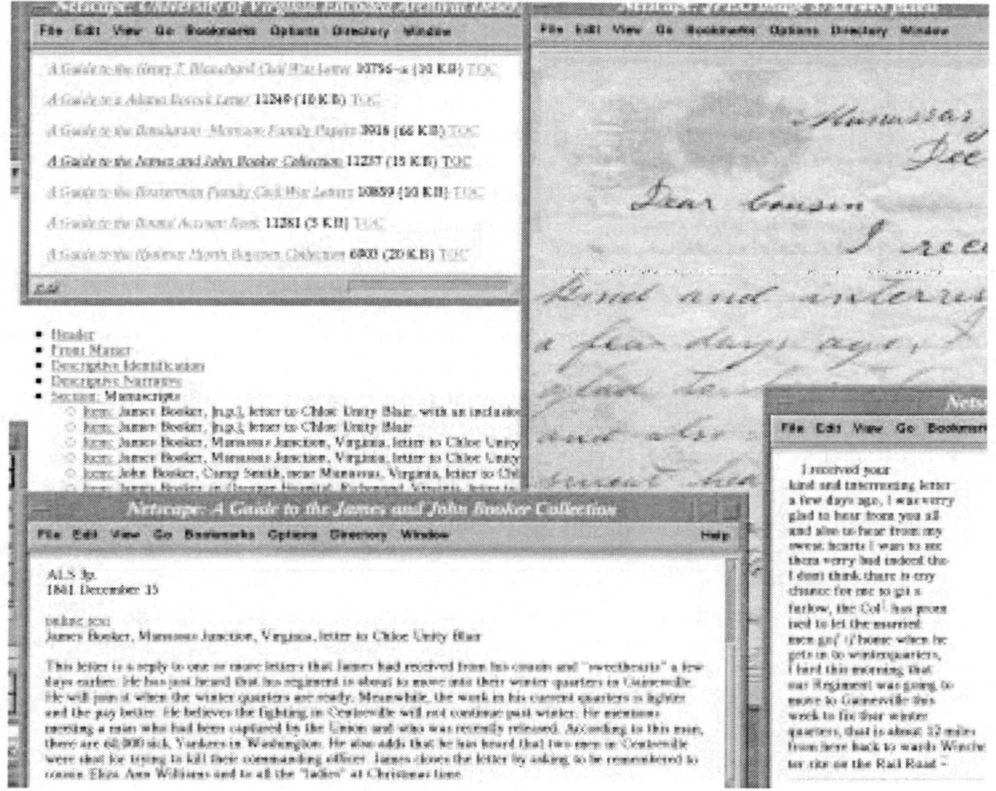

Figure 3. Search results (full-text and image items) demonstrating use of the table of contents generator.

- Users on slower connections resent being forced to download an entire document instead of simply the piece of the document—a <c01> for example—that they need. The SGML helper applications do not currently allow one to request a portion of a longer document.

Looking Ahead

The UVa Special Collections are using the current retrospective conversion project to think through very clearly what the shape, format, and contents of future guides created directly in EAD should be, now that we have a searchable, browseable electronic environment in which to place them rather than simply a paper medium. This initial period of EAD creation allows reflection on what the sensible, functional level of markup should be—what the tagging "sweet spot" is—and allows us to experiment with guides that combine EAD summaries with links to digital full-text and image versions of the objects they describe. A good example would be the James and John Booker Civil War letters.[9] The combination of full-text and image items that are available on-line for this collection

[9]See <http://etext.lib.virginia.edu/ead/eadB.browse.html>.

adds to the level of excitement and makes the value of archival description much more evident to nonarchival users (see Figure 3).

We also keep reminding ourselves of the promise of a national union database of EAD guides, and the incredible research potential that would be enabled by the ability to perform high-level national or regional searches. The multi-institutional American Heritage Project is testing this potential in a very practical manner: each of the four institutions delivers finding aids regularly via FTP transfer to Berkeley, where they are being assembled into one large searchable and browseable database.

Conclusion

In conclusion, I offer four suggestions to archivists contemplating implementation of SGML-encoded finding aid systems.

1. Partnerships. Much of what we do at the University of Virginia relies on good working relationships with others in the organization who have skills necessary to the success of our digital library projects, including catalogers, collection development specialists, archivists, and systems specialists. Archivists working in smaller institutions may have to go outside their immediate environment for these partnerships, perhaps by forming a consortium with neighboring institutions.

2. Take advantage of workshops. Working in isolation is ineffective, and one should try to take advantage of conferences, workshops, and professional meetings to learn new skills and share discoveries prior to attempting implementation of a technology such as EAD.

3. Set achievable goals. Take on small projects initially; for example, ones that can be brought to completion in a semester. Such an approach provides the benefits of a quick result for demonstration purposes, as one tries to raise user awareness and interest while pursuing local and national funding opportunities. Such small projects also can be useful for working out local data creation or conversion processes.

4. Remember that SGML is your friend. While learning and implementing EAD is not a trivial undertaking, it is a manageable one, as is witnessed by the rapidly growing numbers of institutions taking on EAD projects. The investment in EAD over plain ASCII text or HTML is repaid quickly as one starts searching and delivering the guides, notwithstanding the current paucity of good, cheap SGML tools. With WordPerfect's support of SGML, and with important advances such as Extensible Markup Language (XML) on the horizon, there is a firm sense that the use of SGML DTDs other than HTML is entering into the mainstream, precisely because of the longevity and explicit nonproprietary data structure that have led to SGML's growing adoption by libraries and publishers over the past decade. An EAD guide may not have any more tags in it than does an HTML version, but the tags are descriptive of the nature and structure of the data rather than simply describing its appearance.

In all of this, it is salutary to remind oneself that we are still working in something of a "frontier culture" (the work reminds you of this with some frequency if you forget), not in a settled environment, and there will be moments of frustration along with the warm glow of EAD success.

CHAPTER 12

EAD and the Small Repository

ELIZABETH H. DOW

EXCEPT FOR A CERTAIN genetically driven pig-headedness,[1] I think I'm fairly typical of other small repository archivists and librarians.[2] I know my way around a computer, the world of databases, and the Internet in a more than casual but less than expert way. I have no programming background beyond the concepts of command stacking in Dialog, SPSS[3] query structures, and HTML coding—all pretty pedestrian stuff. But as soon as I saw finding aid markup using EAD, I thought it important that Special Collections at the University of Vermont have this technology as quickly as possible, and I knew it would be my responsibility to make it happen. Unquestionably I've done this the hard way, but I didn't see any alternative at the time. To tell this story, I will describe Special Collections at the University of Vermont and the process by which we developed the EAD Project. I will then address some of the issues the conversion project raised.

Special Collections at the University of Vermont

The University of Vermont (UVM), founded in 1791, is the largest institution of higher education in Vermont, enrolling 7,500 undergraduates, 1,125 graduate students, 375 medical students, and 1,150 nondegree students, led by 850 full-time and 150 part-time or research faculty. The three libraries on campus hold about 1.25 million volumes.

The Wilbur Collection of Vermontiana, located in the Bailey/Howe Library, ranks among the largest collection of Vermontiana in the state. It holds approximately 80,000 books and pamphlets, 200,000 pictures, 7,500 maps, and uncounted thousands of items of ephemera. The collection also includes more than 7,500 linear feet of manuscript materials in some 700 collections, of which 40 percent have been fully inventoried, approximately 40 percent have been arranged, and about 20 percent await processing. Boxed collections range in size from single five-inch boxes to 400 one-foot containers.

N.B. "EAD and the Small Repository," by Elizabeth H. Dow, co-published simultaneously in the *American Archivist* (The Society of American Archivists) vol. 60, no. 4, pp. 446–55; and *Encoded Archival Description: Context, Theory, and Case Studies* (ed.: Jackie M. Dooley) The Society of American Archivists, 1998.

[1]According to my baby book, the first complete sentence out of my mouth was, "I do it *myself*." That sounds like a pretty sophisticated sentence for a toddler, but who am I to doubt the historical record?

[2]Case studies usually reflect the work of teams, and so most reports on case studies use plural pronouns in the course of describing the project. The implementation of EAD at the University of Vermont, however, came about because I decided to do it, knowing that a shortage of staff in the department would make it essentially a one-person project. In writing about it, therefore, I thought plural pronouns sounded royal, if not actually stilted, so I wrote in the first person, generally using the singular pronoun.

[3]*Statistical Package for the Social Sciences*, SPSS, Chicago.

As with most collections of this sort, patrons and staff alike find it difficult to access the contents of all but the published materials. The primary finding aids to the boxed manuscript collections consist of about ten linear feet of inventories created between 1970 and the present, ranging in size from one page to more than three hundred pages. More than half were created with a typewriter, and no one seems to know the whereabouts of the computer files for all but a few of the rest. The quality varies, as the inventories were prepared by students, interns, and professionals with a broad range of skills.

The Wilbur Collection also has fifteen card catalog drawers referencing smaller manuscript collections. Catalog information for about one hundred of our collections has been submitted to the *National Union Catalog of Manuscript Collections*, and about a dozen have been entered into the university's on-line public access catalog (OPAC). We also have a card catalog for maps. Fewer than half our broadsides are listed in the OPAC, and there is no other finding aid for them. We published guides to our manuscript collections in 1986, to our photographs in 1992, and to our American Civil War manuscripts in 1994.

We have nearly four thousand vertical files of clippings and a wide range of short, incomplete runs of defunct serials and other periodical publications such as annual reports, high school newspapers, manufacturers' catalogs, and the like. While none of these has national interest, all could have high appeal to our primary patrons at UVM if they knew about them, but most have no intellectual access at all.

Why EAD?

A basic pessimism drives my enthusiasm for EAD: I see a dismal future for small repositories that don't establish a presence on the Internet. This pessimism gained support on August 14, 1997, when twenty or more messages on the ARCHIVES Listserv[4] (a large proportion of the traffic that day) consisted of members from all over the country recounting discussion and/or confrontation with researchers who want access to materials discovered via the Web. Undoubtedly, many researchers express diminishing patience with both paper finding aids and the detective work they once accepted as part of the research process. Because of the potential of the Web, they want intellectual access tools, and the actual documents, on-line and searchable. Long-term survival strategies for small repositories must include a Web presence which provides at least a catalog of holdings, preferably inventories for larger collections and probably portions of the collections themselves, because it seems clear that researchers will go to those sites that do have these resources.

My pessimism combines with my desire to achieve a standard of professional service which I cannot provide today but which I see the use of EAD making possible in the future. For decades the archivist's human memory has served as a major tool both for identifying and evaluating collections the researcher should consider. As a result, patrons receive uneven service, depending on who is serving them and how nimbly that archivist's memory functions during the reference interview. From one month to the next, I may or may not remember that some of our Vermont governors' papers have materials on solid waste and landfill issues, but once the computer ''knows,'' it will never forget. While I don't think computers can ever adequately evaluate the ''goodness of fit'' between a research question and an archival resource, without a doubt they do a much better job of

[4]Dean DeBolt, et al. (14–15 August 1997), ''Reference Services—Common Complaint [Discussion],'' ARCHIVES listserv, available at <http://listserv.muohio.edu/archives/archives.html>.

initial identification. Turning our finding aids into searchable databases using both MARC records and SGML documents relieves archivists of the brute memory work and allows us to apply our knowledge of the collections to the scholar's tasks by helping determine what comes closest to his or her actual need.

EAD at UVM

I had worked in Special Collections at UVM for less than two months when I saw Daniel Pitti's demonstration of the Berkeley Finding Aid Project at the annual meeting of the Society of American Archivists in Washington, D.C. in 1995. When the session ended, I was so excited I literally left the hotel and walked around the block a few times to calm myself and to comprehend the full potential of what I had seen. I had already planned a MARC database to handle item-level and collection-level records, and Pitti's project demonstrated the solution for the manuscript inventories. I knew that I had to make EAD implementation possible for UVM, but that I couldn't expect much assistance from other members of our small department; nobody had the time.

The staff of Special Collections consists of two library faculty, 2.9 FTE staff, and undergraduate work-study student help that totals sixty hours per week during the academic year. The staff maintains a public service desk in two locations for eighty-four hours a week during the academic year; this cuts back to fifty-six hours through the summer. While the library's technical services department handles most processing and cataloging of our print material, all work on archival materials must be done in Special Collections.

A few months after the Pitti demonstration, I learned from a colleague at the university's computing center that Inso Corporation would grant a full suite of electronic publishing software, called DynaText, DynaTag, and DynaWeb, to educational institutions that present an "interesting, innovative, or unique" project with which to use it.[5] My colleague from the computing center and I each developed project ideas, I wrote the proposal, and in mid-summer 1996 we got word that we had received the grant. In September, the two of us were joined by the library's head of systems for a week at Inso headquarters learning to use and administer the software. As soon as I got back from the training, I spent six weeks developing, test-running, and writing an Ameritech/LC American Memory grant proposal[6] full of ideas about how we would use this wonderful new software to post the George Perkins Marsh inventory and selected papers to the Web. In November 1996, I finally got down to work on EAD.

The Inso software will read and display SGML documents but does not have authoring capabilities. As it happened, just as I was learning the Inso software, WordPerfect went public with a beta version of its SGML authoring tool, which we purchased; we later bought a full version of WordPerfect 7 with its SGML authoring module. I started on two documents: 1) a contents list for fifty-six cartons of newly received unprocessed papers from Madeleine Kunin, a former Vermont governor on her way to serve as Ambassador to Switzerland, and 2) the inventory of the eighteen-carton Marsh collection. The Marsh inventory had been created on a typewriter, and we hoped that conventional wisdom would prove wrong and that we could convert it to ASCII text with optical character recognition (OCR) software. While the front matter scanned well enough, the container lists, set up

---

[5]For more information about Inso and its products, see <http://www.inso.com>.

[6]Library of Congress/Ameritech, *National Digital Library Competition* (Library of Congress, 1997), available at <http://lcweb2.loc.gov/ammem/award/>. We did not receive funding.

in a tabular format, did not. One software package resolved the problem caused by the container list tables by stacking the columns one after the other. The second preserved the columns by including a lot of proprietary codes which the SGML authoring software couldn't work with and which conversion to ASCII completely destroyed, turning the document into a jumble of alphanumeric characters. In the end, I had a student rekey the inventory in WordPerfect while I worked on encoding the Kunin inventory, which a student had already created in WordPerfect.

I had only WordPerfect 7's authoring software and a hard copy of the EAD Document Type Definition (DTD) to guide me. To learn to interpret EAD, I went to the stacks and pulled the library's three or four books on SGML. I quickly discovered that: 1) I lacked the background to make more than the foggiest conceptual sense of them, and 2) they were written for people about to write a DTD, not for those of us trying to use one. I longed for Laura LeMay to write a manual on EAD as she had on HTML.[7]

With that thought, I decided to compare the HTML DTD to LeMay's instructions on using it. I expected the comparison would demonstrate how to translate the code into English, and it did. While the subtleties of the EAD code remained obscure, the general structure easily came clear, and I started generating EAD markup in WordPerfect 7, trusting the software's validator to rap my knuckles when I erred.

I stepped my way through the front matter successfully, but when I came to the container lists my heart sank. We needed to apply the following set of tags to 3,500 folder labels: <c03><did><unitloc>Folder 53</unitloc><unittitle>Campaign Contributors, Caledonia County,</unittitle><unitdate>1988</unitdate></did></c03>.

I inquired about macros, but nobody I talked to had any experience with WordPerfect macros in a Windows environment, and the documentation wasn't helpful. We slogged on by hand. I had six hours of student help per week, and through the long dark Vermont winter the students and I took turns at markup duty. Talk about mind deadening! But, as spring 1997 rolled around, we finished the markup and I moved on to style sheet creation.

A readable SGML document requires three modules: 1) a marked-up document, which defines how each element relates to other elements; 2) a style sheet, which tells the browser how to display the marked-up document and; 3) a browser, which provides the actual display. Web browsers in 1997 can read only HTML markup, not other SGML DTDs. DynaWeb does an "on the fly" conversion from EAD to HTML, so after I created the EAD style sheet, I mapped the EAD tags to HTML tags. Such mapping can be a fairly simple process of equating a tag in one tag set to a tag in the other (e.g. unitloc = h4; unittitle = h4; unitdate = h4), but it can also be a lot more complicated. When I finished tag mapping, our systems department set up the DynaWeb server, we loaded the files . . . and it worked. I can't imagine that any corner of the Earth failed to hear the shouting!

After a rush of exuberance upon seeing our first finding aid on the Web, I found myself overwhelmed by the enormity of the task of converting all the old to the new. Although our collection inventories generally resemble one another, when you get down to the details, they contain enormous variations and are occasionally highly idiosyncratic. Though the EAD developers consciously included enough flexibility to accommodate

[7]Laura LeMay, *Teach Yourself Web Publishing with HTML in a Week* (Indianapolis: Sams Publishing, 1995), with an update, *Teach Yourself More Web Publishing with HTML in a Week* (Indianapolis: Sams.net Publishing, 1995), and a second edition (*Teach Yourself Web Publishing with HTML 3.0* (Indianapolis: Sams.net) in 1996.

many such variations, each of us who use EAD must decide how to deal with variation on a case-by-case basis.

By late spring I keenly felt a need for contact with others working on similar projects, so I registered for Pitti's class in EAD at the University of Virginia's Rare Books School. His pre-course reading led me to the Berkeley SunSITE, which I had vaguely known about but had ignored. There I found the American Heritage Virtual Archive Project, and the EAD "Retrospective Conversion Guidelines."[8] The American Heritage Project joins Stanford University, the University of California at Berkeley, Duke University, and the University of Virginia to create "a prototype 'virtual archive,' integrating into a single source, hundreds of archival finding aids . . . from collections . . . held by four major academic research libraries."[9]

When I compared what I had done to the American Heritage Project guidelines, I discovered that I had created valid, but thin, EAD markup. WordPerfect wouldn't let me do anything illegal, but it didn't prompt me for optional but important elements that I had overlooked or ignored. I had created "Stranger in Paradise" when *Scheherazade* was called for.

Determined never again to subject myself, or the students, to marking up container lists by hand, just before I went to Virginia I contacted a programmer I had worked with in another department of the university; he had retired because of medical disability, needed some diversion, and found this new area of work a challenge. When I returned from Virginia, he had completed the alpha version of the first of what will become a set of utilities for container list markup.

Thanks to those utilities, UVM now has six inventories on-line.[10] At this point I've stopped to reassess everything I've done, to revisit all decisions and assumptions I've made, to work with Alvin Pollock at UC Berkeley to create a template for our "front matter," and to document the final decisions which will establish the UVM standards for further work. That's where the project stands at this writing.

Lessons Learned

How do I think we did? To answer that question, I'll make a variety of observations from an evaluation stance.

What Effect Did the EAD Project Have on Department Workflow?

At UVM, the major workflow change came about when the university hired a librarian (me) to succeed a historian/bibliographer. As someone with a history of building databases in archival repositories in Vermont, I was asked specifically to bring Special Collections into the twenty-first century. The EAD project consumes about 30 percent of my time, as well as six hours weekly of student time, enhanced by the efficiency supplied by a volunteer programmer.

---

[8]University of California at Berkeley, EAD "Retrospective Conversion Guidelines" (1997), available at <http://sunsite.berkeley.edu/amher/upguide.html/>.

[9]<http://sunsite.berkeley.edu/amher/proj.html>.

[10]Special Collections, University of Vermont, *UVM Special Collections* (University of Vermont, 1997), available at <http://sageunix.uvm.edu/~sc/>.

What Stand out as Successes?

1. That I can publish finding aids on the Internet at all feels like success.

2. That I involved our systems people; they know what the project involves, they support it enthusiastically, and they respond promptly to my needs.

What Would I Do Differently?

1. I would begin using the Inso software immediately after completing the training in its use. As I designed the Marsh project for the LC/Ameritech reviewers, I learned a lot that I'll eventually need to know when we reach the point of attaching full documents and illustrations to the infrastructure provided by the inventory. In the course of sorting all that out, however, I forgot a lot of detail about the Inso software. Consequently, I found I had to relearn much that we had covered at Inso.

2. I would work less independently; I succumbed too much to my ''do it *myself*'' mentality. If I weren't so independent, for example, I might have pushed the macro issue harder. I now know that I should have gone from the computer-types I asked about macros to some top-notch secretaries who had worked intensively with WordPerfect. If I didn't now have a programmer, I'd be furiously writing keyboard macros in WordPerfect. Further, if I hadn't been so independent, I might have found the Berkeley SunSITE earlier and monitored it more closely.

What Problems Continue?

1. Working alone obviously has its drawbacks. I monitor the EAD and the Inso Listservs, but the phenomenon of the ''teachable moment'' comes very much into play. I frequently failed to comprehend the importance of discussions and information posted there because I lacked a context for it. Invariably some months later I would reach the ''need to know'' point and then would have to go back and dig it out of the listserv archives.

2. I have decided to adopt the American Heritage Project protocols. That consortium has experts to debate the details and establish a range of acceptable practice; I see little reason to second-guess its decisions. Even so, the American Heritage guidelines provide a range of practices, not a set of rules. I face many decisions that require knowledge of the software, the DTD, and the document I'm working on. I make those decisions alone, because I have no choice, but I wish I had someone locally to discuss them with.

3. SGML depends heavily on indirect logic and references to external files. SGML browsers expect to find those external files precisely placed on the system. Loading and managing files takes more time than I ever imagined.

What Changes or Refinements has EAD Brought to Inventory Creation?

1. As Pitti points out in his introduction to the American Heritage Project's EAD ''Retrospective Conversion Guidelines,'' using EAD does not in and of itself ensure that machine-readable finding aids will function well in a union database. Inventories and other finding aids in union databases will need to share a degree of uniformity to make them easily intelligible for users moving from one institution's documents to those of another. More fundamentally, they will need to share a degree of uniformity so that computers can manage them; this uniformity applies to both intellectual content and markup protocols.

Therefore, as I look forward to entering our inventories into a union database in the future, I must stay current with new developments.

2. I first directly translated the look and feel of the paper inventory into two electronic documents we marked up, which means that I included the box number only once—at the top of its container list—followed by folder numbers only. This approach works poorly on-line, because SGML display technology in 1997 does not retain the box number at the top of the screen the way typists do when they carry over information from page to page. Unless the display includes the box number on the screen with every folder number, the patron quickly loses track of which box an item resides in.

3. Most of our finding aids blur the distinction between intellectual and physical arrangement. EAD was designed to give primacy to intellectual organization, and so as we convert our data from paper to electrons we have an opportunity to reorder the inventory to take advantage of this. I think that is the right thing to do from a theoretical point of view, but I question whether taking the time to rethink and reorder every inventory for conversion will yield enough benefits to justify the cost of the process.

4. I would like all my data to work using one style sheet. While conceptually easy to understand, the minute detail necessary to develop a good style sheet takes a lot of time and a considerable amount of expertise. I would prefer to spend that time just once. Given that inventories do have unavoidable variations, however, I may have to develop up to three: one for collections processed in classic series/subseries order; one for those processed in chronological and/or physical location order, and one for totally unprocessed collections.

What New Considerations has EAD Brought to the Inventory Creation Process?

1. Collection inventories contain lists of names associated with political or ideological action/causes, and the folder labels make the location of those lists quite clear, as in my earlier example for "Campaign Contributors, Caledonia County, 1988." In theory, despite publication on the Web, nothing about this finding aid has changed. The inventories direct researchers to the contributor lists and are public information, as they always were. But in reality, before the Web, the public could not so readily access that information. It was confined to a notebook in our reading room which was open to the public only about a third of the daytime hours each week, and so the information simply didn't fall into the hands of anyone who didn't consciously, and at some inconvenience, seek it out. On the Web in a searchable inventory available every minute of the year, the information is now easily and globally available. After Web publication, the probability that someone will find and use membership or contributor lists, benignly or otherwise, increases substantially. I have begun to wonder what responsibility, if any, we have for people's privacy when we make such information globally available. This can be particularly troubling in collections acquired before global availability even seemed possible, and our deeds of gift say nothing about this sort of information dissemination.

2. With Web publication, a paper inventory becomes a searchable database, necessitating good database maintenance practices. EAD includes protocols for controlled access points at all levels, but is it worth the time it will take to include them? On the other hand, can we, in good conscience, *not* include them? How much should we gear our markup toward the search engine? Should we begin standardizing our folder label language? What about authority control for proper nouns? If we're looking to produce one or more union catalogs of finding aids, we cannot simply ignore vocabulary issues. Nor can we each arrive at our own conclusions independently.

3. At about the same time the Berkeley Finding Aid Project started to develop EAD, a group of digital library researchers, Internet networking specialists, content specialists, and librarians—all concerned about absence of librarianship on the Web—started to develop what has become known as the Dublin Core, "an ongoing effort to form an international consensus on the semantics of a simple description record for networked resources. It is expected that a simple and widely-understood set of elements will promote interoperability amongst heterogeneous metadata systems and improve resource discovery on the Internet."[11] Like anyone who has used any of the Web search engines, I applaud the effort to develop such a protocol, but it's not yet clear to me how to integrate the EAD and Dublin Core elements.

4. Repositories process collections for three reasons: First, going through the materials and storing them in a tidy manner in archival enclosures helps preserve them, identifies items of particular value, and brings to light items that need conservation. Second, a well-ordered collection brings like materials together, making them convenient to present to patrons. Third, an inventory of the collection provides intellectual accessibility. Given that UVM fully processes manuscript collections only when we have special grant money or other beneficial circumstances, there is no real hope we'll ever truly process many of our collections. Therefore, I see creating and publishing the existing container lists in "raw" order as a way of providing at least some intellectual access where there would be absolutely none otherwise. I can hear the real archivists among you bemoaning the devaluation of the neighborhood, and I sympathize. Granted, all of us would be better served if collections were fully processed. However, in a world in which that may not happen, a searchable finding aid makes the collection *usable* without full processing. Further, tracking which unprocessed collections get repeated use can give us data for choosing those collections on which we will spend our scarce processing resources.

5. As Richard Szary has suggested, the introduction of EAD has served as a catalyst for discussion of fundamental issues regarding what a finding aid is.[12] When does a MARC record adequately serve as a finding aid, and when do we need something more? When do we need individual MARC records, and when can we represent our holdings more efficiently but just as effectively through SGML-encoded lists? I've created a half dozen or so MARC databases for materials such as our vertical files, uncataloged town reports, photo files, etc. What is the relationship between our on-line public access catalog, the website on which we publish SGML finding aids and these databases? The UVM library system will soon move its public catalog from a mainframe computer to a client-server system. When that's in place, of course we will link the MARC records and the published inventories, but it is unclear how we can blend all aspects of our intellectual access tools into one integrated user-friendly system for the patron.

Conclusion

EAD implementation at UVM began when it did because one faculty member took complete responsibility for it and received total support from the administration at both the departmental and library levels. Within the next few years we will convert all our

[11] "The 4th Dublin Core Metadata Workshop Report," *D-Lib Magazine* (June 1997), available at <http://www.dlib.org/dlib/june97/metadata/06weibel.html/>.

[12] Richard Szary, "Improving Access to Finding Aids: The Encoded Archival Description Project," *NEA Newsletter* 23 (October 1996): 4–8.

inventories, as well as container lists for many of our unprocessed or semi-processed collections. We also have lists of holdings, such as nineteenth-century newspapers, diaries, ledgers, and other materials, for which the list constitutes the finding aid, and I'm not sure how to handle these. Should we load them into a database, mark them up in a perverted EAD, or take on TEI,[13] a DTD more suited to general documents such as lists? After we've published the inventories, to what degree do we want to link scanned images of the documents? We don't know, but when we reach the point of addressing those questions seriously, we'll find answers—probably by watching what others have done.

If the University of Vermont is a small repository, the state of Vermont is dotted with micro-repositories. Virtually every one of the state's approximately three hundred municipalities has a historical society or library or municipal office with a collection of locally important historical documents. Some have materials of much broader importance, but the holdings of most remain totally inaccessible. Having begun my archival career in one of them, I care about these repositories a great deal. Although UVM Special Collections would face marginalization without a Web presence, it would not face extinction because of its position within the university. Vermont's micro-repositories, however, have no such institutional insulation. Many struggle to survive now and will surely follow the town band into oblivion as the users and financial supporters on which they depend completely come to rely on repositories like UVM that can serve their needs by remote access through the Web.

EAD is quickly becoming fundamental to the Web presence of a historical repository. I'm very grateful for the work large repositories have put into EAD, and their willingness to share their tools and insights with those of us in small repositories. Despite my illusions of having done it "myself," I know that nothing this large, or even my own little success, can happen with only one person or one institution's efforts, and that we as a profession still have huge questions yet to address. The workable answers to the questions raised by the authors in these case studies will require all of us to relinquish some of our more idiosyncratic practices for uniform standards that will serve us all. Comprehending and adhering to those standards will come hardest to the small- and micro-repositories around us, because we are largely understaffed, underfunded, and poorly trained. As I have benefited from the direct and indirect help of UC Berkeley, the University of Virginia, Harvard, and Yale, I must now reach out to Vermont's micro-repositories.

[13] *Text Encoding Initiative*, a project to develop guidelines and an SGML DTD for encoding electronic texts for scholarly use, available at <http://www.uic.edu/orgs/tei>.

Contributors

Nicole Bouché *is Head of the Manuscripts Unit at the Beinecke Rare Book and Manuscript Library at Yale University. She directs the Beinecke's implementation of EAD and is actively engaged in the further development of the Yale Finding Aid Project site and related digital library initiatives at Beinecke. From 1987 to 1993, she was Assistant Head of the Manuscripts Division of the Bancroft Library at the University of California at Berkeley. Her chapter is a somewhat revised version of a paper given on 29 August 1997 at the annual meeting of the Society of American Archivists held in Chicago.*

Steven J. DeRose *has been working with hypermedia document systems starting with the File Retrieval and Editing System (FRESS) hypertext system in 1979. In 1989 he completed his Ph.D. in Computational Linguistics at Brown University and co-founded Electronic Book Technologies. He designed DynaText, the first SGML on-line delivery engine, and other EBT products and served as the SGML expert on the Bentley Library fellowship team that developed EAD. He is now Chief Scientist for Inso, EBT's parent company, and also serves as Adjunct Professor at Brown University. He has written many papers and two books:* Making Hypermedia Work: A User's Guide to HyTime *(with David Durand) and* The SGML FAQ Book.

Jackie M. Dooley *is Head of Special Collections and University Archives at the University of California at Irvine. She has been involved with the development of Encoded Archival Description as a member of the 1995 Bentley Team and as a member of the Society of American Archivists' EAD Working Group. She serves on the University of California's Online Archive of California Advisory Working Group and as chair of the Online Archive of California Metadata Standards Working Group.*

Elizabeth H. Dow *is Public Services Librarian in Special Collections at the University of Vermont. Some of the opinions and text in her chapter have previously appeared in the July 1996, December 1996, and August 1997 issues of* SAA Manuscript Repositories Newsletter. *Her chapter is based on a presentation made on 29 August 1997 at the annual meeting of the Society of American Archivists held in Chicago.*

Michael Fox *is Head of Processing in the Minnesota Historical Society's Division of Library and Archives. A member of the EAD development team and SAA's EAD Working Group, he has been both an early implementer and an instructor for numerous workshops on EAD.*

Steven L. Hensen *is Director of Planning and Project Development in the Special Collections Library at Duke University. He is the author of* Archives, Personal Papers, and Manuscripts *and of numerous articles and papers in the area of archival description and standards. He is a Fellow of the Society of American Archivists and has been a member of its council. He was a member of the SAA National Information Systems Task Force, the Working Group on Standards for Archival Description, the 1989 Airlie House Multiple Versions Forum, the Bentley development team for EAD, and other groups, and has conducted numerous workshops and consultancies in archival cataloging and description and the use of the USMARC format.*

Kris Kiesling *has been Head of the Department of Manuscripts and Archives at the Harry Ransom Humanities Research Center at the University of Texas at Austin since 1990. Prior to that she was a manuscripts processor in the Department of Rare Books and Special Collections at the University of Michigan and at the Social Welfare History Archives at the University of Minnesota. She is currently chair of the SAA Committee on Archival Information Exchange, of CAIE's Working Group on Encoded Archival Description, and is an instructor for numerous workshops on EAD. Her chapter is a revision of a paper given on 30 August 1996 at the annual meeting of the Society of American Archivists held in San Diego.*

Mary A. Lacy *is an archivist in the Preparation Section of the Manuscript Division of the Library of Congress and serves as the division's liaison to the National Digital Library Program. She has been active in the digital conversion and distribution of Manuscript Division finding aids since 1995 and has participated in the library's testing of EAD and encoding efforts during the last two years.*

Dennis Meissner *supervises the arrangement and description of manuscript collections at the Minnesota Historical Society and has been closely involved with the repository's EAD planning and experiments. He directed the internal task force that reengineered the MHS model for archival finding aids. A preliminary version of his chapter was presented on 30 August 1996 at the annual meeting of the Society of American Archivists held in San Diego.*

Anne Mitchell *is a cataloger of pictorial materials with a specialization in architecture, design, and engineering collections in the Prints and Photographs Division of the Library of Congress. Prior to her participation in testing the use of EAD for pictorial collection finding aids, she completed an eight-year project to arrange, preserve, house, and catalog architectural drawings relating to the Washington, D.C. metropolitan area. Her chapter with Mary Lacy is a revision of a paper given on 30 August 1996 at the annual meeting of the Society of American Archivists held in San Diego.*

Leslie A. Morris *is Chair of the Harvard/Radcliffe Digital Finding Aids Project and Curator of Manuscripts in the Harvard College Library, Houghton Library, Harvard University. Her chapter is a slightly expanded version of a paper given on 29 August 1997 at the annual meeting of the Society of American Archivists held in Chicago.*

Daniel V. Pitti *is Project Director at the Institute for Advanced Technology in the Humanities at the University of Virginia. Previously, he was the Librarian for Advanced Technologies Projects in the library at the University of California, Berkeley. Pitti is the principal architect of Encoded Archival Description.*

Janice E. Ruth *is both a writer/editor and an acquisitions archivist in women's history for the Library of Congress Manuscript Division, where she also has held positions as a reference librarian and processing technician. She was a member of the EAD development team convened by Daniel Pitti in July 1995 and continues to monitor and contribute to EAD's progress as a member of SAA's EAD Working Group. She also serves as a member of SAA's Committee on Archival Information Exchange.*

David Seaman *is the founding director of the Electronic Text Center at the University of Virginia. This library service, open since August 1992, combines an on-line archives of thousands of SGML texts and digital images with a center housing equipment suitable for the creation and analysis of text. Seaman has taught e-text and Internet courses at the annual summer Rare Book School at the University of Virginia and has a particular interest in the application of computer technologies to special collections and museums. An earlier version of his chapter was presented on 29 August 1997 at the annual meeting of the Society of American Archivists held in Chicago.*

Index